POSTCARDS

from Elsewhere

TRAVELS IN A CHANGING WORLD

Barbara O'Shea's collection of stories is stark, searing and deeply moving. Perhaps it could make us just that bit more caring and compassionate and inspire us to want to do something to change the often awful circumstances she describes so well.

(Archbishop Desmond Tutu)

Postcards From Elsewhere is a powerful book, written with a rare combination of historical knowledge, political acumen and unsentimental compassion. Avoiding polemics and statistics, the author simply records what she herself has observed and describes several of the outstanding characters she has met. She reveals how life is lived by the majority of human beings – and why it must be so lived. Using extraordinary skill, Barbara O'Shea sketches in the historical backgrounds to her travels – briefly, yet without oversimplification. In laconic, memorable phrases, she captures the cultural and social significance of tiny details and provides striking vignettes of landscapes and cityscapes. Now, when the controllers of the global economy are working hard to conceal many of the sources of our Rich World's affluence, *Postcards From Elsewhere* is an urgently needed book.

(Dervla Murphy)

A wonderfully descriptive book that is difficult to put down once started. … provides an incisive insight into the lives of peoples in faraway lands that often remain hidden from view. It is a testimony to the courage and tenacity of the human spirit in a vastly changing world.

It is a must both for the armchair and physical traveller.

(Tom Hyland – East Timor Ireland Solidarity Campaign)

POSTCARDS
from Elsewhere

TRAVELS IN A CHANGING WORLD

BARBARA O'SHEA

MERLIN
PUBLISHING

First published in 2004 by
Merlin Publishing
16 Upper Pembroke Street
Dublin 2, Ireland
Tel: +353 1 676 4373
Fax: +353 1 676 4368
publishing@merlin.ie

ISBN 1-903582-58-X

A CIP catalogue record for this book is available from the British Library.

5 4 3 2 1

Typeset by Gough Typesetting
Cover Design by Faye Keegan Design
Printed and bound in Denmark, by AIT Nørhaven A/S

For Betty and Joe O'Shea

BARBARA O'SHEA worked as a radio producer and reporter with RTE (the Irish national broadcaster) for several years and travelled in Asia, Africa and Latin America for the programme *Worlds Apart*. She lived in New York, freelancing in television, video and radio production. She later lived in Cambodia, working with the United Nations on the elections that followed the peace agreement, and has monitored elections in a number of countries. A graduate in Development Studies and International Human Rights Law, she lectures in human rights and lives in Dublin.

Contents

Foreword

Nothing existed until it was gazed on by European eyes: the Americas and Lake Victoria. I had an African friend who as a small boy went to school under the high snow-capped peaks of Mount Kenya. He remembers sitting there and being told of the mountain's discovery by the European missionary explorer Ludwig Krapf on December 3, 1849. He wondered as he looked out and up at its great mass, did my ancestors not see it, did the mountain hide itself from us and only reveal itself when a white man came? It puzzled him; it didn't occur to him at the time that the teacher could be wrong.

When it did occur to him, as he grew older, he questioned everything.

This books lays open a lot of questions about the world we live in and the relationship between the countries in the rich north and those in the poor south. I had the good fortune, through working with RTÉ and the UN, to travel and meet people living – in Africa, Asia and South America. I met and spoke with them in their homes, hospitals, prisons, refugee camps, feeding centres, schools, orphanages, farms, workplaces, pagodas, churches, polling stations, offices and government ministries. They gave their time willingly. Many felt that if people knew their situation then they would do something and the interviews were sometimes by way of an appeal. The more I saw and heard, the more I felt outrage. The shadow of countries in the North bore down over their lives – the legacy of colonialism, the structure of the international political and economic order, globalisation, the virulent arms business and the support given to cruel, repressive regimes.

Radio is a wonderful medium, but a transitory one, so I decided to write down their stories to put them more firmly and permanently on the record. Among the captured faces and captured voices are the gazes of old women, innocent children and worn out soldiers; stoical Prudence, the Guarani tribe from Brazil, the Subaanen from the Philippines, the Rwandan orphans, the slender Cambodian dancers who survived the Khmer Rouge, the bonded labourers from India, the children on the Manila dumpsite, the Zimbabwean taxi driver, the East Timorese grandmother and her hidden tea-set. The stories they courageously told were of displacement, conflict, exile, famine, sickness, poverty, AIDS, struggle, survival, and in the midst of it all, the human capacity to survive.

I started to write. As I began I remembered the day the doorbell rang and, on opening the front door, there before me – a little damp because the overcast day had turned to a soft rain – was the smiling, genial face of Jose Lopes.

East Timor

Jose's Homecoming

2000

When Jose Lopes headed for home after seven years he wasn't able to send word to his family in Manatuto because of the war, the bad roads and there being no working telephones. He just showed up.

As Jose walks down the dust-covered road towards his house, he sees his elderly father coming towards him. Around the scorched plain, some buffalo scratch at the scrubby earth. Little by little, the two men move towards each other like a pair of uncertain gunfighters. As they draw closer his father suddenly turns around, goes back down the track road and into his house.

'I didn't know what to do', says Jose, 'I expected him to hold me and welcome me home.' Instead Jose stands there, hands on hip, then takes a deep breath and walks more slowly towards the house.

His father comes out, squinting at something in his trembling hand. His eyes narrow to look closely at Jose, his now tear-filled eyes go back again to the photograph he is holding.

'It's me, papa, Jose', says the young man.

'No,' rasps his father, 'you are Jose's spirit come to tell me that Jose is dead'.

'Papa, it's me and I'm alive.'

With no words the old man's weathered arm, bare, dry as parchment, reaches out and firmly presses the muscle in Jose's shoulder – real flesh and bone; then his thin hand wanders up to the handsome young face. Cracked worn fingers touch the cheek, the thumb brushes over the eyelid causing Jose to close his eyes and the hand ends up touching his hair. With a yelp, the old man fiercely pulls Jose to him, holds him and welcomes him home.

* * * *

'Did he kill the Manatuto pig in celebration?'

'No,' laughs Jose, 'but he did kill two buffalo'.

Jose, back in Dublin, is in the conservatory talking about his homecoming. 'And you know,' he says, 'my father took a big risk all those years keeping that photograph; because I had been deported, the Indonesians might have killed him if they had found it.'

'My father, Francisco Lopes, was chief of the village, Malushun, in the sub-district of Soibada, when Indonesia invaded East Timor in 1975.' The island of Timor is at the south-eastern end of the Indonesian archipelago, a little less than five hundred kilometres north of Australia. Following the aroma of sandalwood, Portuguese and Dutch explorers arrived and eventually divided the small territory into east and west; these boundaries still separate East Timor and West Timor. As a Portuguese colony for four hundred years, East Timor was different to the rest of the archipelago, which had been formed into the Dutch East Indies. The Portuguese language was superimposed on native dialects; Christianity overlaid the traditional animist culture, although these beliefs are still there, beneath the surface. Dili, the capital, has an immediate feel of a Portuguese past with its colonial architecture, especially along the waterfront. Running through the centre of the island is a rugged mountain range and, in the hills, old traditional villages offer cool relief from the hot humidity of the coast. Surrounding this coastline are clear, turquoise waters.

Jose's village rests on the southern side of the rugged mountain range that runs through the centre of the island. The regional town is Manatuto, fifty kilometres away on the coast.

In 1975, eight hundred families lived in the village; three hundred survived the occupation.

'My mother had ten children and I was the second youngest. I was three years old when Indonesia attacked with fighter jets, but I remember the loud wailing noise overhead. I saw people lying on the ground and I thought they were pretending to be asleep until it was over. When they didn't wake up I asked my father why and he told me that they were dead.

After the invasion, my eldest brother joined the resistance group, the Falantil, and was killed three weeks later in a gun battle with the Indonesian forces. Our entire village of eight thousand left for the safety of the mountains because they were afraid of the army. Within months three of my sisters and three of my brothers, aged from seven to twenty-two years, had died from sickness and hunger. I hardly knew them. As each one died, my father laid the body under a tree and marked the bark with a cross so that he could return and bury them properly.'

For three years the villagers trekked from place to place and across the mountains, just ahead of the Indonesian patrols.

'We grew cassava and corn. These crops could be dried and carried while travelling but there were many crops and nutritious plants we couldn't sow. As well as cassava and corn we ate wild fruit and monkeys, deer, wild pigs and goats. Everybody carried supplies of food. I remember always dragging a load as I walked.'

The whole village became a nomadic tribe of eight thousand with the Falantil guerrillas at the rear for protection. As the villagers sowed, harvested and moved, the bodies of his children preyed on Jose's father's mind, especially the thought of animals devouring them. He tried to get back to the marked trees but with the military all around it was impossible. It still upsets him to talk about this. After independence in 1999, he erected one memorial for his six dead children.

It became more and more difficult to escape the military and capture. One morning, looking up through the forest trees, the people saw helicopters hovering. Letters were thrown out and landed in the undergrowth. Loud megaphones blared instructions to surrender, to give up and integrate with 'the Great Nation of Indonesia'. The siren voices and fallen leaflets promised a better life than the jungle and the temptation of good food instead of the meagre helpings of dried cassava and corn.

'When my father read one of the letters,' says Jose, 'he realised that if the village did not surrender they would be mercilessly attacked from the air.'

Three thousand villagers had already died through hunger and disease, especially tuberculosis and malaria. Only five thousand were left. Jose's father decided that the village must surrender and resist the occupation from inside. He persuaded the guerrillas to allow them to leave the forest. He went into the town he was told to go to and said, 'I have come to surrender the whole population of this village.'

The Indonesians had built a compound and each person was given a tin of food, a novelty that they enjoyed at first. After two weeks they were taken to a new village because there were too many Falantil fighters near the old one. Each family was allocated a house. Travel was curtailed to three kilometres and they were told that if they went beyond that limit they would be shot. The villagers started getting on with life under the occupation and began cultivating again, but there were tensions. The people of a nearby village that favoured integration with Indonesia insulted them when they went about their business in the market, calling them the 'leftovers of Freitilin', the political movement that had wanted an independent East Timor, and taunting them that they should have stayed with Freitilin.

'As they settled into the new village the Indonesians arrested my father,' says Jose, 'and they tortured and questioned him about the resistance fighters. When my father told me about this during our reunion he cried so hard that I stopped him; it was too painful for him to speak about and for me to listen.'

Francisco Lopes told his interrogators that he had no connection with the guerrillas and that he had brought his people in from the forest, as the Indonesians had demanded. At sunrise he was put standing, his fist held in the Falantil salute, until sunset. He stood all day in the thirsty heat, watched by two soldiers holding guns. By midday his eyes had given up, no longer able to withstand the glaring sun. They promised to release him if he them gave information about the resistance movement.

'I was then six years old,' says Jose 'and I crept into the trees and hid there crying as I watched my father's pain and humiliation and powerlessness. That evening he was allowed home, his eyes red from the day in the sun.'

The Indonesian occupation of East Timor was violently repressive and bloody; over two hundred thousand Timorese lost their lives. Declassified documents in the United States show that on December 6, 1975, the day before the invasion, President Gerald Ford and Secretary of State Henry Kissinger met Indonesian President Suharto in Jakarta and indicated that there would be no great fall-out if Indonesia took control of the small island. That control, seized the following day, became a stranglehold. By 1989, despite Timorese resistance, the Jakarta government felt sufficiently in command to allow some opening up and a Papal visit to the Catholic island was arranged. During the visit it was important to present an air of normality and show that the Timorese had accepted integration with Indonesia. Francisco's villagers were allowed back to the old village. They returned to a ghost village, to houses that hadn't been touched since their abandonment fourteen years before, and started working the neglected, overgrown fields. Settled back in the old place, they renewed contact with the Falantil and supported them in whatever way they could. Letters from the guerrillas in the field were passed to the villagers, put into a cylindrical bamboo container filled with rice and transported on to the leaders in East Timor's capital, Dili.

'When I was eight years of age,' says Jose, 'I was sent to school in Dili and when I was older I became involved with pro-independence students who met secretly after school hours.

Indonesian spies were everywhere so we devised a system of hand signals and code words to communicate with each other.' At school Jose's generation of Timorese were taught in Bahasa, the official language of Indonesia.

The school was beside the Santa Cruz cemetery, a small, enclosed burial ground. In November 1991, sixteen years after the invasion, students gathered there to commemorate Sebastiao Gomes, who had been murdered by the Indonesians a few weeks before. During the memorial service, Indonesian soldiers surrounded the cemetery and started shooting at the crowd.

'I was at Santa Cruz the day of the massacre,' says Jose, 'and when the Indonesian military came in I ran to the back and jumped on the wall. The others crouched among the graves; there were screams and gunshots from soldiers firing M16s. I was very frightened so I jumped off the wall and ran. That night I hid in a friend's house while the military went to the hospital and killed the wounded and searched the town for those who had escaped.'

Two hundred and seventy one named people died in the massacre but the number of dead is said to be closer to four hundred.

'At daybreak I got a bus to Manatuto and on to Soibada. The only person I told about Santa Cruz was my father, no one else. My father decided it wasn't safe for me to stay in East Timor so I left and enrolled at university in East Java.'

At university Jose continued secretly meeting with students who supported independence. In November 1994 the Asia Pacific Economic Conference was held in Jakarta and since world leaders, including US President Bill Clinton, were attending, the students saw an opportunity for media attention about Indonesia's brutal repression. The students around Java decided to go to Jakarta and hold a demonstration. When they got there the railway platforms were full of armed troops and police.

'As the train pulled into the station,' says Jose, 'I saw military uniforms through the grilles covering the windows. I wanted to stay in the carriage but my family got off and I went with them.' Some were arrested, others got through because of the crowds in the noisy, chaotic station. Twenty-nine students showed up at the arranged meeting place and took taxis to the American embassy. Outside they unrolled the banner with its message: *INDONESIA OUT OF EAST TIMOR NOW* and shouted slogans.

After five minutes they heard sirens. The police arrived first; then soldiers and tanks came and surrounded the embassy. Trapped by the Indonesian military, Jose and his friends started to climb the twenty-foot high wall that guarded the embassy, helping each other clamber up and jump into the grounds. Immediately, US guards ran towards them shouting, "don't move or we will shoot!" The students stood still. Indonesian soldiers came in and tried to push them out, screaming that they had to leave. The embassy guards stood there and did nothing.

'Someone shouted, "hold hands, hold hands so they can't get us out!" We held hands and argued with the soldiers that they had no right to force us out of the embassy; that it wasn't Indonesian territory.' After half an hour the soldiers left and the students stayed.

'The staff at the embassy told us we had to leave,' says Jose. 'We said no, we weren't terrorists; we only wanted to tell the world about East Timor. We reminded them that the US had supplied some of the weapons that had killed our people.'

Word about the stand-off in the embassy went around the international journalists covering the summit and they took pictures of the protesters through the spiked iron railings of the embassy. Outside, the Indonesian military fumed at the international mortification and hissed, 'we know who you are, we know where your families are; they will pay for what you have done'.

'At first the embassy refused us food saying that we would have to go outside. In the heat we became dehydrated and some of us collapsed.'

The students said that they would stay until the last one died rather than be handed over to the Indonesians. Finally the embassy was given instructions to provide food, water and medicine, and was told not to forcibly hand anyone over to the Indonesians.

After two weeks, Portugal, the former colonial ruler in East Timor and still the recognised sovereign power, offered the students sanctuary in Portugal.

Some of the refuge seekers were delighted. 'But' says Jose 'I wondered why we should go to Portugal. I wasn't Portuguese, I couldn't speak Portuguese and I had no wish to go to a country that had controlled and exploited East Timor for four hundred years. I wasn't going to the other side of the world, so far away from my family. My home was East Timor and I wanted to go back. My family didn't even know I was in the embassy. My friends argued with me and said I was crazy, the only place I was going to was a prison cell; Suharto would make us pay for the embarrassment we had caused him and his regime. I finally decided to leave with the others.'

The students were taken in Red Cross vehicles to Jakarta's international airport and flown to Portugal. They left in the clothes they were standing in, never returning to their lodgings to pack, or to their family and friends to say goodbye. The protesters became exiles.

In Portugal, they were given accommodation, language classes, full citizenship and a passport, which allowed them to travel around Europe. In exile they continued to campaign about East Timor. After two years Jose and another exiled Timorese, Dino Gandara Rai, met Tom Hyland from the East Timor Ireland Solidarity Campaign and he invited them to Ireland to raise awareness. They arrived in September 1996 to another foreign country speaking another foreign language, and began to learn English and work with the solidarity group.

The most poignant memories I have of Jose in Dublin are those of September 1999, just after East Timor voted in a United Nations supervised referendum to be independent. His face was used on posters, a stark black and white photograph of a serious-looking Jose with a bandana around his forehead that said 'Freedom'.

In East Timor, almost eighty percent of the people voted for independence. The result was rejected by pro-Indonesian militias, who went on the rampage destroying everything and forcing the population once again to flee to the mountains for safety. Jose drew more and more into himself, barely able to speak. He could get no news about his family. In a bitter irony, one of the leaders of the militias was Eurico Gutteres, a good friend who had sat beside Jose at school. Once a strong supporter of independence, Eurico was taken away one day, detained, tortured and beaten, and when he came out was militantly pro-integration with Indonesia. Inducted into the grey world of the paramilitary gangs organised by the Indonesian military, he became a leading figure in the destruction of East Timor after the independence vote.

The campaign office in Dublin was busy organising demonstrations and lobbying for UN peacekeepers to be sent in to restore order. Jose came to all the protests but could barely function. Perhaps the worst night was when we were all in the office watching the evening news on the old clapped-out black and white portable television and suddenly there were pictures of Manatuto in flames. Jose stared at the screen stunned, then without a word buried his head in his hands. Even after the peacekeepers went in, it was weeks before he heard that his parents were still alive.

Then in December 2000, after seven years, Jose, with Dino, took the flight from Dublin to Darwin, onto Dili, the capital of the first new nation in the new millennium. Then he caught the bus home to Manatuto and met his father.

Tea with Marta

2000

As Jose headed off for Manatuto, his friend Dino was being reunited with his family of mother, sisters, brothers, several aunts, uncles and cousins. When Dino was very young, his father, a leading member of the Falantil, the resistance movement, was killed. Like Jose, Dino had been sent into exile after protesting and occupying a foreign embassy in Jakarta.

I went to East Timor only days into the new millennium to record material for radio. It was three months after the militias had looted everything they could, and burnt and destroyed anything they could not. The island was dotted with villages of ashes, where villagers slept under large plastic sheets provided by humanitarian organisations. Charred remains of village schools smouldered; not a trace was left of the buildings, not a blackboard, not a pencil; the Indonesian teacher gone back to the safety of Jakarta.

Having come from inspecting Dino's family home in Dili, a house so gutted that even the tiles on the floor had burnt out, we went on to visit his Great Aunt Marta in one of his relative's homes that had not been ruined. The old woman poured tea with swift jerky turns of the wrist and the porcelain cup clacked on the saucer. Small and spry, with rapid delivery and defiant, feisty tone, she talked about the militias coming to her hometown, Los Palos. Reaching forward to take the tea, I was drawn from the bird-like face with its narrow intense eyes to the china tea set. The manager of the Hotel Turismo in Dili – the hotel itself had fared badly in the days following the vote –

had shrugged and offered a smoke blackened room without breakfast, as neither coffee nor cup were left in the kitchen. Proudly, Dino's Great Aunt Marta thrust the chinaware into our hands, where it glistened unbroken and pretty against the shattered backdrop of a devastated East Timor.

The devastation began on a bright September day in 1999. The referendum result on whether the small island should be part of Indonesia had been announced – an overwhelming vote for independence. Celebrations were muted for fear of the militias, trained by the Indonesian army in the event of the vote going against them. Marta dos Santos was working in the rice fields near her home in Los Palos when the result was announced. The word spread quickly through the terraces of rice, the same terraces where during the occupation the rice planters murmured to each other the name of Xanana Gusmaõ, the resistance leader (now the President of East Timor) until it became a national mantra: 'Xanana is our Mandela'. Word ricocheting around the terraces of rice on that September day was that the militias were coming, killing and destroying everything.

Hearing the news, Marta remembered 1975, when the Indonesians invaded, causing terrible destruction and loss of life. She survived the brutal regime that followed, when many of her family suffered and were killed. This part of her story is no different than that of most East Timorese.

Now, Marta, working the fields in the September sun, told her neighbours as they hurried towards the mountains for refuge that she would follow. She ran back to her house, gathered up her china tea set, dug a hole in the ground and buried it.

The attack, she says, was the most ruthless she had experienced in her life, even worse than the 1975 invasion. The militias and army were chasing them and shooting. The noise of gunfire was everywhere. She was terrified and her heart was pounding. Even though she was old, she had to keep running. She ran into a militiaman who had been given a gun by the Indonesian army. Fortunately he was a relative, and she remembers him saying to her, 'oh my grandmother, you must run to the mountains or they will come and kill you'. She went to the mountains and the militia relative accompanied her to protect her.

The Timorese hunkered in the mountains for three weeks while the gangs of marauders rampaged throughout the countryside terrorising the population, killing livestock, looting or burning everything. Children scuttled over rocks as if chased by the bogeyman, eyes full of fear and incomprehension, big as saucers. Surviving on berries and fruits, young boys shimmied up the coconut trees and shared their bounty with Marta, sleeping on the hard ground below. She was afraid of getting sick or dying in the mountain. This, she recalls, was her main concern. She also worried about her family, spread out around the country. Afterwards, she discovered that some were among the six thousand that sought sanctuary at Bishop Belo's house in Dili. The house was surrounded and finally attacked by the militias.

One of Marta's relatives puts down his teacup and tells us he was there at the Bishop's house. He saw a ten-year-old girl shot through the forehead; a man plead for his wife's life before his head was chopped off with a bayonet; a young boy dying on the altar used to celebrate Mass.

After three long weeks, the United Nations sent in blue-helmeted peacekeepers to restore order. Marta returned home to no house and no animals. She dug up her precious, unchipped china tea set and carried it to Dili where she stayed with relatives. Later, international aid agencies came to assist in the rebuilding of East Timor. To raise money, they portrayed the East Timorese as victims.

Marta dos Santos is no victim.

Rosary

2000

The cadence is immediately decipherable to anyone who grew up in Ireland in the fifties or before. The first half of the prayer of two halves is said in an increasingly rapid monotone by a single leading voice and ends in 'the fruit of thy womb, Jesus' with a vaguely relieved but definite full stop. Then a surge as the supplicants respond with a loud rising inflection, chanting in unison 'Holy Mary'.

As the prayer is repeated fifty times it settles into its own rhythm. The sound of the rosary is the same wherever you hear it and whatever the language. Rare in Ireland now, it is still said regularly, and with familiar indifferent gusto, in East Timor. As afternoon faints into evening you can hear it sung by the kneeling orphaned children as you walk past their dwelling in Dili. If you can't hear it live it is transmitted at six every evening on the radio.

Cambodia

The Dancers

1999

Cambodia's lush, tropical countryside basks in the natural bountifulness of banana trees, mangos, papayas, coconuts and sugar palms, while the artistic skilfulness of the Khmer people has found wondrous expression in the famous temple city of Angkor Wat. More interesting is the resilient population: women with the traditional sarong styled sampot hitched up, ankle deep in the wet paddy fields or seated on the dusty ground beside clumps of fruit and vegetables at the market; or slight sturdy men hauling heavy containers up and down the makeshift port; or fishermen casting large webbed nets on the Mekong River while buffalo cool down and children scream and jump from the bank, their legs bent like tadpoles. The Khmer people have survived bombing by the United States during the Vietnam War, the brutal regime of the Khmer Rouge, civil war, and international isolation because of Vietnamese backing of the Phnom Penh communist government.

The end of the Cold War galvanised international support for a peace agreement between the four Cambodian factions. The United Nations sent a peacekeeping mission to organise an election and Cambodia's transition to a multi-party democracy. Photographs of the time show mobile teams outdoors in villages registering curious voters and later, lines of voters on squatted haunches waiting patiently in the hot sun. A particular memory I have is a UN soldier from Uruguay at a water pump, offering a bowl of water to a small boy.

Having left in 1993, after working for a year on the election,

I returned to Cambodia in 1999 to record some radio programmes. Backstage in the Chatomuk Theatre in Phnom Penh I met a handful of dancers, just finished performing the Ramayana, who had survived the Khmer Rouge. Since around ninety per cent of Cambodia's dancers died, this is no mean feat.

Surviving meant dissembling, shuffling, avoiding notice, unlearning gracefulness, dirtying fingernails to scupper telltale hands; it meant stifling the need, resisting the urge to perform. Lean limbs, sore after long sweltering hours working the fields, ached to dance. Some risked slipping away, quietly limbering up to remember the steps and to keep their bodies supple. Others practiced in their minds, mentally sorting through the dances without flexing a muscle, mutely expressing the desire, much too afraid to physically realise the moves. Many died of sickness and starvation, unable to withstand the callous treatment. Those that were killed, sensing no harm, had told the Khmer Rouge truthfully that they were dancers, or else frightened villagers had pointed them out. Sometimes the elegant way they held themselves or their smooth manicured hands betrayed them. The dancers that survived lied and said they were farmers or petty vendors who could not read or write. As an ancient tragic chorus, the dancers told their tale:

'The Khmer Rouge were very strict, they follow our activity all the time and want to know our origins, what we are and where we are and some we cannot hide and so ninety percent die. Ten percent survived, fifty out of five hundred professional dancers.'

'During the Pol Pot time we are not allowed to dance, if they know you are a dancer they will kill you.'

'During that time we are slaves and work in the rice fields like everyone else. I could not let anybody know that I was a dancer.'

'We hid our real profession. So many of my friends had the same problem. In the village some people who love our art and artists told me please hide your real profession, say you are from the poor classes and that you are the small seller of bread. The whole village helped me to hide and that is how I survived.'

Cambodia has one of the oldest artistic traditions in Asia and about twenty art forms, including dance, musical theatre, shadow puppets and circuses. Classical dance has been around since the eighth century, cultivated when the Angkor Empire of the Khmers spanned all of Laos and Southern Vietnam, much of Thailand and part of Burma and Malaysia. Under the rule of the Khmer kings, who governed until their defeat by Siam in the early fifteenth century, the illustrious temple city of Angkor Wat was built. The dancing apsaras, female figures carved on the famous temples, were heavenly dancers who entertained gods and kings. They were created during the Churning of the Ocean of Milk, or so the story goes. Gods and demons churned the ocean of milk for a thousand years trying to skim from it the elixir of immortality. With help from the God Vishnu and another thousand years of churning the magic liquid appeared, together with the seductive apsaras.

At Angkor thousands of engraved apsaras are flaunted on grey temple stone, dancing to the music of a carved orchestra, flying over impressions of rural living and hunting, enjoying the water festival, fluttering on an imprinted bed of lotuses. The apsaras' fleshy, earthly counterparts were the temple dancers who served the ample line of Khmer kings, moving with them when the court left Angkor, finally settling at Phnom Penh. Out of this tradition the royal ballet was nurtured, performing and teaching classical dance at the palace. The dancers went in as children and lived reclusively in the cocooned world of the court. Some became part of a royal harem until Sihanouk disbanded it when he took the crown. On a visit to Marseilles in 1906, when Cambodia was part of French Indo-China, the sculptor Auguste Rodin sketched the flowing, lissom movements of the troupe and murmured when they left that they had taken away the beauty of the world.

Away from the luxurious, silken court at Phnom Penh, and throughout the countryside, the traditional dance loved by the people and handed down from age to age celebrated rural life, the work of the fishermen and farmers.

The Khmer Rouge's attack on Cambodian culture was sustained and barbaric. Killing the artists, leaving musical instruments to rot in the rain, burning and tearing up books, emptying the national library in Phnom Penh to rub out the country's documented memory; all part of the plan to snuff out the old society and make ready the new beginning from year zero. The court was an icon of the corrupt, affluent ruling class and an enemy; the royal ballet as part of the court and as a body of artistes was another enemy. Lopping at the roots of Khmer culture and identity, the radical revolutionaries meant to pull down the essential social relationships in Cambodia; to usurp that intangible, shared heritage that binds people together, the tales, sagas, myths, names, cycles and rites that seep through each generation and that people simply know. Even the courteous Khmer greetings and ways of addressing each other, complemented by intricate rules of language, were forbidden. To submit to the new, people must disremember the old. Among illiterate people, artists are the community memories, recalling and passing on what cannot be written to keep tradition alive. This is why the Khmer Rouge killed them, to induce a national forgetfulness, and this is why the dancers took risks to remember, coveting what they knew as a fretful mother hoards what she can against the day she has to discharge a debt. The graceful embodiment of an old, treasured culture, the dancers were too awkward for the new.

The discharging of the debt came in 1979 when the Khmer Rouge command collapsed. Some of the survivors made radio announcements calling together any dancers who were left. When they met they shared what they remembered. Sometimes just one dancer recalled all the moves of a particular dance. Only one old dressmaker survived who could tailor the specially figured costumes that are sewn piece by piece onto the dancers before a performance. The troupe were in bad shape, weak and hungry after more than three years of starvation, but the survivors worked to mend their health and revitalise the dance.

They searched especially for the scattered children of the dancers who had died; some of the young ones had never even seen Khmer dance. Finally they gathered together and started training almost four hundred new pupils. Now, in the rainy season, when the South Western monsoon brings humidity and heavy rain, they learn. Then, in the cooler dry season, they perform. The dancers explained:

'We lacked every material thing but by the effort and sacrifice of the survivors who worked hard day and night we slowly started to rebuild.'

'We have influence from Buddhism; vengeance is not so good. We do not tolerate the man who made the killing field. First of all we must condemn him but vengeance will not help us rebuild our country.'

'After 1979, like the plant after the dry season, the rain comes down and the rain revives. Now we have many plants.'

The saplings can be seen practising in the mornings at the School of Fine Arts in Phnom Penh. Strolling along the avenue, with classrooms on both sides, is a lift to the spirit. In one of the rooms, young girls in coloured silk stand like cranes, extending slim, brown fingers into stylised hand movements, the teacher pushing fingers back with a bamboo stick until they almost touch the wrist. A delicate writhing of a finger can mean a bud, a flower or a fruit. A finger to the sky means today; arms crossed over the chest say very happy; a hand up means dead; a hand down is alive. In another room an ensemble of *pinpeat* musicians bang on drums, gongs and xylophones and twang on strings; in another a small troupe learns the fisherman's dance, a dance about love and courtship, created from the movement of fishermen casting their large nets on the Mekong River; a teacher beats out rhythm, *muey pii bey,* one two three. The morning is getting hot. Since the rooms have no electricity or fans, the doors are kept open to catch any breath of breeze, and musical notes stray out onto the avenue.

The Royal Palace, still intact despite the years of war and

once again home to King Norodom Sihanouk, glimmers beside the gentle breezes of the Mekong River as it flows through Phnom Penh. Close to the palace, at the more recently built Chatomuk theatre, old and young dancers perform together before a packed house of business people, office workers, government officials, students and foreigners. On stage are the traditional *pinpeat* instrumental ensemble, narrators and performers costumed as comics, giants and monkeys. In bare feet the dancers present the Khmer version of the Ramayana, the story which during the last two thousand years swept through India, Pakistan, Bangladesh, over the Himalayas to Nepal, across the Indian Ocean to Sri Lanka, down into Burma, Thailand, Laos, Cambodia, Vietnam and across the South China Sea to Indonesia. The able bodies, sewn into the glimmering lamé costumes so that they arch and flow smoothly, pick over the epic tale of gods and demons, of good and evil. Faces formal, impassive, powdered, masked, showing no emotion. As for the hands, they make the same exquisite gestures customised by the Angkor sculptors and hardly altered in over a thousand years.

* * * *

The revival of the dance was evident when I went back to Cambodia three years later for the local government elections. Beneath a honeyed-moon night sky in Kratie in the north-east of Cambodia – one of the earliest places taken by the Khmer Rouge – hundreds of people sit or squat in a field in rapt attention. A large stage dominates, festooned with the garish costumes worn by travelling players who continue the myths of humans, gods and messengers. The stillness of the balmy night and the brightness of the star-filled sky enhance the illusion of celestial beings and easy passage between heaven and earth. For local teachers, farmers and market sellers it is a magical break from the blackboard, the planting of rice or harvesting of tobacco or the selling of bicycle parts, reams of cloth or dried fish. They are away from the nightly torpor of the stilted houses built either from wood or bamboo, or the huts of the very poor made from weathered palm fronds plaited together. Barely furnished with mats, hammocks, pots, pictures of relatives, dead ancestors and of King Sihanouk and his wife, there is little to do when the sun dips away at about six o'clock, all year round.

Children skip and flit, delighted with the theatrical diversion. Old women chuckle, toothless and red-mouthed from chewing betel nut. There are a few ex-soldiers with dishevelled stumps for arms and legs, but not so many since the prosthetics unit opened at the local hospital. A woman with fine cheek bones, tolerated but avoided for her reproachful insensible mumblings in her nocturnal walks through the town, has wandered into the performance where she continues her low level, cross remonstration. She is said to be the widow of a rich man and to have lost everything when he died, but nobody knows her story for sure. On the fringes of the crowd vendors have improvised a little night market, quietly offering sugared confection, charcoaled bananas, sweet gluey rice wrapped in banana leaves, sticks of raw sugar cane, coconuts with crowns cleanly macheted to coax out the opaque milk, fruits such as papayas or pineapples pressed by attractively painted hand contraptions and added to palm sugar and crushed ice to make delicious juices.

Another evening in Kratie, at Wat Kapor pagoda, a wide white screen separates the animated audience from the puppeteers directing the silhouetted movements of the paper dolls. The frail shrouded figures look larger when projected and appear funnier, angrier or braver. Commune elections are coming soon. A sketch telling people how to vote and assuring them their vote is secret is included in the programme, the effort of a fledgling human rights group to counter the intimidation and petty chicanery of political parties reluctant to loosen their power over the community. This local power effects everyday life here much more than national politics, as the commune chief decides who gets work, or a market stall, or emergency rice when the floods come, as they do now to Kratie almost every year.

The black velvet sky leaves the pagoda in darkness, although the impression of its shape with its distinctive roof and columns can be inferred. Through the tall coconut trees, in a corner to the right, an amber glow secretes from a small wooden hut. The air around the hut carries the warm, earthy scent of burning incense. Half a dozen monks, orange robes draped over one shoulder, leaving the other bare, are sitting in scant candlelight, unperturbedly meditating or smoking, resurrected from the ashes of the Khmer Rouge regime and the Vietnamese occupation and once more an important part of village life.

The dancers, through memory and stubborn survival, have revived Cambodia's artistic tradition but they are now competing with other attractions. In the small provincial town of Kratie one street, unpaved, is given over to a strip of open-door bars where karaoke machines and televisions blink and screech out into the night. Some have four screens showing different noisy channels simultaneously to entranced, vacant looking patrons seated at rows of formica topped tables. The young beer girls working the tables are on commission and on these sultry nights measure how much flirtation, how many promise-laden hints are needed to sell enough to make a decent livelihood. Having lived through the Khmer Rouge, the dancers wonder if they can withstand the threat of cultural globalisation, the sky messengers of westernised television, now seen in every village, plying clothes, habits and attitudes. Can they survive the dullness of pretty boy bands with mimed spins and swivels or the unseemly mores of the karaoke bars, because what can ever be seemly about ill-using poor, young, naïve girls?

Still the artistes believe in Cambodia and Khmer culture. As the country grapples with its divisive past the dancers believe that they have a role in helping to restore Cambodia's shattered national identity. The fractious world of Cambodian politics is still sour and factionalised. The artists bring to their society the reminder of what is shared, valued and agreed rather than what is discordant and bitter.

'The temple dancers we believed were messengers to us from the sky. The dance was to satisfy the God and for the well being of the country. If the country was in starvation or war, the dance was to make the situation better. The dancer is a peace messenger right now. Culture is a bridge to understand each other, to rehabilitate and reconcile our nation. Dance or culture is the national soul and identity of each country. The role of the artist is to repair the broken spirit.'

A short time later, just as their agile ancestors had in the days of French Indo-Chine, the Khmer troupe danced in Paris. Like a moving river of sparkling gems they took centre stage and were resplendent at the palace of Versailles.

Sokha

2002

The stories of those who survived the Khmer Rouge slip out quietly in unlikely moments, often as a hint to be probed. With Sokha, an interpreter that I worked with, it was the matter of fact way that he said, 'I don't eat beef'. We were in Snuol, in the eastern part of Cambodia, near the border with Vietnam. Snuol is thick with jungle and rubber plantations and famous for pepper. The district had a reputation for lawlessness but this has improved since a government scheme traded promises of local development for the handing over of weapons. We had sat down at a local eating stall on Snuol's one wide street, dry dusty red because of the heat and the soil found in the region, and were having a couple of cold beers while deciding what to eat. Occasionally a big-wheeled ox cart rumbled by, laden with sacks of rice for market or chunks of timber for building, the spokes spewing sporadic spools of crimson dust in their wake. The 'menu' was the display of fresh vegetables, meat and fish that was beside the large wok resting on the charcoal burner. 'Chicken and pork *qat panhaa*, no problem,' said Sokha, 'but I do not eat beef since the Khmer Rouge times'.

April 1975, when the Khmer Rouge emptied Phnom Penh, is indelibly pressed into Sokha's memory. He is thirteen years old, one of five children. His father is a clerk in a government ministry. Khmer Rouge cadres arrive at the house and tell his mother to leave, that the US are going to bomb the city. His mother packs only food and pots and pans and they set out to join the hundreds of thousands of others leaving the capital.

April is the cruellest month, the hottest time of the year for a journey. As they walk through the streets they see the burnt out houses, the ransacked shops, the overturned tables in the small cafes. The exodus shuffles slowly in the heat, carrying bundles and makeshift biers with the infirm; pushing motorcars, handcarts and loaded cyclos – the three-wheeled hooded cycles traditionally used in Phnom Penh for transport. After a few days the mass of migrants are told to go to their place of birth. For Sokha's parents this is Takeo, a district south-west of Phnom Penh where they still have relatives.

With so many on the move the trek takes weeks. Sokha remembers people being sick and giving up and dead bodies along the road. People are frightened, confused and distressed. One rich Chinese man, Sokha says he will never forget him, carries a sack of money. It is all he has taken from his house, and he stands on the roadside crying and offering all his riel for some rice. The money is worthless since the Khmer Rouge is abandoning currency for a barter system, part of the plan to return the country to a simple agrarian society. The taciturn soldiers in black carrying AK-47 guns and drinking cola confiscate watches, cameras, radios and tape-recorders.

Outside Phnom Penh the countryside is wasted from the war. Huge craters made by the bombing from the air leave deep impressions in the earth; the sugar palms that fringe the paddy fields are destroyed. The displaced Khmer scuffle on, moving through phantom villages, stumbling in cracked earth. Sokha's mother does her best to keep the children calm and over night-fires cooks the food she has brought.

When they arrive in Takeo the family is broken up. Sokha's parents are sent to one camp with the two youngest children. He and his brother and sister are sent to another. They work during the day, their clothes now in tatters, weeding and watering the rice paddies; their stomachs are always empty. When darkness falls they go to school but the endless hours of criticism and propaganda stretch on until after midnight. Only a few hours slumber and they are up again in the cool dawn, still hungry and sometimes so tired Sokha can hardly walk. The children, pure and untainted by the past, are the hope for the revolution. They are educated to be good, unthinking comrades. Sokha is thirteen years old and is told night after night, like a bad bedtime story, that individuality, play, friendship and feelings are wrong. He must relinquish the old relics of intimacy. The only joy is the revolution, the only loyalty to the Angka – the organisation. Sokha feels lonely and friendless and he misses his mother terribly. He sees her only on the few occasions a year when the Khmer Rouge allow families to visit each other. He hears news that his father has been killed; that is all he hears, he has no idea how or why.

At fifteen Sokha has another job taking care of the oxen, now common property and needed for ploughing the fields, for transport, for meat and for manure. According to the radio, the breeding of oxen and buffalo is very important; as an aid to agriculture, to produce strong animals that can pull the plough and the harrow.

Like the people, the oxen are hungry and overworked, pulling plough to granulate the land until they die from exhaustion. Sokha feeds them what he can and carefully washes them down with sheaves of grass. He has become especially fond of one pair of oxen and he strokes them and whispers to them when no one is around; he pours his young love into them. One morning he wakes to find that one of the pair has died and he is upset. To his surprise he discovers that the surviving ox is bereft. Sokha swears that the ox moaned for one week, heaving a humped lament for her lost partner, and when he checked on her there were tears wetting her flaccid cheeks. The tears, he says, touched him so tenderly and moved him so deeply; that the oxen should have such feelings for each other, even more than humans, and that she could express it with such abandon without having to hide it away.

Seated at the stall in Snuol twenty-five years later Sokha, now a father of two little girls, half-smiles. 'During the Khmer Rouge time', he says, 'you ate anything you could find'.

Afterwards, when he had a choice, he stopped eating beef. As a tribute: with an ox's grief he kindled his humanity.

Foot Soldiers of the Khmer Rouge

1999

After meeting the dancers, I visited a group of old demobilised Khmer Rouge soldiers living in the countryside outside Phnom Penh. These were the grunts, the foot soldiers of Division 305 to be exact, not the ideological thinkers and leaders of the notorious Khmer Rouge. The sun was setting, throwing a warm light on the wooden pagoda. With the surrounding mango trees the scene looked almost pastoral. The group of old men with shaved heads coming and going added to the air of harmless domesticity. They were dressed in the traditional loose-fitting black trousers and white shirts that old people in Cambodia who live around pagodas wear. The red and white check kramar was worn easily around their necks, as it had been for centuries by Cambodian peasants. The Khmer Rouge leadership wore it when they promulgated their agrarian revolution and, theoretically at any rate, glorified the peasant. As information about the atrocities came to light it became the macabre symbol of a confused, crazed, paranoid, inhumane regime.

The raggle taggle bunch of old men from Division 305 was based in Kompong Speu, sixty kilometres outside Phnom Penh. Illiterate, uneducated peasant farmers, perhaps idealistic, they had joined the Khmer Rouge in the 1970s as young men, believing, they said, that they were fighting for freedom. They obeyed orders from the commander and instructions that came from Brother Number One, Pol Pot. They could not move around as they wanted, but were ordered from province to province, to places like Kompong Thom and Siem Reap. When the Khmer Rouge took charge of the country they worked building canals in the soldiers' group. To increase the country's rice yields the Khmer Rouge set as a priority the control of water from the grand Mekong River and the great freshwater lake the Tonle Sap. Everybody laboured on the canals and dams. In this they looked back to the glory days of the Angkor Empire when the people were mobilised to create an elaborate water system made up of huge reservoirs linked to a network of canals, dykes and moats. It was later destroyed by foreign invasion. Even the orange-robed monks dripped sweat on the shadeless land, their bodies worn out hauling and digging to build the dams; the temple pagodas were destroyed or profaned and the statues of Buddha smashed. The pagoda was part of the rhythm of Cambodian village life; the cultural and social centre where children were educated and festivals celebrated. Now the monks were bloodsuckers, imperialists and oppressors: the only wise man was the man who knew how to grow rice.

When Division 305 was routed in 1979 the soldiers receded into the jungle, hidden by the dark, lush foliage, crouching through the thick brown undergrowth to fight the Vietnamese troops of occupation. The Kompong Speu landscape is flat but has a mountain with a water source. They hid and lived in the mountain, as it was difficult for the government troops to go there.

The fighting was seasonal. In the dry season, armed with weapons from China, they made military raids on the government soldiers and then waited for the counter-attack. The routine of attack, withdrawal, counter-attack became predictable. In the wet season they got through the long days of monotony and boredom, sinewy limbs dangling from the green worn hammocks strung up between the trees, like sagged shadow puppets resting between shows. Fingers bent around triggers in the dry season now lazily pulled on a cigarette. Card games were played but with only half a heart; the players afraid of using up the luck needed to gyp death in the next battle. Occasionally they slipped away for furtive visits with their families who lived in town or in the neighbouring province. The message that they were coming was transmitted secretly so that no one would know that the women were Khmer Rouge wives. Some never saw their wives in all those years. Like a feudal band they followed the commander and depended on him for food, although there was never enough. Sometimes they found bamboo shoots, leaves and roots or hunted an animal that they came across in the forest. The wounded suffered particularly and were an added burden for the other soldiers because they had to be carried to the Khmer Rouge clinic in Pursat, many kilometres away, for treatment. In some Khmer Rouge areas, deep in the jungle, they were left alone with their families and survived for years on subsistence farming; the young reared there knew no different and were uneducated and unskilled for anything else.

The winds of peace rustled the leaves of the forest in 1991 and the foot soldiers nearly left after the leaders signed up to a peace agreement in Paris. During the Cold War each side in the Cambodian civil war had international backers. With the end of the Cold War the backers wanted Cambodia off their agenda and put pressure on the factions to reach agreement. In the largest and most ambitious undertaking yet the United Nations came, with battalions of soldiers and civilians from Africa, Asia, Europe and the Americas, to disarm all the factions and to organise elections. Initially the Khmer Rouge command issued instructions to the units to prepare to demobilise troops, but as mistrust between the factions grew they withdrew their co-operation. Instructions were given to the foot soldiers to suspend demobilisations, attack villages, cut communications routes, demolish bridges and prevent the UN entering their zones of control.

Division 305 had minor successes, at one point even boldly firing at the UN helicopter that hovered over their area in Kompong Speu. The month before the elections they were ordered to disrupt the arrangements. Small teams, armed with light weapons, carried out clandestine activities around the villages where polling stations were planned so that election officials would be afraid and would leave. Villagers noticed new unrecognised faces at this time as they lurked in from the forest. A week before the elections a new directive ordered all units to stop the attacks and soldiers were instructed to wait and see if the UN could ensure the elections were free and fair. Afterwards the guerrillas were ordered to stay in the jungle hideouts while their leaders parleyed for a place in the new government, but the talks in Phnom Penh bore no fruit and the Khmer Rouge held on in the forest.

Some of the soldiers deserted because morale was low; they were hungry, tired of fighting and wanted to go home. The government came up with a scheme to help defectors join the new national army or enter civilian life, but when the deserters returned to their villages they risked retribution from the Khmer Rouge still active in the area, and might even be executed. Sometimes they rejoined their comrades because they could not make a living outside.

The first dry season arrived and the government troops started a military campaign against them, which ended in disaster. The fresh hostilities meant the planting of more landmines, the loss of human life and serious injuries; towns and villages were bombarded and set on fire, crops pillaged or ruined, reconstructed roads, bridges and railways were wiped out. The Khmer Rouge was outlawed and returned to the seasonal fighting until negotiations began again to bring them in from the forest.

* * * *

In the late afternoon light, Division 305 looked neither hardy nor fierce, just old, weary, skin and bones. Their eyes, they complain, are no longer any good. While the leaders bargained for an amnesty in the capital, the foot soldiers and their families were granted a small amount of land for clearance, although the only tools they got were hoes, and they were given no livestock. The area had landmines, but since they had laid them, they say, they knew where to find them; the only victims so far were unwitting animals. The veterans now plant trees, which they proudly pointed at, and have started a plantation of sugar cane, which was already showing off its tall leaved stalks. They eke out a frugal livelihood as rice farmers, lacking resources to develop the land any further, but they have begun planting cashew and plan to grow banana and coconut trees. Wild forest pigs were a nuisance and sometimes devoured the harvest. Wells were needed for water and they were seeking assistance from non-government organisations; improved irrigation would help them produce rice in the dry season.

Some of the men make a living from woodcutting, the wood transported by oxcart, or from selling charcoal. Travelling to market means ten kilometres on a bad road, which deteriorates even further during the heavy rains. In a couple of places deep crossings of dry creeks make the road impassable in the wet season and bridges are needed. The houses they have built are simple and made from local thatch and woven leaves. They fend off the mosquitoes the best they can because they have no medicine to treat the scourge of malaria. The government built a school but the teachers receive no regular pay and depend on donations from their pupils.

Hanging around the yellow walled building and waiting to go to a writing class were young demobilised Khmer Rouge soldiers. They wore the fresh uniforms of the newly formed national army, an attempt to integrate the soldiers of the four civil war factions and foster loyalty to the state. The young men were a marked contrast to their bedraggled older relatives and were harbingers of a more hopeful future. There is little sign in the village of the millions of US dollars that the Khmer Rouge leadership earned extracting hardwood and gems from areas under their control, although the commander has a white saloon car, wears gold jewellery and lives in a nice wooden house with an aluminium roof and electricity. He still holds sway here.

His men defected because their commander, in his forties and with a pleasant smile, decided it was time to leave the forest and join the government forces. The current negotiations in Phnom Penh are uneasy and Khmer Rouge leaders Khieu Samphan and Ieng Sary, fresh from their stronghold in Pailin, say that if they are not given an amnesty they will go back to fighting. The men from Division 305 laugh and say that Ieng Sary can go and fight by himself. They are getting old and do not have the strength or the stomach for it anymore. As young men, they say, they believed the politicians' lies, not understanding that they just wanted power, but they know that now. As old men they had come to realise that for nearly thirty years, the years for loving, fathering, nesting, gathering, they were used, pawns in a game for power and riches which benefited others and which had little to do with freedom.

The old foot soldiers had built a small wooden pagoda, without any hint of irony. The pagoda, they say, is for when people marry or die, for celebrating the Khmer New Year, and for practising Buddhism. Next-door is a small house for the monks, and saffron robes hang across the wooden veranda. In old age, Division 305 had emerged from the shadows and wanted to live in peace in the gentle, waning, forgiving light surrounding the small pagoda. The day was shutting down the way it does in tropical countries, as a shopkeeper pulls down the blinds, business-like, no fuss, a silent signal that the work of the day is over. It was the end of the day, the end of their lives and the end of the Khmer Rouge.

Watermelon Monk

1992

I have a copy of a photograph that I took of a monk on the top step of the pagoda at Ksach Andett, Cambodia as he pours a basin of water over a younger laughing monk who is there bathing. It resembles the Christian ritual of baptism. The photo is one of several that were taken of the Buddhist community at the monk's request and he has the originals. During the 1993 election I lived and worked in the pretty district of Chhlong in north-east Cambodia. The district wound its way around the Mekong River, the magnificent waterway that begins on the Tibetan Plateau and flows on for over four thousand kilometres through China, forming the border between Burma and Laos and part of the border between Laos and Thailand. It continues on down through Cambodia and into Vietnam where it spills into the South China Sea. Around sixty million people depend on the river's richness for their survival and livelihood.

Since the dirt roads in Chhlong were impassable, myself and my Norwegian colleague travelled by boat. Setting out at early light we never entirely knew how the day would unfold. Working to prepare the district for an election meant that much of our day was spent liasing with the community, local politicians, administrators, police and military and with the pagoda monks. One morning we headed downstream towards the commune of Ksach Andett. From the water the bamboo huts appeared so close to the river's edge that they might tumble in at the gentlest of pushes. Arriving at the pagoda, delightfully situated along the slow bend of the river, young monks produced what seemed an ordinary watermelon, large, green, plump and very inviting in the drowsy heat. With a sharp knife the elder orange-robed monk cleaved it down the middle revealing not the usual luscious pinkish inside but a cheerful yellow centre. It was mouth-watering and tasted sweet and refreshing. The melon, the surrounds, and the scenery seduced us into an easy feeling of well-being. The monk looked about eighty years old and had lived a varied, experienced life. He had been married and raised six children; when they had grown up he decided to become a Buddhist monk. He was shrewd and intelligent and although cloistered in the pagoda he knew what went on in the local villages.

We had come to talk to him about the election. The pagodas were neutral venues and the hope was that the monks would allow the UN to use them as sites for registering the population and then later as polling stations. The monk at Ksach Andett was very positive about the election and happy to help. The pagoda could be used and he would ring the bell for summoning the people on the first morning of registration. Agreement reached, we finished the watermelon. With the generous hospitality out of the way, and genuine co-operation assured, the monk very gently began the understated subtext of negotiating a possible quid pro quo. He asked us to follow him into the monks' sleeping quarters and pointed to a bed which had blankets piled high on top of it. It was his bed and the problem, he told us, was that he needed something to store the blankets in so that he could sleep in the bed. With an engaging smile he asked if the UN could help. We said that the materials for the registration had come in large aluminium trunks, and that afterwards we could maybe give him a couple to meet his storage requirements.

He gave a slight nod that seemed to indicate that he was satisfied, said farewell and that he looked forward to seeing us again when registration began.

At Ksach Andett the watermelon monk rang the bell as promised and enjoyed watching the lines of people form for registration. Registration sites were set up in the village pagodas, the monks being among the first to register and effectively giving their imprimatur to the process.

At one point during the registration Electoral staff working at the Ksach Andett pagoda began experiencing difficulties. They were sleeping at the pagoda and heard shooting outside, disturbing the hush of night. Local police said that in the hours of darkness the Khmer Rouge came in from the forest, scattering and stealing the scrawny chickens from the villagers.

We visited the watermelon monk the next morning. He took another watermelon, sliced it in half with his knife, again the same yellow inside and we all had a piece. We then told him what the local police had claimed.

'The information from the local police,' he said, 'was nonsense'. The Khmer Rouge had come nowhere near the area. The shooting came from the local military who were robbing the people. They used the Khmer Rouge as an excuse, either as cover for their own criminal activity or to keep fear alive in the population, a reminder that they were the only army equipped to deal with the notorious guerrillas. It was a clever election ploy, given that the other main political parties were tainted during the civil war by their involvement in a coalition that had included the Khmer Rouge. The monk then asked how the registration was going and when it would be finished so that we could bring the promised trunks. We assured him that we had not forgotten.

Registering the population went on for several weeks. Because of the years of war, the Khmer registrars were effectively devising an electoral roll from scratch. The lack of documentation and high rate of illiteracy meant that the procedure was slow and time-consuming. Besides the registration sites in the village pagodas, mobile teams of registrars facilitated those who lived in remoter areas or who were unable to travel. It was an enjoyable time and there was lots of good-humoured banter as Cambodians lined up to have their photograph taken, for many it was their first time to see themselves shrunken into a small black and white square. Many of the pictures on the registration cards had a slightly surprised look, captured as the camera flash went off. The other novelty was the thumb printing of those who could not sign their name. This was considered such diversion that we later discovered some people who could read and write pretended otherwise so that they could be thumb-printed instead. (This shattered the confidence of one UN official in Phnom Penh who had hoped to devise literacy statistics based on registration information). Some struggled to remember the year of their birth and the registrars became adept at converting the year of the rat, or the rabbit, or the tiger into the Gregorian calendar.

A couple of weeks after the end of registration we again took the wooden boat back down the Mekong to Ksach Andett, hauling two of the shiny silver cases up the riverbank like Medieval princes from a distant land bearing gifts for a royal personage. The trunks gleamed in the sunshine and as the monk cut open a watermelon, he eyed his new possessions. While his young disciples ceremoniously carried them into his bedroom, the monk, with the same winning smile, invited us to walk alongside the bank of the Mekong with him. As we did he explained that during the rainy season, when the broad brown ribbon of water rose, brimming over its banks, the pagoda flooded. Pointing across the river he asked if the UN could build a dam to save this yearly hardship. We apologised and explained that providing a dam was completely outside our ability and resources and was not a gift we could bestow.

He smiled; we smiled back, thanked him for the watermelon and clambered down to our chuntering boat. As we chugged up the Mekong, looking back at the riverbank the silhouetted figure of the monk had turned and was heading back to contemplative repose.

The Vote

1993

While the registration of voters had gone relatively smoothly, by election time the security situation in Cambodia was extremely tense. The Khmer Rouge had decided to boycott the election and there were fears that they might attack polling stations. In spite of this threat almost ninety percent of the population turned out to vote.

It was nearing the end of the day in a polling station in Chhlong when a young woman came in. It is her first time to vote and having dropped her ballot paper into the box, she makes her way over to the presiding officer.

'My grandmother wants me to vote for her, to cast her vote for the King.'

The presiding officer explains that it is not possible; her grandmother must be there in person.

'If she comes to the polling station you can help her mark the ballot paper.'

The young voter persists.

'She can't come. We live three kilometres away. My grandmother is very old, blind and can hardly move. She has rarely left her bed for many years. She wants Sihanouk's party to win and rule Cambodia.'

The polling officials murmur among themselves, keenly watched by the agents of the political parties present to observe that the elections are conducted properly. Still, everyone is curious about the elderly woman who has survived Cambodia's brutal history and wants to vote in the country's first multi-party elections since the Paris Peace Agreement; even the agents from the opposition parties show concerned interest.

The granddaughter pleads: 'She's not able to come and she's waited so long for today. She will be very disappointed.'

The election officers mutter searching for a solution.

'We're not supposed to, but if we send the UN vehicle to pick her up and bring her here can she come?'

The young woman shakes her head sadly and walks away down the dusty track wheeling her bicycle. The staff shrug, 'what could we do?' The UN police and military providing security for the station agree that it is unfortunate but nothing can be done.

Around the faded yellow walls of the building, normally a school, are brightly coloured posters that set out the voting procedure and remind people that the ballot is secret. The plain desks in the room itself are laid out as in the poster, with each election official scrupulously in place, ensuring that the voters go through every part of the process in an efficient circular flow.

The polling day winds down; only an occasional voter dwindles in. A scrawny mongrel dog with moulting coat wanders in from the wilting heat, casts a disinterested look, and limps out again. A lumpen lizard lazily slithers across the election poster's line of smiling voters. Seated behind his neatly arranged table, the presiding officer checks the time, determined to close on the exact hour according to the regulations. The party agents on the narrow wooden benches behind the polling officials also check the time. One idly caresses a single loose dark hair growing from a mole on his chin. The clerk in charge of the register yawns widely and stretches. The woman in charge of the ink covers her mouth with a slim, limpid hand and with the other uses a toothpick to winkle out the small pieces of rice lodged there since her last meal. In between voters there is leisurely chitchat.

Then on the horizon, through the shimmering heat haze, a young woman is seen frantically cycling. As she draws near, her two legs jerk out on to the ground to help the brakes stop the bike. Panting hard she forces out the words:

'She'll come,' she says, 'if the UN takes her, she'll come'.

Two of the UN police from Colombia grin broadly, hop into the pick-up truck with the granddaughter and take off down the scorched surface as if responding to an emergency. There is a triumphant laugh from everyone. Suddenly the torpid afternoon has found energy. A little while later they return. The policemen from Colombia reverently open the truck door and, as if she were their own mother, gently ease the old, stooped blind woman onto the ground and take her into the polling station. The presiding officer attends to her personally and outlines the process. Her grainy finger is dipped in ink to ensure that she will only vote once. He explains that he is handing her a ballot paper.

'King Sihanouk,' she hoarsely whispers at him.

The granddaughter carefully takes her behind the cardboard screen, marks the paper and hands it back so that her grandmother can have the satisfaction of placing the vote in the ballot box herself. As they emerge from behind the partition the old woman's unseeing eyes and toothless smile radiate contentment. Her granddaughter is close to shiny tears. Leaning her bony frame on the younger woman, the elderly voter is led over to the ballot box where her granddaughter takes her shaky, wrinkled hand with the marked paper and directs it into the narrow slit. As it drops she raises her puckered face and says again 'King Sihanouk' then makes her way out of the polling station. Gingerly the old woman is helped back into the truck, which drives slowly away in deference to her age and condition.

The granddaughter picks up her bike and says: 'That was her first time out of bed for years and that was her first time ever in a motor vehicle' and speeds off after the truck.

The General in His Departure

1993

The General was departing from the provincial town and hurrying back to Phnom Penh. The guard of soldiers stood erect in immaculate uniforms, right hands stiffened just beneath their forelocks in the salute position. The General had taken time away from the capital to come and visit his peacekeeping troops in the field but his time was precious. His determined face and brisk gait as he strode through the double row of impassive men said so. His job – boosting the morale of the rank and file – was done. All that remained for his commanding presence to do was to board the waiting helicopter. We civilians, standing nearby in an easy slouch, watched the scene of exemplary discipline unfold.

As the whirring noise of the white helicopter, with the letters UN painted in black, started up, the General stepped resolutely into the metallic machine. Familiar enough now with the reddish brown cloud of dust and typhoon-like wind that a helicopter throws up in this dry terrain, we pushed back covering faces in scarves and holding on to baseball hats; all except the saluting men. The helicopter blades turned and the transporter took off from the dusty ground, generating a shower of soil filings as it rose into the air. Down below, the steadfast soldiers held firm, ending up powdered from head to toe in particles of the ruddy earth. Whether or not the General noticed such unflinching loyalty is hard to know. The dusty men had kept ranks, the General in his departure leaving behind an obedient line of terracotta warriors.

Bangladesh

After the Flood

1999

The women are rebuilding their houses after the flood. Bangladesh is home to one hundred and twenty million people who daily get through lives of hard work and poverty in a territory about twice the size of Ireland. The country is an expanse of lowland. Two major river systems, the Ganges and the Brahmaputra with the lesser Meghna River flow through Bangladesh and form the largest delta in the world. Carrying with them snowmelt from the Himalayas, the rivers, added to the monsoon rainfall, make the flat country prone to floods. Bangladeshis are used to this seasonal challenge and have very capable methods of coping. The floods in 1998, however, lasted too long and these resourceful people were put to the pin of their collar.

When I visited, the floods had subsided and rehabilitation was underway. The torrential downpour had lasted two full moons and a crescent and left devastation. When the rains came the rice was just ready and the harvest was washed away; with everything under water Bangladesh seemed afloat. Beneath the blanket of wetness, petitioners perched on the roof of the submerged mosques and prayed for merciful relief from the inclement weather.

The women are an unlikely construction crew, bare-footed and dressed in saris of green and pink and indigo with threaded borders. Pearls of perspiration from the work and heat edge their faces; the day gives no brush of wind for respite. Broad smiles unveil wide gaps in their teeth as they stand on the curved bank. Raising smooth, slender arms, they bring them down to hack at combs of packed earth that look like sodden turf; a thud as slabs of clay are tossed into baskets. Now and then the builders throw a good-natured yell at each other.

The emergency over, the water subsided so all that is left is a landscape of soggy sponge, it is time to rebuild. Under the immense blue pristine sky their muddied feet squish the puddled narrow track the riverbank. Spattered robes swish as they carry the baskets brimming with the raw material to make the mud floors for the new houses, the old ones having being swept away by the deluge. In the rain-washed sunshine they have thirty-one houses and a school to erect. Each dwelling will have an earthen floor, bamboo walls and a tin roof. It is hot, hard, backbreaking work and going on throughout the countryside. As the women toil, they keep an eye on the young children they have brought to the site, who revel in delight and self-daubed muck. During rest-time some of the labourers playfully shape the moist clay into small round bowls and soft dolls, and leave them to bake in the sizzling sun. Others bend over, and mindful of the evening meal, sift slowly through the brown sludge with their fingers, searching the silt for sunken fish.

In the distance the men are throwing ball, checking that the cricket field is alright.

A Bank of One's Own

1999

The women sat side-by-side on the wooden benches outside the bank and waited. Their coloured dress, bright against the glare of the sun, sweetened the surroundings; a few of the women wore the all-black chador of their Muslim faith. They had come to make short financial transactions; small sums perhaps, but they opened a door to some small measure of independence. The modest building was a bank, the waiting clientele poor rural women. All of the branch's two thousand one hundred and seventy customers were women and, more unusually, were the owners of the bank.

Just beyond the bank were planted paddy fields. Around the corner the clamorous market sold local produce and attractively painted rickshaws transported people through the town. Inside the unassuming building was a hive of activity as it was the day for giving out loans. Officials worked a manual system with dexterity, flicking through cards, peeling off and counting out banknotes.

This was a local, rural branch of the Grameen Bank, established by economist Muhammad Yunus expressly to give loans to the millions of poor throughout Bangladesh. His idea was revolutionary and kicked against conventional wisdom: that the poor were a bad risk, that they had neither the wherewithal, skill, or education to handle finances, and that they simply could not be trusted with money. When Professor Yunus established the Grameen Bank he proved traditional institutions wrong and set up a system of micro-banking that spread beyond the Bay of Bengal to other countries with impoverished communities.

As they waited in the bright sunlight, the women spoke openly and with pride about how they had turned their borrowings into tiny plots of land, milch cows, poultry or sewing machines to generate income for better food, housing, furnishings, clothing, medicines or schooling for their children. One had used the money to buy paddy, which she crushed and sold as rice at market. Another had used the loan to buy rice and pulses, which she sold from home, and had given money to her husband to go to Saudi Arabia to work in construction. With a nod to modern times some had started mobile phone enterprises. Several had been with the bank for years and over time had taken and paid back a number of loans. They all felt that their lives had substantially improved by being given money and access to credit.

The beginnings of the Grameen Bank go back almost thirty years when Professor Yunus was teaching economics at the University of Chittagong in Bangladesh. Struck by the fact that the textbooks had little relevance to the realities of the people actually living in Bangladesh, he began investigating conditions in the villages. He selected a village close to the university campus, the village of Jobra. There he met Sufia Begum, squatting on the dirt floor of a run down house and plaiting strands of bamboo cane to make a stool. When he spoke to her he discovered that to buy the bamboo she had to take money from a middleman and then sell the stool back to him at the end of the day for very little profit. With this arrangement she earned fifty paisa, or two cents, for her day's work. The trader paid Sufia a price that covered the materials and just a little more so that she could stay alive but had to continue borrowing from him. The alternative was to get the cash from a moneylender at an exorbitant interest rate. The professor realised that what Sufia needed was credit so she could sell her stools at market and make a better profit.

Professor Yunus got one of his students to make a list of the poor in Jobra who were borrowing under these disadvantageous conditions. The list showed that forty-two families had borrowed eight hundred and fifty-six thaka – twenty-seven US dollars. The idea that forty-two families lived in misery, unable to break out of the cycle of poverty for the sake of twenty-seven dollars, shocked him. They were able-bodied, hard-working and skilled at what they did but no financial institution would give them a loan. He lent them twenty-seven dollars, freeing them up to sell their products on the open market for a better price. They were to pay him back when they had earned enough from their sales; as soon as they got on their feet the borrowers settled up with him.

The village of Jobra and Sufia Begum taught him that what the poor need is access to very small amounts of working capital. He also learnt that poor people have myriad skills, especially women in poor households and he realised that they often do not want to depend on charity or begging; they simply want to earn a living from their work and live with dignity. Since they have nothing to offer as collateral they have no access to capital to create their own jobs and are vulnerable to exploitation by employers and moneylenders. They work hard creating wealth for the benefit of others but remain destitute. Professor Yunus discovered that extending credit facilities to dispossessed men and women could create opportunities for self-employment that would help them break out of the trap of poverty, debt and exploitation.

The professor began developing the credit experiment and spreading it out to other areas in Bangladesh. In 1983 the project became a bank, the Grameen Bank (Grameen in Bangla means 'of the village'), essentially a rural credit delivery system targeted at the poor.

From the beginning the rules were different at Grameen. The new bank reversed conservative banking practice by providing credit to the destitute of rural Bangladesh without collateral. The bank focuses strongly on women – they are around ninety-four percent of its customers.

When a person is identified as a potential member she has

to fulfil basic eligibility criteria to prove that she is very poor. Two measures are applied: the first is land ownership. Anyone who owns more than a half an acre of land is not entitled to a loan; anyone who owns a quarter of an acre is more suitable than someone who owns half an acre. A person who does not own any land is the most eligible. The second measure is income. Anyone whose income is more than what they would earn from owning one acre of land is disqualified.

Grameen does not tell the borrower where she should invest but the whole group appraises the loan proposal. So if a woman decides to buy a Singer sewing machine to make clothes and sell them in the market, the other members may say 'You have never stitched a garment in your life, what would you do with a sewing machine? Why don't you keep a milch cow instead and you can sell the milk and earn a regular income?' The enterprises that have been successfully financed range across the usual daily requirements and activities in Bangladesh: paddy husking; bamboo works; puffed rice making; cane works; fishing net making; weaving; sugarcane cultivation; betel-leaf cultivation; goat and poultry raising; duck purchase; buffalo raising; rickshaws; barbers; bicycle purchases; buffalo carts; timber; second-hand clothes; peanuts; bangles; biri cigarettes; tea stalls.

The bank's success depends on borrowers paying back at the agreed times. Borrowers have shares and own ninety-three percent of the bank; the shareholder-borrowers elect board directors from among themselves and the board governs the bank. Peer pressure and support ensures repayment most of the time. Grameen believes in a financial system that can gradually become self-reliant and charges customers realistic interest rates.

The reason that most of the bank's 2.4 million customers are women is that Grameen's mandate to lend to the poorest first, nets many women, since they are the most marginalised group among the destitute. The bank has found that changing a woman's economic situation makes more impact on the family. When extra income comes into the household through the woman, children's diet, family health, nutrition and housing improve. Men spend more of their income on themselves than women do. The bank also found that women are a better credit-risk than men and more responsible managers of slender means.

Reaching the women of Bangladesh was initially difficult for Grameen in a society where many women are hidden away in the house and are only allowed contact with males who are relatives. Traditionally Bangladeshi girls have been reared to keep house and have a family; marriages are arranged and take place at a young age. Education has not been a priority; the female literacy rate is less than thirty percent. The Grameen Bank's initial meetings were often conducted using a go-between or from behind curtains or bamboo partitions so that the women would not have to show their faces. Confidence and trust were slowly nurtured. Some of the women were shy or frightened at the idea of money, usually handled by their husbands, and they did not want to get into trouble. They had grown up hearing that they were a financial burden on their families who had to find a dowry to marry them off. Sometimes in marriage they were targets for the frustration of husbands who could abuse or divorce them with ease. Having the temerity to opt for a loan against all the binds of poverty, tradition, and social convention was an act of courage for these Bangladeshi women.

For the women in Bangladesh, having money, 'a bank of one's own', has given them more freedom. Without money a woman is constrained the minute she steps outside her door as to how far she can go and for how long, especially if she cannot read or write. She may visit a friend's home, but even arranging to meet at a stall or a coffee shop requires money. A fine invisible leash always leads her home. To last any time in the public sphere you need currency. The understanding that the woman has no option but to return home affects the domestic power dynamic and can leave her insecure and vulnerable. Creating a public world that needs money, and then prohibiting or limiting women's access to it, perpetuates a form of servitude. From the initial strand of that invisible leash a web spins out, delicate as gossamer. If a woman has no need to negotiate the public world then there is no need to educate her. It psychologically sends the message to women that the world outside the home is no place for them; they have no function there.

Credit loosened this leash and gave women money and the confidence to step into the fresh air of the public space. Going to the bank and beginning a small business brought women out from the private domestic world, and it increased their self-esteem and influence at home and in the locale. Since they earned money they had more say in how it should be spent. This changed their relationships within the extended family. They were now given a modicum more respect; when they spoke during family discussions they were listened to.

Loosening the leash may be the beginning, but shifting power relationships can be complex. Men may enjoy the material improvement in their family lives but in some cases women have met with aggressive attitudes from male relatives who see traditional roles, their reputation and authority threatened. While the loans were intended to help women earn income, some women were pressurised into borrowing money on behalf of husbands or male relatives and left with the burden of meeting the repayments.

The empowering nature of credit was not lost on embedded patriarchs. The Grameen Bank met with opposition from husbands, religious leaders, moneylenders and some government officials. Villagers have been told that Grameen will convert them to Christianity, steal their money, traffic them to slave traders and is part of a Western conspiracy to re-colonise Bangladesh. Palestinian women who sold their goods at the souk in Gaza told me on a visit there that when they joined a credit scheme they were denounced from the Mosque and accused of being in breach of the *Koran*, which forbids usury. The women wondered how the numerous Arab banks, seen on high streets from Gaza to London, observed the Book's holy teachings. These banks manage by a lending methodology that circumvents any possible offence to the Prophet. While charging interest is not allowed under Syariah law, the law does not apply where a borrower is the owner of the bank and both the Grameen Bank and the credit schemes are owned by their borrowers.

On the road back to Dhaka the signs of poverty in this densely populated country were very obvious. The road was full of painted, laden trucks, buffalo pulling carts and people crammed onto dodgy looking buses or into artistically decorated rickshaws. On either side were barefooted children, and women working the paddy fields. There were simple, basic bamboo homes. On the flat riverine plains men and young boys rowed through the thick water hyacinth in traditional wooden boats. Further on were the brick kilns with their smoke spouting chimneys and in the searing heat skinny men and women were making bricks from the red, hot clay.

Grameen has inspired about seven thousand micro-finance operations around the world, catering for twenty-five million poor clients. Systems have evolved and built on the original concept that the poor are bankable. The bank has faced criticism and questions have been raised about its repayment rate, reporting mechanisms and operating costs but even its critics acknowledge that the bank has changed thinking. Credit is now regarded as a cost effective way to fight poverty. Yunus himself sees access to credit as a human right; it is the basis for economic freedom among the poor. The professor's and the Grameen Bank's approach help create conditions that enable the poorest human beings of the world to find a dignified way of making a livelihood.

Minority

1999

Back in Dhaka I went to one of the most squalid slums that I have ever seen. It was overcrowded with people who dwell in cheap, dingy housing and outside on the street, open fetid sewers oozed out a bracing stench. Muslim and Hindu communities live uneasily side-by-side here. Two transvestites, effeminate, exaggerated, perfumed, wearing light fancy sweaters, one a canary yellow colour, the other bright pink, minced over. The crowd pressed together, separated by religion but united in contempt.

After a short chat as they pointed out and complained about the conditions that they live in, the transvestites provocatively gavotted indoors; they returned with photographs of themselves dressed up in glamorous regalia. The tight knot of onlookers dispersed with ill-concealed disdain, the more vocal muttering abuse. The transvestites spat back a retort. Their faces had an ochre hue; they explained that it is powdered turmeric and advised that it is good for the skin.

Then, a quick turn on the heels and they were gone.

Rwanda

A Tale of Two Cities: Kigali

1998

One of the most poignant places in Cambodia is the Killing Fields where the bones of the victims of the Khmer Rouge lie. The site is harrowing, especially the gravesite that still has fissures of bone and pieces of cloth protruding out through the dirt. A strip of clothing or a button turns skeletal remains into a human person who washed and dressed every day and had their own life story; for me these very ordinary bits and pieces had more immediacy than the stacks of skulls gathered and arranged in the memorial glass cases. Back then, in 1993, I would have found it hard to believe that such mass atrocities could happen again. The following year Rwanda, the land of the *milles collines,* the thousand hills, was the scene of genocide.

This small, hilly land of only 26,000 square kilometres is the most densely populated in Africa and is bordered by Uganda, Tanzania, Burundi and Democratic Republic of Congo. The landscape of mountains and hills are kept a rich green by copious rainfall. Every piece of earth is needed for intensive cultivation. Up and down the hills are the small farm holdings and homesteads where most of the population lives. This population is eighty-five per cent Hutu, fifteen per cent Tutsi, with a small minority of Twa or Pygmy. Hutu and Tutsi are not simply ethnic identities; they encompass other factors such as lineage or ancestry, traditional occupations and politics, which makes the relationship between them complex.

In Rwanda in 1994 it was the worst of times and the worst of crimes; when the dead were counted they ran into hundreds of thousands. The capital city, Kigali, is a tale of two cities. Two places that are inextricably interwoven, Kigali central prison and Ntarama Church, on the outskirts of the city, tell of the division in Rwandan society and the genocide carried out against the Tutsi population and moderate Hutus.

The *genocidaires* behind the twenty-foot brick walls of the prison are clothed in the prison uniform of short-sleeved shirt and matching Bermuda shorts, in baby pink. The incongruous colour means that in the event of a break-out the escapee could be easily identified as a prisoner. Kigali is beautifully set into gentle, undulating hills and pink was a perfect colour to show up against the surrounding landscape of green and brown – any fugitive would stand out as gloriously as *Priscilla Queen of the Desert*. The sea of pink-clothed bodies with shaven heads crowded together made the prison seem like an over-age nursery of delinquents, of humans not yet responsible.

The prison held over seven thousand prisoners. It had been built to shelter only two thousand. A handful of the Hutu inmates had been convicted, the rest were awaiting trial. The cellblocks formed the prison's exterior wall and faced the open-air courtyard. In the blocks each man had a sleeping cot; clothes, bedding and personal belongings were hung from the roof like permanent lines of washing. Those with no space to sleep in the blocks erected tents of plastic sheeting in the courtyard, which was uncomfortable in the rainy season. The prison had the boisterous routine of a busy town. Throughout the crowded 'streets' were detainees with buckets of water washing dishes, clothes and themselves; there were tables for tailoring and improvised barbershops where the men were shaved, many had shaved their heads.

The detainees ran the town. They had their own police force to maintain discipline, with the power to put an ill-behaved inmate into a holding cell, a justice system within the justice system. The range of skills and occupations of the prisoners was a reminder of the complicity of every social group in the genocide. Prisoners who were doctors and nurses ran the dispensary and administered to the infirm and those with phlegmatic coughs from tuberculosis, or to the mentally ill, who had their own area and no doubt their own world. Squads of detainees assigned to kitchen duty cooked the one main meal; the only other meal was porridge for breakfast.

To pass the day, a large room was given over to different sedentary activities because of a lack of space for more physical sports; the middle of the room held a ping-pong table. If there was little opportunity for exercising all that contained energy, there was at least diversion. There were several clubs that the prisoners could join; in a corner, languages were taught: English, German or Swahili. A blackboard in another corner showed a drawing of a carburettor for a course in mechanics. Various religious denominations had brought prayer groups together.

At the back of the prison were the kitchens and metalwork shops that resounded with banging drums as the workers serviced the large vats and cooking vessels. A truck from outside delivered firewood for the stoves that heated the pots. Supplies of oil, flour and beans were hoarded in the large storeroom. The water reservoir ensured a clean water supply, reducing the risk of epidemics and disease. Outside there were hills of red beans, as tall as the detainees on kitchen duty.

The women suspects, around six hundred in number, were kept in a separate wing. Muslim women were screened off with a piece of blue cloth behind which, at certain times of the day, they could be heard praying. The first nuns arrested and accused of crimes in connection with the genocide were sent here. Activities for the women were basket weaving and embroidery. Since infants under the age of three were allowed stay with their mothers, babies cried, demanding comforting, and a handful of toddlers played gleefully in the yard.

In short, community life was echoed and reflected in the life of the prison. There was an unexpected air of normality, even of geniality, and laughter was heard.

Family visits were once a week and were a clamorous affair. Relatives arrived with packages, which were checked for security reasons, and the visitors were placed in a line at the prison walls. Inside the prison lists of names were read out and those on the list were brought to the visiting area. At the 'off' the families rushed over, said a few words and handed over the parcel, all in a chaotic choreography. The noisy exchange was like a closely run horse race where the steady murmur of the spectators gathers pace at the last furlong, the shouting reaching a crescendo for a few moments. Then just as suddenly it is all over. Just enough time to smile, say hello and pass on the parcel. Since there might be as many as three thousand relatives on visiting day it was like a series of races spread throughout the day, each exuberant upsurge conveying to the inmates behind the wall that another throng of families was passing on hurried bundles and greetings.

The prison was like a hotel compared to the detention centres outside the capital. The *cachots*, the makeshift detention centres throughout the rest of Rwanda, had an oppressive, hopeless air. The condition of men held in these *cachots* was extremely bad. To detain the one hundred and twenty-five thousand suspected *genocidaires* arrested, buildings, schools or factories were transformed into communal lock-ups. In Butare, which had witnessed some of the largest massacres, the men were packed into classrooms, as many as one hundred in one room. There was not enough space for all the prisoners to lie on the ground at the same time, so they slept in shifts. Movement was curtailed; they were confined to the cell room and the day passed with a deadening lack of occupation. They were allowed outdoors only to eat the one cooked meal. The authorities did not supply food, the inmates depended on their families and the provisions brought in were pooled and distributed among them. Non-government organisations provided food as well. When I visited, as a friend of one of the aid workers, the prisoners were cooking up large pots of beans. The lack of food led to malnutrition. They got no exercise and felt fresh air only during the one mealtime. The unvaried diet and lack of air, exercise and sunlight led to poor health. Some of the detainees suffered from a pigmentation disease that caused the skin to lighten in blotches, as though it had been peeled back. Mostly men used to physical work, their once taut muscles now hung wasted, as the muscles of weightlifters do when they grow old and reduce their exercise. The poor sanitation and hygiene resulted in infections, epidemics and gangrene, which sometimes led to the amputation of limbs. They were all men without the company of women.

Since the wheels of justice grind slowly in Rwanda, the prisoners expected to spend a long time in jail before seeing a courtroom. The system had to deal with an overwhelming number of suspects because entire communities were involved in the crimes. Whatever justice system had been there before had been decimated; no judges, lawyers, buildings or furniture were left. Dealing with the aftermath of genocide is something no other legal system has had to do; particularly not one in a poor country with scarce resources. Rwanda's justice system was creaking beneath the burden. A visit to one of the trials in Kigali was discouraging. The court looked like a colonial absurdity. The three judges wore black gowns, the defendant the baby-pink prison uniform of shirt and Bermudas and flip-flops. Although the hearings were open to the public, the plain, wooden benches in the courtroom were practically empty. The prisoner and witnesses spoke Kinyarwanda, which was translated into French; the process looked remote and unwieldy and somehow farcical.

The government was aware how important it was to procure justice for the victims, and was exploring other possibilities to quicken the process, such as the traditional, tribal system. For the country to achieve any degree of reconciliation, justice had to be seen to be done; otherwise vengeance might seep out like an infested sore and manifest itself in individual acts of retribution.

* * * *

The terrible nature and scale of the crimes of which the prison and *cachot* communities were accused was hard to contemplate, much less reconcile. The premeditated genocide was organised by a corrupt Hutu elite reluctant to move towards democratic governance and to share power and privilege with their Tutsi compatriots and Hutu opposition parties. Playing on poverty, ignorance and old fears of Tutsi domination, they incited the population to rid themselves of the root of their problem – their Tutsi neighbours.

The minority Tutsi were traditionally the ruling group in Rwanda and their position had been upheld during colonial rule. The Hutus had first revolted in 1959 – thousands of Tutsi were killed and many had fled to the border countries of Uganda and Tanzania. When Rwanda became independent in 1961 the first president was Hutu; in 1974 another Hutu, Juvenal Habyarimana, seized power in a bloodless coup. The country was a one-party state, politically and administratively tightly controlled.

Outside Rwanda, the Tutsi who had fled in 1959 demanded the right to come home, but negotiations with the Hutu government produced little result. The exiles organised themselves into a military force, the Rwandan Patriotic Front (RPF), and invaded from Uganda. Peace accords in 1993 between the Hutu government in Kigali and the RPF were supposed to end the conflict and allow for the setting up of a United Nations peacekeeping force, UNAMIR (United Nations Assistance Mission to Rwanda).

UN troops were deployed in December 1993 and by January 1994 the head of the UN mission, Major General Romeo Dallaire, was warning that Hutu militia, the Interhamwe, were preparing to carry out genocide on the Tutsi population. He was told to pass on the information to the French, Belgian and US ambassadors and to the Rwandan Hutu government. Nothing else was done. The French in particular continued their support of the Habyarimana government. Many journals and the radio station Radio Mille Collines, which broadcast throughout Rwanda, waged a virulent campaign arousing fear and inciting hatred against the Tutsi.

On April 6, 1994, the President's plane was shot down near Kigali airport killing all the passengers, including the Presidents of both Rwanda and neighbouring Burundi. The planned and well-organised genocide began. Within a week twenty thousand Rwandans were massacred. Major General Dallaire told the UN that with a force of between five and eight thousand well-equipped soldiers he could stop the killing. Instead of increasing troop numbers the UN Security Council, led by the US government who had just lost soldiers in Somalia, reduced the size of the Rwanda force to a mere two hundred and seventy. Up and down the slopes of the thousand hills the killing continued. The worst of the genocide ended when the RPF made its way to Kigali and took the city on July 4.

Ntarama church, just outside Kigali, still shows signs of the horrible massacre that took place there. The church is located in beautiful countryside among trees and birdsong, quiet and peaceful, although occasionally a murder of cawing crows troubles the tranquillity. Thousands of people were killed here. Tutsi, as well as Hutus who refused to take part in the attacks on their neighbours, had fled from the Hutu militia, the Interahamwe, and come to the church for sanctuary, hoping that they would be protected. They were not.

The attackers made holes in the back wall of the church and threw in grenades; the Interahamwe then entered the church and brutally killed the defenceless thousands, with machetes, spears and sharpened sticks while soldiers fired guns. Some of the bodies were left in the same place and in the same position they were in when they were killed. They were now skeletons but still wore clothes and lay amongst the small, everyday things that the frightened sanctuary seekers took with them when they ran: plates, cups, basins, kettles, lamps, mattresses. The juxtaposition of the domestic and the grotesque made what was harrowing even more disturbing, as if the ordinariness of the plates and cups said, this was done by ordinary people to ordinary people. The sight prevented the cold comfort of emotional distance; the faint reassurance felt when something is seen as a monstrous aberration.

The simple altar remained and on top of it was a missal. On top of this had been placed three skulls. The brickwork of the Church walls was marked and bloodied, but the Stations of the Cross were intact. On one wall hung a poster celebrating International Women's Day and equality, peace and development. It was dated 8 March 1994, just one month before the genocide. Underneath the poster were the bodies of women, men and children. The smell of decay incensed the air.

The horror at Ntarama church was replicated all over Rwanda, and those in prison and the cachots were only a portion of the population that had been involved.

Outside the church a young girl, about eleven or twelve years old, was wandering aimlessly. She had a large scar that began at her forehead and covered part of her shaven head, the marks of a wound from a machete. She shied away when approached, shaking her disfigured head.

Rwanda challenged moral certitude; not what is the moral thing to do, but the certainty of how any individual would respond if caught up in the nightmare of such horrible events – join in, resist, go mad?

Lost and Found

1998

The children are like small bundles in a 'Lost & Found' office waiting to be reclaimed. They were lost during the large movements of people crossing the border between Rwanda and Zaire in 1994 and again in 1996. The first movement was after the 1994 genocide when the Hutus massacred their Tutsi neighbours and moderate Hutus. As the Rwandan Patriotic Front (RPF), an army primarily of exiled Tutsis, swept through Rwanda routing the Hutu leadership and militias, the population fled towards the border. A swarm of over seven hundred thousand men, women and children crossed into Zaire, now the Democratic Republic of Congo. In Zaire they settled into refugee camps run by the United Nations and international relief agencies in Goma and Bukavu, living under very basic conditions while the RPF established its authority and a government in Rwanda's capital Kigali.

Some in the border camps were members of the Hutu militia group the Interhamwe, directors of the mass killings. In the camps the Interhamwe re-organised and trained and were determined to control the camp population. The structure of communes and villages was replicated with many of the refugees again living with those local leaders who had issued orders during the genocide. Aid organisations providing humanitarian assistance were in the invidious position of feeding and helping *genocidaires* living in the refugee camps. The strengthening of the Hutu militia was keenly watched from Kigali by the new Tutsi-led Rwandan government. By the following year the armed groups in the camps felt strong enough to begin incursions over the border into Rwanda.

Rwanda's troubles spilled into Zaire, destabilising that country, and the refugees on the border found themselves again in a war zone and a precarious situation. In the same way as they had arrived into Zaire, in their hundreds of thousands, they gathered themselves up from the camps and in the months of November and December 1996 crossed back to Rwanda.

So there were two massive movements of people, one in 1994 towards Zaire and the other in 1996 when the refugees left Zaire and repatriated themselves to their own country.

One thirteen-year-old girl hung on to her family during the first crossing and lived with them in the camps. They got food from the United Nations, beans and maize flour, but she says that she did not like that kind of life. She remembers the sound of shooting as they crossed and lots of people running. Then in the rush back to Rwanda in 1996 she lost her family and ended up on her own.

With the multitudes crossing it sometimes resembled a stampede; there was chaos and confusion. Hordes of bodies pressed together and the elderly, the sick and the very young found it difficult and tiring to keep up. Especially the small ones running beside their families, seeing only rows and rows of thrashing legs and feet; trying hard not to lose sight of mothers, fathers, brothers and sisters. To fall was a calamity; by the time they recovered, everything had moved on like the next scene in a film. There was sheer terror when they looked around and recognised nobody. In the din their tiny voices could not be heard shouting out for their family. Parents worried about the children but could not carry them all or hold all their hands. They struggled to mind them as they ran, but it was impossible. To manage one of these crossings with the whole family intact was difficult, to survive two was a miracle. Thousands of families became separated and children were lost.

A small shy boy of seven is from Zaire. During the war he was parted from his relatives. His parents are dead but he prays that his grandmother and uncle are alive and wants to rejoin them; he thinks they are still in Zaire. He says he feels hopeless because it is hard to go back to his country to find them.

The lost children were found by the aid agencies and taken care of firstly in camps in Zaire. After the movement back to Rwanda some of them were collected and sent to orphanages. The children were found wandering and were taken to a centre in Ruhengeri in north-west Rwanda.

Ruhengeri is a small town with spectacular views of the Virunga Volcanoes. It is a gateway to the mountains inhabited by the famous silver-backed gorillas, the primates most closely linked genetically to humans. As the gorillas overlook the town, fiercely protecting their young, down below are the young of the humans that evolved from them – shattered, vulnerable and huddled together for comfort. The children have been in the midst of a genocide, where they witnessed people being killed or people they trusted and loved killing neighbours. They escaped to another country where they lived in refugee camps. Two years later they had to move back to their homeland where they ended up separated from their families.

The home in Ruhengeri is frugally well run. The sleeping quarters have no beds; mattresses on the ground are pushed together. Missing their kinfolk, the children need affection, and sleeping close to each other helps them feel more secure. They have created their own family.

Outside is a playing field for football and a play area. The children are shouting, laughing and giggling. It's a place of some fun and love in spite of the underlying trauma and sadness. Blankets and clothes on large wash lines tussle with the soft breeze. In the sun they'll dry quickly and be back on the beds in no time. Washing the children is a big job and the older children help with the little ones; in this family the smallest need the biggest to take care of them.

Lunch is outdoors, no tables or chairs but wooden benches on which they sit and eat their plate of food, sociably sharing the meal. Today's dish is maize flour mixed with oil and cabbage; one little boy says it is good and that he likes it. Yesterday they had rice. They all say they will eat every bit. In the kitchen a big open fire roars night and day. Something is always cooking in the large pots; at night the beans cook for the next day. In the garden they've planted banana trees and are looking forward to the first crop. The centre has a happy atmosphere, but behind it is loneliness and the sad, miserable stories.

When the children arrived in November and December 1996 after the massive repatriation, they were unhappy, unhealthy, and never smiled. Since then, the centre has tried to make them content and teach them to love and take care of each other. The staff show them tenderness, talk to them, teach them songs and games to bring out the playfulness in them. The children are so small it is hard for the staff to know what is going on inside their heads, but it appears that they think a lot; it is not usual for children to think as much as they do, and the carers wonder if they are remembering what they have seen. The biggest task is to build a good relationship, so that the youngsters tell them everything. As they begin to trust, the children open up: 'You know I saw that person killed' or 'that person jumped into the water and I never saw them again'. This happened throughout Rwanda when the Tutsi were driven to the river and given a choice to leap in and drown or be hacked to death by machete. Many threw themselves in the river, sometimes taking their children with them.

Any information gleaned may assist with the arduous task of tracking down relatives so that the lost children may be reclaimed. The centre has put a lot of effort into tracing families. On market day the staff go to the marketplace with the children or with lists of names or photographs hoping that someone might recognise them. The older ones, who knew where they lived before the war, are taken to the local authority, which tries to find the family and reunite them. Radio announcements ask parents to come to the centre if they hear the name of their child. Seventeen hundred children have been reunited with their kin in this way. There's great excitement at the orphanage when a parent who has not seen a child since 1994 comes and is remembered by the small boy or girl who jumps up and greets them; parents cry with joy and happiness.

Yesterday a little boy was reunited with his mother. Neighbours ran to her house to tell her that they had heard his name on the radio and she immediately came to the centre. When he saw her, the child leapt up with delight, taking her by surprise. She could only mumble that he had changed so much, and weep.

A young girl of nine, traumatised and withdrawn, always asked for thread to knit, knitting all the time, like one of the Fates, knitting day and night and there was no thread. If there were no thread she would pull the finished work apart and start again. She knew her mother's name but had no other information. The name was announced on the radio, her mother heard it and came to the orphanage. The girl was as usual knitting, but as soon as she saw her mother she stopped and ran towards her crying 'Mama you are going to give me cassava leaves and potatoes and look I have been knitting for you'.

Still left in the centre is a soft spoken child whose parents were dead and who lived in an orphanage before the fighting. During the war, he says, the orphanage was destroyed and they fled to Zaire. In the border crush he was separated from his friends but they found each other again in the refugee camps. They were disbanded when everything was uprooted in 1996 and the refugees came back to Rwanda. Outside of the Ruhengeri centre, he is quite alone in the world.

Over three hundred thousand Rwandan children have lost parents. The family structure has changed. Children now head many households; others live with relatives or neighbours or are fostered, adopted, in centres, prison or on the streets. Many communities have taken the orphaned children into their homes and their hearts. Seeing a woman now with children in Rwanda may not mean that she is the mother; they may be the young ones of dead sisters or neighbours that she is taking care of.

One young girl in the centre had become separated from her mother and her sister in the 1994 border crossing when she was only eight years old; her father was already dead. There were so many people rushing she became befuddled and lost her family. Her brothers were shot crossing into Zaire with her; she saw them being shot but she kept running. In Zaire she found an aunt who was living there and stayed with her, not in the camps. When the war began in Zaire they fled and she lost her aunt; she has no information of her whereabouts or whether her mother and sister are alive.

The children wait to be reclaimed by their loved ones. They need to be reclaimed by a country that has failed them tremendously; failed to physically protect them, to meet their emotional needs or to provide moral guidance. Already they have seen too much. Many of the soldiers in the Rwandan Patriotic Front were children who had been forced to flee Rwanda in 1959 when Hutus, tired of colonial rule and Tutsi domination, massacred thousands of Tutsi. They grew up with their parents as disenchanted exiles in bordering countries such as Uganda, nursing the grievance of being driven from their native soil and vowing to return.

In the orphanage in Ruhengeri they have a song that they sing with strong impatient voices. The words are heartrending: 'We'll go home, we'll go home; when it will be the right time we'll go home.' The children are like small bundles in the 'Lost & Found' office – still waiting to be reclaimed.

Burundi

Cibitoke

1998

South of Rwanda is the small country of Burundi; to the east and south-east Burundi is bordered by Tanzania, to the west by beautiful Lake Tanganyika and the Democratic Republic of Congo. Travelling from Rwanda by car, a border post declared entry into a different state; the similar looking landscape indicated no change. At the busy checkpoint people and traffic waited under the beating sun while slow officialdom leafed through passports and documents. After Rwanda, Burundi is the most densely populated country in Africa. The majority, eighty-four percent of the population, are Hutu; fifteen percent are Tutsi and a little less than one percent is Twa. The Tutsi minority held power until the 1993 elections returned the first democratically elected Hutu president, Melchior Ndadaye. Within months he was killed by a section of the predominantly Tutsi army. His death led to clashes between the two main ethnic groups and civil war. Another Hutu president was appointed but the political power struggle and violence continued for three years until Major Pierre Buyoya, a Tutsi, took power after a military coup. Security improved but the country did not immediately move towards democracy and a return of power to the Hutu majority. Armed elements of that majority were still engaged in fighting the government. Thousands of civilians were suffering and in Cibitoke, only an hour away from Burundi's capital city, people were starving to death.

As I discovered when I arrived in Cibitoke, even if your own country's history tells of the devastation of hunger, nothing prepares you for witnessing famine. Every bone in the body shudders; every sense is jarred, like cardiac arrest; everything is upside down. It is not supposed to happen; it offends the laws of nature. The stomach feels as if it has been gripped by a vice. Famine is an inert eerie stillness; like petrified Pompeii, the emaciated bodies laid out in different poses, lifeless but still alive; like a frieze, a still life, the air drained of energy and all the time the sceptre of certain, inhumane death. Protruding shoulder blades and blank protruding stares, swollen stomachs, women with skeletal fingers weakly holding babies that suck limply at dried milkless breasts, shrunken hollowed cheeks that give a wasted wraith-like appearance, shaky trembling sticks of legs that seem too thin to support the meagre frame. One baby manages a feeble cry; the incantation is a verbal rocking back and forth with a resigned rhythm that suggests the infant does not expect the whimper to get attention or achieve anything. The twelve-year-old orphan girl sitting on the ground is too listless to notice or to manage to swat away the flies that buzz around her in the parched heat. She is covered in scabies and walked twenty kilometres when she heard of a centre to help people who are sick or without enough to eat. Another young girl shows signs of oedema, with badly swollen infected legs; her condition tells that she has been living rough for several months.

The people came from a commune in the hills ensnared in Burundi's civil war, and were running from the conflict, hiding in the forests and eating poorly, unable to cultivate their land. They walked between ten and fifteen kilometres to the feeding centre run by an Irish aid agency; so desperate they risked crossing the lines of war to get here. Ten thousand people made their way to the centre over six months but many more were starving back in the hills, too weak to make the journey. At the centre they are put on a therapeutic feeding regime of high-energy food. When they are strong enough they will leave but many are afraid to go home because of the fighting and because they know that conditions have not improved and the problem of food shortages remains. While the centre is welcome, it is an admission of a country's failure to prevent great hunger.

In this muted place of the famished, a distant hum resonates from a church two hundred metres away. Walking towards the chapel, the sound rises; the sound of melodic, harmonised, rehearsed choral singing. The church belongs to the local congregation and is full, highlighting the contrast in Burundi that among those dying from hunger, and unfortunate enough to live in the conflict area, is a neighbourhood that is doing fine.

Burundi's capital Bujumburu is less than an hour's drive from famine-stricken Cibitoke and is an entirely different world with no sign of starving people. The city is set in a naturally lovely location, built in a plain surrounded by hills and on the shores of Lake Tanganyika. The attractive lake gives the capital a beach and good fishing and in the evening wide-girthed hippos yawn and waddle up from the water. At weekends it seems carefree as its citizens enjoy a swim and children play along the shoreline, but never far away is the knowledge that Hutu rebels hold the surrounding hills. A midnight curfew warns that anyone driving after that hour risks being shot by the army. Cows wander around the city, a reminder of the insecurity outside the capital. Those from the rural areas who escaped being killed but whose farms were taken and houses destroyed, came to Bujumburu with their cattle looking for shelter and protection. So far they have not been housed and are in dispute with the municipal authorities about the roaming animals.

All along the road back from Cibitoke to Bujumburu the images of hunger swim around. Arriving in the hotel it seems that a local brewery is having a beer promotion in a room off the terrace. It is like walking into a mistake, the contrast is so shocking. Here is an elegant cocktail party with well-dressed, well-fed guests. Uniformed waiters carry tinkling trays of drinks and slivers of finger food to nibble. As they glide by the small groups of guests, the food is within easy reach but only occasionally eaten, as happens at this kind of reception. The women are well groomed and bejewelled and smell of perfume and soap; the men have paunched stomachs, well-spread and somehow comfortable looking. During the evening there are polite introductions and short welcoming speeches. The sound in the room is like chattering white noise. It is as though I have walked into a bubble; so cut off that the air itself must be rarefied. Or maybe this is reality and the afternoon was a bad nightmare. Standing there for an imperceptible time, perspective begins to distort. The room becomes a hall of mirrors; everything seems exaggerated and jarring. After the still faces of Cibitoke, ordinary human expressions here seem overstated: the smiles too wide, the faces too animated, even the mildest hand gestures too flamboyant, as if I'm no longer seeing the room as it is but as the pen of a lampoon artist has caught it. The room seems to close in, to lack air.

As the evening tapers off, from a corner of the lit garden comes a deep, trembling rumble that sounds like the beginnings of thunder or a minor earthquake. For the amusement of the invited company enormous drums are pounding out ancestral rhythms, accompanied by chanting, shouting and leaping; the very physical choreography is danced by a performing troupe dressed in tribal costume. Drums are Burundi's national instrument. Traditionally they were played to mark important events in the lives of villagers such as the seasonal cycles, fertility and agriculture. The planting and harvesting of the sorghum crop and praise of the cow, an animal much prized in Burundi, are basic drumming themes. The diverting entertainment celebrating fertility and prosperity seems incongruous when the reality just an hour away in Cibitoke is famine, poverty and death.

Drumbeats in Burundi also beat out ethnic hatred, politically managed by the factions in Bujumburu. Sunday afternoons in the town seem normal. People meet after Church to share a beer and a chat in one of the public houses, but a drive around the dusty crowded suburbs shows the extent of ethnic tension. In one of the richer residential areas with wide boulevards people from both ethnic groups live in villas; some of the homes belong to those who manipulate poorer Burundians for their own political ambitions and incite them to kill on an ethnic basis. They themselves live in wealth and harmony. No houses have been destroyed here and nobody has been killed because of their ethnic group.

The car slows down as it goes through a police checkpoint made from a piece of string stretched across a road at the entrance to Kamenge. This is a Hutu-dominated quarter; the destroyed houses belonged to Tutsis who were chased out and killed after news of the death of the Hutu President in 1993. Driving through another Hutu-dominated quarter, Kinama, there are further signs of the destruction of homes of Tutsis who fled the attack by their neighbours. Other houses were damaged during clashes between the army and the rebels.

Close to the two Hutu quarters is the Tutsi-dominated quarter of Cibitoke, a place which bears the same name as the area of famine one hour down the road. Hutu houses here were destroyed by the Tutsi in retaliation for the destruction and death of their brothers and their homes in Kamenge and Kinama; they hounded out the Hutus living here, killing those who could not escape. The houses of both Hutus and Tutsis in these quarters are poorer, built of stone and brick with roofs of corrugated iron, very different to the villas of the better off.

The politicians eat well, live comfortably in pleasant homes in Bujumburu and drive good cars. Most, an army officer told me, have not been outside the capital to see what is happening in the countryside and the effects of ethnic hatred. Those paying the price are the dead, the shrunken communities and the starving multitude in the nearby hills.

The famine in Cibitoke was not as a result of a natural disaster nor was it climate, drought or crop failure. It was about politics and the failure in Burundi to allow the Hutu majority democratic representation.

For the peasants in Cibitoke the food supply in their territory declined because of the fighting, causing them to flee. They could not plant and harvest the land. They had no means to import food from elsewhere; they had nothing to sell and had lost their produce and their only means of getting money. The starving had no voice and no power to muster the concern of the Bujumburu politicians.

The memory of famine is deeply disturbing and easily triggered for a long time afterwards. Back in Ireland, I went to a friend's home for dinner. They had relatives over who run a restaurant in New York and there was a very competitive conversation about food and cooking. I couldn't engage; I could barely taste. It wasn't their fault and I wasn't being fair; normally it would be okay. I said I was jetlagged and left.

Democratic Republic of Congo

Flight

1997

On the Red Cross flight from Kinshasa, the capital of the Democratic Republic of Congo (formerly Zaire), the aeroplane stopped at Mbandaka to pick up Rwandan refugees who had pushed across the country from eastern Zaire. They had fled because the events following the genocide in Rwanda had destabilised Zaire and the country was at war.

I first remember the word 'flight' from school when we learnt about the Flight to Egypt when the holy family – Mary, Joseph and the infant Jesus – fled to safety from Herod's murderous assault. At the time I never made the connection with aeroplanes, which were entirely outside my experience. The next time I remember the word flight was when we were told in class about the Flight of the Earls, when the Irish nobility fled to the continent of Europe leaving the running of the country to the English. I still have these two images: a man walking alongside a donkey, bearing a woman and her baby; and a group of cloaked men hurriedly leaving the homes of their ancestors, vowing to return. The word flight has that early resonance of people fleeing – from something bad.

The passengers on the Red Cross flight had been living in the refugee camps in eastern Zaire when Laurent Kabila and his Alliance troops revolted against the Mobutu dictatorship. Hundreds of thousands of those in the camps crossed back over the border and into Rwanda. Among the refugees were the perpetrators of the genocide, the Interhamwe, who had controlled the camps. This militia fled into the interior of Zaire, joining the fighting against Kabila's Alliance. As they moved into the interior they used some of the refugees as a human shield and scattered to forested, remote, inaccessible areas. Pushed ahead of the approaching army, many of the refugees were killed; others walked several hundred kilometres across the country, some even reaching Kinshasa, the equivalent of walking across Europe, almost from Warsaw to Paris. It was a dreadful journey; there was nothing to eat, no medicine, no transport and they were vulnerable to attack by bandits. Along the way people died of hunger and malaria and other illnesses. The others survived on bananas, which they took from the trees, and sugarcane and berries that they found along the way.

Laurent Kabila finally took the capital, Kinshasa, and power. Hungry, ill people emerged from hideouts and wanted to go back to their villages. The passengers we picked up on the plane from Mbandaka were some of the refugees who were being repatriated to Rwanda. The flight would end in Bukavu in eastern Zaire and the twenty-five men, women and children would be transported by road to a transit point and then onto Rwanda.

Sitting beside me on the plane was one of the men who had been displaced. He needed help with the strange contraption – the seat belt. He seemed to be on his own. He was quite tall, handsome, with dark hair, beautiful teeth, and stocky. He still looked strong even though he could not have eaten properly for several months. His eyes had a slightly wild look, a look that was in no way threatening, just bewildered, as if his soul had left his body and taken the subtlety and nuance of expression that only the eyes can manage. A bible in German, black leather with a tarnishing gold cross etched on the cover and with pink edged, well-thumbed pages, was the only thing he carried. This he anxiously showed me, flicking through the pages of densely arranged words; there were no pictures. 'Sprechen Sie Deutsch?' I asked. He looked blank. 'Parlez vous Francais?' 'Oui.' 'Parlez vous Deutsch?' 'Non.' He did not speak German yet he clutched, clung to the German tome like a precious relic.

My French was weak and he spoke too rapidly for me to have any real conversation with him. I sensed, perhaps wrongly, that coherence had left him.

On his feet he wore flip-flops. I was amazed to see that one of the grimy white thongs that fit in between the toes had come away, and I wondered how he had managed to walk in them. He had dark shorts, which went half way down his thighs, a faded red t-shirt, ragged and dirty. His feet in the flip-flops had tough, calloused skin with old scrapes and scratches. I wore runners and had a couple of spare pairs of shoes in my bag; my light travel bag contained more than the small bundled belongings of the displaced passengers. I looked at his chafed feet and tried to gauge if the runners would fit.

The flight was particularly quiet. No one spoke. There was occasional coughing, as heard during a solemn Mass. For the travellers, poor subsistence farmers, the airflight was no doubt a first. It was hard to know if the silence was because they were in awe of the experience of moving suspended in the sky, high up among the clouds, or if they were simply non-plussed, exhausted from the years of killing and running, too used to the commonplace being turned topsy-turvy. A woman in the seat behind sat nervously throughout. As the plane began to land the others teased her, and when it finally hit the ground she shouted, 'Mon Dieu!'; everyone laughed.

When we left the plane in Bukavu I took off the runners and offered them to him. His life was not a fairytale and the shoes did not fit. Seeing this, other bare feet were thrust out, but he held the shoes into his chest and indicated that if he took them he could swap them or sell them at the next market place; they had some currency. So he delightedly kept them, more gratitude than grumbling disappointment at his ill-fitting luck. I wished him *bon chance* as he headed with the others towards the pick-up trucks that were waiting to take them on to a transit camp.

Already the travellers were getting news that they could expect to go back to houses that had been looted and damaged, and some heard that relatives who had stayed at home were dead. The local radio broadcast messages from family members who had been separated in the fleeing. One man, desperate to meet up with his young son, left this plea on the radio: 'I heard that you are somewhere and that your situation isn't good. We can't sleep until we see you again. I am looking for how to trace you. I trust in God.'

Now I have a third image of flight: I see him in the faded red t-shirt standing in the back of the pick-up, the shoes hanging around his neck by the laces he had tied together, the beautiful smile, the dust flown up as the truck took off and the wave goodbye as he headed off to his uncertain fate.

An Intake of Breath

1997

Laurent Kabila's rebel forces entered Kinshasa, the capital of Zaire, on May 17, 1997; Mobutu Sese Seko had left the day before, ending his thirty-two year reign. There was some gunfire, but the takeover was about as peaceful as you could imagine the takeover of a city inhabited by over five million to be. The demoralised government troops had retreated with little resistance, pulling off their uniforms as they ran and merging with the civilian population. There were cheers to see Mobutu gone; there was hope that the guns in Zaire were now silent and that a period of peace, prosperity and democracy would set in.

Kinshasa showed little sign of war because by the time Kabila arrived it was all over bar the shouting. What they found, according to the new Minister of the Interior, Mwenze Kongolo, 'was a state of statelessness, no state, no responsible government, everything was actually collapsed. So we started from scratch and we're trying to build something out of nothing. Corruption was everywhere, decay as far as morals are concerned, the economy was completely absent, as a matter of fact the big bank across the street was empty, very high rate of joblessness, so everything was collapsed. This was the legacy of the dictatorship that was in this country where the dictator was piling up money for himself and nothing for the people.'

When I came to Kinshasa two months after Mobutu's departure and Kabila's arrival, it was like entering a snapshot, a moment in time. Everyone knew what was on the old roll of film: Mobutu, dictatorship, brutality, fraud, embezzlement and poverty. The roll of film before that showed colonial rule, brutality, exploitation and poverty. In the snapshot were the newcomers but how would the new reel unfold? In short who was Laurent Kabila and what kind of administration was now in charge of this huge African country?

While Kinshasa showed little sign of fighting, there were palpable signs of impoverishment. Ndjili airport was grim, although I emerged without my bag being rifled or without being pressed to palm money, as was usual in this city known for its grafting officials. Outside the sky was grey, overcast, the climate heavily humid. Taking the badly-kept road towards the centre the city shouted neglect; it was dirty, open sewage ran through its streets, its citizens were poorly dressed. Few soldiers were about; they were boyish and grinned gratefully when offered cigarettes. They had come from rural eastern Zaire and seemed wrong-footed patrolling the nation's capital.

The city was businesslike: taxis plied their trade, markets and shops were open and cassettes of the vibrant music that Zaire is famous for blared out onto the street, small stalls engaged in selling, women carried firewood or baskets of freshly baked baguettes on their heads. The cost of living had rocketed. To supplement a meagre income, the police stopped motorists on the slightest pretence and were paid off. Along the way, amongst the tropical vegetation, were shantytowns with homes of concrete boxes and corrugated roofs. There were intermittent churches, Roman Catholic and Evangelical. The billions of dollars that Mobutu had allegedly stashed away in Swiss banks could do a lot here or could ease the fourteen billion-dollar national debt that he left behind. The most visible form of his exported wealth is the various chateaux, villas and properties that he owns in different African and European countries.

The vast country of the Congo stretches across a terrain the size of Western Europe. At its furthest points it is twelve hundred miles wide and the length from north to south is twelve hundred and fifty miles. Forty million inhabitants form themselves into two hundred and fifty ethnic groups. The soil has abundant deposits of copper, zinc and uranium as well as cobalt, gold and diamonds. In spite of such rich natural resources, the annual per capita income is less than two hundred dollars.

The country's fight to win independence from the Belgians in 1960 was fraught: shortly afterwards the mineral rich region of Katanga and the diamond area of Kasai tried to secede and civil war erupted. The United Nations intervened; the first democratically elected prime minister, Patrice Lumumba, was killed. In the aftermath Mobutu took control and began his thirty-two year dictatorship. The country was renamed Zaire under his plan for Africanisation; Leopoldville, on the River Congo, became Kinshasa. Despite flagrant corruption and human rights abuses, Mobutu's anti-communist line ensured weapons and military training from the United States. With the end of the Cold War, the courtship of the Zairean dictator became less important and aid declined. Calls for democratisation and riots in the capital forced him to legalise opposition parties in 1990. The unpopular Mobutu haggled with the opposition, and appointed Etienne Tshishekedi to form a coalition government, but sacked him within a week. Subsequently the dictator resisted any real attempt to move the country towards democracy. The World Bank declared Zaire insolvent and the country was suspended from the International Monetary Fund.

The creaking Mobutu regime came under more pressure after the genocide in neighbouring Rwanda. When several hundred thousand Rwandan Hutu refugees crossed the border, they altered the ethnic composition in eastern Zaire. The military elements among the refugees, in collusion with units of the Zairean army, began killing Zairean Tutsi who had lived there for generations. In September 1996 the Tutsi Banyamulenge were ordered to leave the region. The Banyamulenge tribe resisted and a coalition emerged with the aim of overthrowing Mobutu. It was called the Alliance des Forces Democratiques pour la Liberation du Congo-Zaire (AFDL), led by Laurent

Kabila, a one time Maoist who in later years ran a business trading gold and ivory. The Alliance had outside support from Uganda and Rwanda; Mobutu's support for the Hutus motivated the new Tutsi government in Rwanda to help replace him with a more sympathetic government in Kinshasa. Within months, Kabila's Alliance had swept across the country and the long thirty-two year reign of Mobutu Sese Seko was over.

* * * *

Two months after Kabila came to Kinshasa the ambience in the four-hundred-room Intercontinental Hotel was surreal. It was a luxurious air-conditioned liner in a sea of uncertainty. The new administration was berthed at the hotel, the best in Kinshasa, and had set up offices. Down long corridors government ministers and military personnel slept behind locked doors. The lobby was stranger than fiction and befitted a scene from a Graham Greene novel. It smacked of African Cold War – men in suits, intrigue, men in jackboots and camouflage. Pamphlets in French about *la revolution* were on sale. Civilians and military mingled together; youngish, clean-shaven entrepreneur types abounded, some perhaps genuine, others using business as a cover for their true role of advisor to the new government, such as a keen-faced Ugandan lawyer who told me that he was here 'looking at investment opportunities' and who was now earnestly talking to a man in military fatigues. The eager 'tea merchant' from Rwanda was more likely here courtesy of his own government. Undoubtedly *bona fide* entrepreneurs had arrived too. One US businesswoman enthused and advised 'the opportunities are fantastic; they're unlimited. This country has real wealth and its resources are pretty much untapped as yet. Very little competition, very few taxes, it's highly attractive. You should stay, and make lots of money.' It resembled a gold rush and up for grabs were not only the country's enormous natural wealth and potential but the tantalising prospect of power. The new prospectors would have their work cut out because there was virtually no infrastructure, no decent roads or communications. No proper banking system operated and the previous day the hotel had put up a sign that it would not accept payment of bills by credit card.

Here was a two-month-old government replacing a thirty-two-year-old regime. With Mobutu gone everyone wanted to believe that at last the new Democratic Republic of Congo would make a successful transition to peace and democracy. Encroaching on this desire to believe in a better future was the uneasy feeling of people out of their depth. The government were settling in to run this vast, imposing country of Congo with, it seemed, more enthusiasm than experience. The waitress in the hotel coffee shop, which served an abundant array of French pastries and delicacies, says she is 'waiting to see what change brings, but the security situation is not good, especially at night'. This is the general feeling; since Laurent Kabila only took over in May it is early days and there is still great relief at Mobutu's departure.

It is as if everyone is in the middle of taking a deep breath; having breathed Mobutu out, with bated breath they wonder what they are about to breathe in. Other African countries watch with interest. There is reluctance among more neutral spectators, such as the aid agencies and the European Union, to criticise the new government. Activity, meetings and conferences fill the hotel but are punctured by a sense of confusion, of political vacuum. Whatever is being decided at these meetings, the air lacks clarity, decisiveness or strong stewardship.

At one press conference the new government announces the three-year plan for the reconstruction of the country. They want to start with rebuilding the roads, which are in an appalling condition and non-existent in many places. The plan is presented amidst rumours that they are about to ban political parties and have a clean-out of the public service. 'Foreign investors are welcome but we'll rely on ourselves', the Minister tells the gathered journalists.

People had been prepared to give the new transitional government the benefit of the doubt, to wait and see. After two months it seems that 'wait and see' is on the turn, and impatience and demands for change are increasing. This is partly due to the exigencies of Congo politics. Kabila has inherited a country with an expectation of democracy.

For the Congolese, Mobutu's downfall was the result of a two-pronged attack. One prong was Kabila and his Alliance's military victory. The other prong was Tshishekedi's non-violent opposition group, with its strong grassroots movement throughout the country, which had been spreading democratic ideas for years. Kabila was hardly known when he started his military campaign last October, but endorsed by Thishekedi he gained popular support as he crossed Zaire. In return, Thishekedi and his party expected to be part of the new administration, but they failed to reach agreement with Kabila. According to the Minister for the Interior, a cousin of Kabila's who lived in Philadelphia until a few months ago, it's been: 'very tough, very tough, things are settling down now but at the beginning it was very tough with people. We found too many unhappy politicians here who were pushing each other to try and find some place in the political realm but we decided that we should not give them that opportunity which made them very unhappy and started turmoil. Now I believe they're very tired and things are getting normal.'

The tired politicians are those of Thishekedi's party who were chagrined to find that when he finally reached the capital, Kabila was not prepared to hand over the crown to the prince in waiting – Tshishikedi; he wanted it for himself. Kabila has also given himself wide-ranging powers and banned all political activity. The other problem is the popular perception that his government is made up of outsiders, people of Rwandan or Tutsi origin, or Congolese who had been living abroad. Refusing to include the opposition parties makes it harder for the Kinshasa politicians to feel part of the revolution.

One of Tshishekedi's advisors still smarted at the upstart

Kabila's failure to include them in the new government: 'What he was saying when he was far from Kinshasa and what is happening now is not the same. We understood that there would be sharing of power, otherwise we are going in the way of Mobutu. We are all members of the one team. You know, on the soccer team we have eleven players, when they are scoring it's not the whole eleven who are scoring, one can score. Kabila did it. He scored but the cup is for the whole team, the power is for everybody, for all opposition members.'

The Kabila government was in transition but the transition was hardening into repressive measures. A smaller opposition party, Partie Lumumbista Unifie (PALU), were realising how far the new government were prepared to go to discourage opposition. At their office they were still visibly shaken as they pointed to worn shirts with bullet holes and bloodstains. The old days of brutal repression seemed to be back. The party had held a demonstration in Kinshasa, afterwards government troops fired outside their offices, killing one man and injuring several others. 'Yes, there have been shootings here, and there is some evidence as we can see, empty cartridges, and over here is a shirt stained with blood. We arrived at the president's palace and we read our petition but it was later, when the demonstration was over, as we were going past the foreign ministry, that troops suddenly started shooting into the crowd, which is evidence enough that they don't want people to express themselves, they don't want to hear the truth and they don't want people to claim their basic rights.'

The Minister for the Interior confirms that: 'Demonstrations are not allowed; any political activities have been suspended until the transitional period is done and the reasons are first of all security reasons – this city is not secured enough at this point. We try to avoid a situation, which was in this country for seven years, where people, all they did was argue all day long and not accomplish anything. Therefore we think that should be banned for a while, so that we can put the country back on track. The people expect actions, change in their lives and not those long political arguments.'

The long political arguments that the Minister for the Interior finds so tedious can be heard on Kinshasa's street corners. On a tree-lined boulevard, under a large, leafy, mango tree, an informal group of interested commentators, the *parlementaires debouts*, the standing parliamentarians, meet. They claim they do not belong to any political party, that they are a gathering of the people and are here to share ideas about change. They have stood arguing under the same tree since the early 1990s and at any time of the day can be heard discussing politics. Members drop by on their way to work or at lunchtime; the participants are ever changing, although they are always men. The women, I was told, have to sell in the market to feed their families. The group is a sign of how ideas of democracy, freedom of association and free speech have taken root. In Mobutu's time they stood here and grumbled about him; he tolerated it but from time to time sent in the troops to scatter the speakers or arrested and threatened them. 'Mobutu leaving, and he should stay away now, is a big relief for we the people.'

These days they complain about Kabila and keep the rumour machine going. 'We standing parliamentarians think that things are not going well here. Mr Kabila has ignored the people who have supported him. What we want is the rule of law in this country and so far we don't think that we have achieved that. He should work with other leaders of the opposition who represent the people. They should get together and set up a government that would include all forces of the opposition who have fought for change in this country, namely Mr Thishekedi who represents the people in Congo.'

Did anybody here have a different opinion about Mr Kabila, I asked. A deep groan, 'non, non,' and another voice adds 'we all share that view. This is a hard core to resist any dictatorship. It's a coalition of different forces here. It's a mosaic; it's composed of different people from all walks of life. You will find here medical doctors, you will find unemployed people, you will find lawyers, you will find almost anybody here, you'll find bank employees, here is a bank employee who hasn't been paid for a long time, there are students.

'If Mr Kabila is going to turn himself into a dictator we are going to fight him the same way we fought Mobutu.' Since it is only two months I wonder if they will give Kabila a chance. 'On condition he respects democratic principles. We had MPR, that was Mobutu's party, which was the single party in this country and look what's happening, the Alliance claims that status again, would like to be the only force in the country.'

But the Minister for the Interior, I point out, says that there has been too much talking in this country about politics, too many people under trees talking. Kabila's people took action and what they want to see is action in politics here, not just talking.

'Look, if Mr Kabila is thinking that he's not a son of this country, he should acknowledge that we paved the way for him. We had weakened Mr Mobutu at the roots and if he has come in with his forces it's because we opened the gate for him, he should not ignore that.'

The lack of information about Kabila himself has sprouted rumours under the tree, some worthy of any tabloid.

'We know very vaguely about his family.' Amidst laughter, 'we wonder why he has never officially introduced his wife if he has one, but it is rumoured that he lives with a number of Rwandan women which might explain why he has such close ties with Rwanda, those would be concubines rather than official wives.' For those who believe he is in bed with Rwanda, it is a rumour relished because it has the added deliciousness and intrigue of political metaphor. 'Rwandans are opportunistic and Kabila is letting them loot his country and take away weapons and luxury cars.'

If the standing parliamentarians are a straw poll of public opinion, a local research institute carried out a more scientific survey to measure what people thought of Kabila's first thirty days in power. The poll showed that most people would define the Kabila government as a dictatorial regime. Asked which leader they admired, almost sixty five percent chose Thishekedi; fifteen percent selected Kabila.

* * * *

Nine countries curve around the Democratic Republic of Congo's borders. A number of African states have pledged support for Kabila. The new government is styling itself as a democracy, important to keep the Europeans and donors onside. The European Union has sent a high level delegation that can be seen working its way around the Hotel Intercontinental. The EU's position is that Kabila needs help and support; he inherited a catastrophe, a tragedy of immense proportions, and should not be left isolated.

The aid agencies are thin on the ground and not sure what to do in the changed circumstances. When I met one international representative in the hotel lobby, he shifted around in his chair, uncomfortable and nervous. They will, after all, have to negotiate and work with the newcomers yet information from the field is not entirely reassuring. Another international aid organisation felt vulnerable, accused by the government of being the source of allegations that Kabila's troops were involved in the massacre of Rwanda refugees. The November before, six hundred thousand refugees crossed back to Rwanda, but several thousand are still unaccounted for. It is alleged that as Kabila moved across the country his soldiers killed large numbers of the refugees. The serious charge is very damaging for a new government trying to establish its credentials with the international community.

The Minister for Foreign Affairs, Bizima Karaha, put up a robust defence when the matter was raised. My hotel phone had rung at six in the morning with a curt message: 'Mr Karaha will see you this morning; a car will pick you up in thirty minutes.' The Minister was waiting on the patio of a villa, seated beside the swimming pool. I wondered was this one of the homes abandoned by a Mobutu aficionado who had fled across the river to Brazzaville and sequestered by the new cabinet. Karaha, who looks older than his twenty-nine years, was a medical practitioner in South Africa before joining the Alliance.

'The real issues', he says are, 'Why did these Rwandese leave their country for our country? Who forced them to come? Why were they armed? Why were they not disarmed? Who continued to arm them? Who gave them the privilege of being called refugees, because as you know ninety percent of those Rwandese who were in our country were innocent civilians who had been taken hostage by ten percent of former soldiers, the Interhamwe, people who had committed genocide in that country? So there were clear distinctions between genuine people who had been taken hostage and criminals involved in genocide. The international community watched for two and a half years these two groups living together in the same camps and they just decided to give them the same name of refugees with the same privileges.'

* * * *

I left Kinshasa on a Red Cross flight that was travelling to Bukavu in Eastern Zaire, near the Rwandan border. For a short time Bukavu and Goma were household names because the refugee camps were here. The area now shows no sign that thousands of people lived in such difficult, overcrowded conditions. It is empty and in this steamy hot tropical climate the thick vegetation has quickly grown back. The town of Bukavu itself is beautiful, the outskirts licked by Lake Kivu, although it now looks war torn. It was once a holiday retreat with lakeside villas for the Belgians and then for Mobutu's self-aggrandising, venal elite. If tourist guidebooks once described Bukavu's attractions, now there are few amenities; banking and postal services are defunct but a small commercial enterprise operates a telephone service. Non-government organisations are still here dealing with the declining number of refugees and displaced persons.

An eyewitness in Bukavu, covertly and behind a locked door, described what happened in a refugee camp near his village. In November, when the Alliance troops were in Bukavu town, they went to the refugee camp. It was in the afternoon, he says, when they grouped the refugees on a hill and then opened fire on them. The following day they went to the villages to get young people to help bury the refugees. Young villagers were forced to bury some who were alive because there was no way to save them. Petrol was poured on the corpses in order to burn them and put them in the holes.

'The operation to burn the corpses took a long time and it made the village smelly. In that camp those young people who helped the soldiers of the Alliance dig got a present of a cow; the soldiers then made the refugee camp their own camp.'

Later in Bukavu, retracing steps with another eyewitness, we drove on the potholed dirt roads outside the town. It is painful for her to recall what she saw. 'All the refugees were running away carrying their babies on their back. I was very curious to know what was happening and I asked them and they told me that RPF soldiers of Rwanda were in the camp and they were killing people. I went into the camp and I saw with my eyes the massacre. And then we were afraid and we decided to turn back. When we arrived at another camp we saw now the corpses of the refugees, the corpses of babies, old men and old women. I can't say that I saw machetes but the soldiers were using guns and bullets, they were shooting at whatever was moving.'

We get out of the old rattling car and walk on the grass, footsteps crunching on the fresh countryside: 'Here are graves of refugees but unfortunately villagers are starting cultivation on those graves.'

Villagers passed us going about their farming business, carrying machetes with which to plant and harvest. The UN and the government are agreed that a UN team should be sent to investigate, but if villagers cultivate over graves, evidence may slowly disappear or prove difficult to gather.

Mobutu Sese Seko's regime had been breathed out but the

fresh intake of breath, the administration of Laurent Kabila and his government, already had an unsavoury taste.

A year later, August 1998, Kabila dismissed his Rwandan advisors and war broke out. The war drew in other African countries. Laurent Kabila was assassinated in January 2001 and his son Joseph Kabila became President. Efforts to allow the Democratic Republic of Congo to emerge as a democratic state and to realise its full potential continue.

Indonesia

A Strange Bloom

1998

Although it was the dying days of the thirty-two year rule of Indonesia's President Suharto, when I met Indonesian writer Pramoedya Ananta Toer in his house in Jakarta he was still under city arrest. Pramoedya lives in a modest, comfortable house on a narrow street in one of Jakarta's crowded districts with his wife, Maemunah Thamrin. Their home was taken from her when he went to prison and she built this one from money put aside by making and selling cakes. He is small and wiry, with thin wisps of white hair and dressed in traditional sarong and casual shirt.

One hand holds a clove cigarette; the other is cupped behind his left ear because of his damaged hearing. His young grandson darts around the room and Pramoedya's eyes brightly follow him, delighting in watching his play. He has an easy smile, believing that a smile is an antidote for stress and feelings of hopelessness, that even as it relaxes one's muscles it serves to soothe one's nerves.

Outside the house the bell and voice of a street vendor can be heard. On other Jakarta streets there is anticipation, excitement and fear as students shout their demands for *reformasi,* democratic reform, following the crumbling of the country's economy. The financial collapse was the collapse of the lie that economic development would come first and civil and political rights would follow. Now the lie is turned over, and underneath is corruption, cronyism and political repression. What we are hearing is the clarion call for the end of President

Suharto's reign, this nemesis who has cast a long shadow over Pramoedya's life.

* * * *

Thirty years earlier, on the prison island of Buru in Eastern Indonesia, Pramoedya spins out the story by word of mouth, like a thousand Arabian nights. The inmates on the remote, desolate isle are not allowed writing or reading materials, except for some religious texts, and so he has a captive audience to whom he recites the saga measured out in daily episodes. Each day he recounts the tale for the handful of hostages in the isolated part of the camp, to ensure that it will not be lost if the chance to write the manuscript ever comes, and he hopes that the story will lift the morale of his fellow detainees. The latest instalment is whispered on, like a chain gang Pramoedya's words pass from one political prisoner to another. Most of the men are Javanese with a strong tradition and natural talent for storytelling. The tale is skilfully told and re-told finally reaching all the units and all twelve thousand detainees – men filled with fear and whose hopes of release fade with each setting sun. Jailed without trial, the prisoners do not know if they will ever leave or see their homes again, because not having been tried they do not carry a sentence for a determined period. Time may stop still here, this is the part that crushes, numbs or embitters.

Cowed by the killings and the cruelties that they witness, Buru's prison inhabitants feel hopeless. Pramoedya needs to lighten these dark times and their burden, to lift up their spirits by creating a character that can provide a model of resistance and courage. From the loom of his imagination he fashions the figure of Nyai Ontosoroh, a native woman who stands up to the injustices of the Dutch, the colonisers of the archipelago of diverse islands that became the Dutch East Indies. Nyai is born one day after eleven prisoners are killed and everyone is dejected. If she can fight injustice, Pramoedya tells them, so can they. The rich, human, entertaining stories help the men survive the harshness of their incarceration. So the captives are the first to hear the vivid, labyrinth comings and goings of Minke, Annelies, Nyai, and the scores of other characters that will in the future sparkle the pages of the Buru Quartet and make Pramoedya a renowned international writer.

One day Pramoedya gets permission to write and is given paper and a typewriter. His friends share his prison work, provide him with onionskin paper and extra food rations and build him a small room to write in. He writes continuously to retrieve the stories from memory. The austerity and toughness of prison life is not disagreeable to his creativity. In fact it seems to clear his head and ideas pour out like a dam bursting. Before his arrest in 1965, when he was a lecturer in Indonesian history and literature at the University, he and his students had gathered material about the Indonesian national awakening. He had considered presenting it as a scholarly historical work but decided that he could reach a much wider readership through the pages of a novel. Buru Island prison camp now gave him the opportunity to produce his four-part novel, whose outline was inside his head even before he was imprisoned.

Prison leaves Pramoedya with time to himself without the escape of family and friends. Pramoedya Ananta Toer grew up in the village of Blora, in central Java, where he was born in 1925, with his teacher-activist father, his hard-working mother and his eight siblings of whom he is the eldest. He grew up amidst the wonderful stories told by his mother that stimulated his lively imagination, the influence of the religious teachers and the superstitions that thrived in the village. One old woman peered at his palm and predicted, 'you are a flower, my boy, a strange bloom that will be loved by half of the people and despised by the other.'

After his mother's death in 1942 he moved to Jakarta. When Sukarno declared independence in 1945 he took part in the struggle against the Dutch. Two years later he was found carrying anti-Dutch political documents and had his first bite of prison. In jail he wrote *The Fugitive*, a story of the fight against colonialism, establishing his reputation at the age of twenty-four. After independence in 1949 he was released, wrote several novels and short stories and lectured in history and journalism in Jakarta. For a while he lived in the Netherlands and he visited China and the Soviet Union.

There have been soft and hard personal moments for Pramoedya: his father's death, the struggle to make a living as the economy collapsed, the end of his first marriage, but then his second marriage and the birth of his children.

These were tumultuous years in Indonesian politics, with Indonesia's first President Sukarno trying to keep the country together as the Cold War intensified in Asia. Pramoedya liked Sukarno's vision and was an honorary board member of Lekra, the cultural wing of the Indonesian Communist Party, but he was never a member of the Party. He liked Sukarno's politics but sometimes disagreed with him, for example with his treatment of the ethnic Chinese. That was why in 1960 he wrote a history of the Chinese in Indonesia, in an effort to shift people from their blind prejudice about this ethnic group. The text was seen as too sympathetic to the Chinese, especially their role in the creation of Indonesian nationalism, and Sukarno had him jailed for almost a year.

The coup in 1965 led to the end of President Sukarno and the coming to power of the right-wing Suharto, supported by the United States. Suharto's New Order government, Pramoedya reflects, 'was built on a foundation of mass murder'. Suharto directed the persecution of Indonesian communists, killing hundreds of thousands and jailing an estimated one and a half million people.

The night they took Pramoedya from his home in Jakarta he had just settled in to edit a collection of short stories. Soldiers banged on his door offering to lead him to safety from a throng of anti-communists that had gathered outside his house under the cover of darkness, wearing masks and brandishing knives. They were taking him in, the soldiers said, for his own protection. His hands were tied behind his back and the rope that bound his wrists was looped around his neck. In the early days of the Indonesian revolution that kind of knot was a sign that the captive was to be killed. The crowd roughly ransacked the house as the soldiers stood by. They destroyed his library and a huge archive he was collecting for an encyclopaedia of Indonesian history and culture. In the dark, shards of charred paper circled above the streets like fireflies as the masked mob set alight thousands of pages of unpublished manuscripts. He begged them to spare his papers, even asking that the government take charge of them, but the writings were destroyed. His pleas to save his books were met with a blow on the head from the butt of a rifle that left him almost deaf.

That night began fourteen years of imprisonment without Pramoedya ever going to trial. He was never told why he was arrested. Three months passed before his family learned where he was. In the first torturous years he was shunted across Java from one jail to another. Then in 1969 he was shipped to the island of Buru, off Sulawesi in the Moluccas, one of Suharto's string of penal colonies. The camps were to wean political prisoners from their misguided ideas. In reality they were excuses for arbitrary brutality, to strip people of their basic human rights and to crush their spirits into acquiescence.

The conditions on the hot, steaming gulag of swamps and savannah are barbaric. Prisoners are beaten, tortured and killed. The men must feed and house themselves and if they are sick find their own cures. All the buildings, from the smallest to the largest, and the household furnishings are made by the prisoners. They fight off starvation by eating eels, snakes and lizards before seizing thousands of acres of land from the jungle of thorny rattan thickets and the island wilderness. While the island is uncultivated, it is home to a semi-nomadic indigenous population whose way of life is disrupted by the arrival of the prisoners and their farming activities. Traditionally the nomads lived off sago, made from palm sugar and wild deer and boar; now their savannah hunting grounds are becoming fields.

The farm is up and running and the prisoners have to

provide food to the soldiers who stand guard, despite the murders and the mistreatment that they inflict. None of the prisoners weighs over one hundred pounds and they go around with thin limbs and bloated malnourished stomachs. Many have died of starvation and disease for want of basic medicines. Forced labour, torture, humiliation and capricious cruelty are commonplace. The most contagious of the diseases on the island is terror. Like a skilled epidemiologist Pramoedya prepares the antidote and continues his stories of hope, courage and resistance.

Some of the men begin to make their own musical instruments: violins, guitars, cellos and drums. Others catch the island's red and green cockatoos and keep them for company. They construct an arts building and sometimes amuse themselves with theatre, music or comedy shows.

Among the prison inhabitants are young children who had searched the jails of Jakarta for their missing fathers. When they located them, they would not be separated and ended up going into exile and serving their indeterminable sentences with them. One young boy, asked by his mother to find his father, went from one detention centre to another until he found him. He did not want to leave and stayed with him in prison. Later the father was released, but not the boy; he had been registered as a political prisoner and sent on to the island of Buru.

Pramoedya writes letters to his own children at home. Counsel from their absentee father: an admonishment to Yudi that he can go fishing provided it does not affect his studies; registering pleasure that Yana likes music but hopes it is music of good quality; an instruction to Rita to read newspapers and magazines; a letter to Tieknong for his twenty-first birthday telling him not to cry about his father and to know that his father loves him; urging Anggraini to get on with her stepmother. He knows that he will never be allowed to send them so he finds somewhere to hide the advice-laden epistles. Later he will try and smuggle out the letters and records of conditions on the island so that his eight children will know his story in case he should die on the island and might understand why he is a truant father.

One day he is surprised to receive a letter from President Suharto, who asks him to reflect on his mistake in judgement and find the true road. Mr Suharto, in proper Javanese non-speak, does not say what the mistake was. Pramoedya politely replies that his parents had taught him that the magnanimous soul will forgive mistakes just as the strong will extend their hand to the weak; there the argument is left.

With the new writing materials Pramoedya begins his masterpiece, spanning twenty years, fifteen hundred pages and a plethora of characters. The story enthralls and captures twelve thousand prisoners on Buru island and later many millions more outside.

Set at the turn of the twentieth century when the archipelago was colonised by the Dutch, the Buru Quartet is an epic about the rise of Indonesian nationalism. At the centre is the novel's narrator, Minke, an eighteen-year-old Javanese youth, and from the thread of this personality a tapestry of characters and stories unfurls. Minke, a very bright native, is educated by the Dutch to be part of the government administration. Impressed as a young man by the scientific progress and modernity of the West, the story follows Minke's personal awakening and his struggle against being integrated into and identifying with the colonists' civilization. His illusions about the superiority of Western ways are shattered. Pramoedya holds up to the light, in all its painful clarity, the arrogance of colonial rule. Through the eyes of Minke we discover the suffering of the people under Dutch colonialism, its cruel, unjust, greedy inhumanity. Minke's turning away from Western influences, towards an appreciation of his own society, mirrors the beginning of an Indonesian national identity based on its own social, religious, cultural and political values.

The character of Nyai Ontosoroh, she who gave such encouragement to the prisoners, is the tragedy of a young native woman sold by her ambitious father to a Dutch businessman, and her determination to maintain her dignity in the face of racism and discrimination. The novel teems with an array of colourful personae that swirl through the pages under Pramoedya's compassionate hand.

One sunny day there is a rumour going around Buru that Pramoedya is to be sent home. Prisoners appear from all corners of the island having travelled on foot beneath the scorching heat, through jungle, muddy paths, crocodile-infested rivers and elephant grassland, to bring him gifts and say goodbye. Write about us, they plead, so that the most vital part of our lives, which have been stolen from us, will not be forgotten. It is only a rumour and afterwards a young man says that it is kind of nice that Pramoedya was not freed, at least they still have someone who is a father to them.

Another day a priest came to visit, who had previously smuggled carbon paper into the camp, and he walked out with copies of the Buru Quartet. Five books were secreted out but six others were discovered and destroyed by prison guards.

Once the manuscripts are out of Buru, photocopies are made in Jakarta and quickly sent abroad. Storing them in Indonesia is too dangerous for both the manuscripts and those hiding them.

Despite the guards' indifference to life at the Buru camp, Pramoedya stays sane and does not mentally fragment. His writings and his refusal to submit to the oppressor see him through his years in prison and enable him to suppress what he describes as life's disappointments.

The years crawl by on Buru Island until 1979 and the inhabitants are finally leaving. Pramoedya always believed that if their freedom came it would be because of the West. The President of the United States, Jimmy Carter, has refused aid to Indonesia unless something is done about the political prisoners. Before departing they must declare in writing that they will not spread Marxism, Leninism, Communism and that they have been treated properly on the island. By the pier, where the ship is ready to board, five hundred of the last group departing for Java have already left the shore. A dozen or so are left, including Pramoedya. When they board the ship they are separated from the others and before arriving at Jakarta, the dozen or so are taken off at Surabaya, to be put away on another prison island off the coast of Java. The international press makes a fuss and they finally reach Jakarta, but to limited freedom. Pramoedya is confined to the borders of Jakarta, effectively under city arrest.

Under city arrest means that he cannot leave Jakarta for any other part of Indonesia without the permission of the local military command. Just one month free from the island and Pramoedya and another Buru prisoner, a former newspaper editor, seek out the home of Joesoef Isak and ask him to join them in setting up a publishing house. The first priority is to publish Pramoedya's novels from Buru Island. Months after they meet, part one, *This Earth of Mankind*, is published.

Overnight Pramoedya's book is a sensation and a popular success. His books are sought by all sections of society: ordinary people, students, journalists, even government officials. Then suddenly, during its sixth printing and the first printing of part two, *Child of All Nations*, the Attorney General bans both books. The books are alleged to be spreading the teachings of Marxism-Leninism and of causing unease in society. The same reasons are given when later books are banned. Pramoedya's editor, Joesoef Isak, considers that the ban is the result of authoritarian arbitrariness and idiocy; a combination of fear of a ghost that they created themselves and the race between officials to prove to their superiors that they are more anti-communist than anybody else.

They do not dare to directly harass Pramoedya, but the Attorney General questions the publishers and printers. Kafka could have written the encounter that followed. The editor, Isak, suggests to the interrogator that they organise a scholarly symposium to discuss objectively whether or not there really is Marxist propaganda in Pramoedya's books. The proposal is rejected on the basis that the interrogator's understanding is better than anybody else's and he is convinced that *This Earth of Mankind* and *Child of All Nations* are Marxist literature. The authorities then ask Isak to point out the lines of the books that contain Marxism because although they cannot find the subversive lines, they feel that they are there.

After the interrogation the face of the interviewer lights up with a smile. He puts his hand under the table; Isak glances underneath and sees the thumbs up sign. The interrogator whispers, afraid of other prosecutors hearing him, that the books are fantastic and asks him to send a copy to his house because his wife has not read them yet. He explains that he is only acting on orders.

Isak decides that there is little point looking for some rational reason behind the policy of banning Pramoedya's works. Pramoedya had to be silenced, that was all. An influential, well-known writer at the time of his arrest, he had his own ideas of what nationalism and independence ought to mean for Indonesians. His ability to connect with people made him a dangerous commentator who had to be stopped.

Isak thinks too that Suharto wants to make sure that the publishing house does not become a large and powerful company. This seems possible; based in Isak's house and garage, with Pramoedya's books becoming best-sellers, they can imagine moving to spacious offices like the big Indonesian publishing companies and having capital to build up the business. Unable to defeat him politically, Suharto and his bureaucrats set out to economically destroy him. When the government denied Pramoedya freedom of expression, they also denied him and his family an economic livelihood. Pramoedya's family and siblings suffer, the publishers go to jail, those caught discussing, reading, or distributing, are penalised; student Bonar Tigor Naipospos, charged with possession, serves five years of an eight-year prison sentence.

In spite of the banning, Pramoedya keeps writing, because that is what he does – he is a writer. The matter of writing is an individual matter, he feels, you do not consider whether it should be banned or not, you just have to write. Literature itself is not a danger to the State but writers disturb powerful elites afraid of losing their hold over the people.

He finishes the last two parts of the Buru Quartet: *Footsteps* and *House of Glass*. Then in 1995 Pramoedya takes the papers that he smuggled out from Buru island, the hidden letters never sent to his children and writes *The Mute's Soliloquy*, woven from essays and letters; a memoir of repression written from the salvaged remains of Buru. In the final segment he adds a table of the dead and missing which lists his fellow prisoners and their cause of death on the island – shot dead, crushed by falling trees, dehydration, drowned in the Apo river, malaria. This is probably the only record of those who died on Buru Island.

Pramoedya, just seventy, decides to publish *The Mute's Soliloquy* himself. The printer returns the manuscript; he fears that he could be jailed and his business closed down. A band of young journalists help, and deliver the published book just as the invited guests are gathering at Pramoedya's house for the official launch. The printing quality is not so good, the paper is the cheapest newsprint, many pages are printed out of order, but everybody is pleased to see it published, despite the flaws.

The Attorney General quickly bans the book. The irrepressible Pramoedya makes the government pay for the privilege of imposing the ban by refusing to submit copies for the censors' approval. The officials end up having to buy the books from the author in order to ban it.

* * * *

Pramoedya is a respected icon of dissent, even among the younger generation, because of his consistent call for open debate and political change. He has enormous regard for the young, without the condescension of old age. When Suharto finally went in May 1998 as a result of the students' relentless protesting, Pramoedya cheered them on their victory:

'Congratulations to you and your struggle!' and told them, 'I'm with you.'

He addressed them again the following year:

'Courage! Again: courage! For the youth in particular courage is the greatest of all capital. Without courage, as I have often said, you will be treated like cattle: deceived, herded from here to there and back again or even herded ready for massacre. It is only courage that can make a firm character.' The elderly dissenter has lived to see one of his wishes fulfilled – the end of Suharto's New Order regime.

For Pramoedya, having the courage to fight oppression is everything. At the end of the first novel in the Buru Quartet, *This Earth of Mankind,* the main character Minke feels defeated, but Nyai Ontosoroh reminds him that they fought back with honour.

And Pramoedya ends the second novel of the quartet, *Child of All Nations,* with Minke's response that they fought back – even if it was only with their mouths.

A Night of Theatre

1998

Ratna circled the stage inside the theatre, striding like a lean tigress. 'Show me the paper,' she challenged the military officer standing before her.

He looked back at her, like an uncertain trainer who realises he has entered the cage without his whip.

'Show me the paper forbidding the performance,' she demanded again, this time flashing out her empty left palm and stealing the space between them.

The officer took a quick step backwards.

'Go away. I won't leave this stage until you show me the paper, a legal paper and a reason that I can accept. You can kill me, you can do anything to me. Go find the paper.'

He replied that it was for her security.

Ratna laughed and said that she felt safe from the audience and that she would perform that night. Ratna Surampaet, a popular actress in Indonesia, was in Sumatra as part of her tour with her one-woman show about the young factory worker, Marsinah.

Back at her house in Jakarta, Ratna re-enacted her encounter with the military officer. A committed actress, on the grounds of her home is a small theatrical space.

'Did you notice that you were watched coming here?' she asked.

'Is that dangerous for you?' I replied.

'Actually it sometimes keeps you safe if you have a profile and they see foreigners calling.'

Ratna Surampaet's play *Marsinah Accuses* is the story of twenty-five-year-old Marsinah, a factory worker who was brutally killed by the Indonesian military. On May 8, 1993, her body was found in a shack at the edge of a field near her home in East Java; she had been battered, strangled and raped.

Days before, Marsinah had been on strike for the minimum wage as required by law, an increase in the daily pay of the workers in the watch-making factory to US$1.25. The workers also wanted to form an independent trade union and opt out of the state-controlled union. Negotiations took place between a workers' delegation that included Marsinah, representatives from the company, the official trade union and the armed forces; where there is any dissent, even labour disputes, the Indonesian military is never far away. The matter ended peacefully with the company agreeing to improve pay and conditions.

The next day, military personnel summoned thirteen workers involved in the strike and ordered them to resign, or face charges for holding illegal meetings and for incitement. Some were beaten; one was threatened with death.

That evening, Marsinah went to the local military headquarters to look for her colleagues, and to protest about the harsh treatment of her fellow strikers. Afterwards she was seen being forced into a white mini-van and she disappeared. Her body was found three days later.

Labour activists and human rights groups forced the police to investigate the young factory worker's death. Military intelligence became involved; the authorities denied that Marsinah's death was related to the labour dispute and attempted to obscure evidence of military involvement.

In November 1993, nine employees of the watch factory and a military officer were charged with the murder and brought to trial. The ten defendants were accused of plotting to murder Marsinah because she had questioned the dismissal of her striking co-workers and threatened to go public with allegations that the company was producing fake designer labels. The suspects were detained for nineteen days without access to families or lawyers and were forced to confess to involvement in the murder.

In April 1994, Indonesia's National Human Rights Commission released a report on Marsinah's death, suggesting that some of the defendants had been tortured, their basic rights had been violated by the military and that other parties could have been involved in Marsinah's murder. During the trial, the civilian defendants retracted their confessions alleging that they had been given under duress or torture. The trial continued and the nine civilians were found guilty of crimes connected to the killing. Prison sentences were handed down ranging from seven months to seventeen years, the longest to the director of the company for allegedly master-minding the murder. Subsequently, Indonesia's higher courts overturned the convictions. The accused military officer was tried before a military court and convicted of failing to report a crime, despite evidence that he may have been in the vehicle used to abduct Marsinah; he was sentenced to nine months' imprisonment.

According to Ratna, Marsinah was different to most Indonesian factory girls; she had a kind of dignity, the self-confidence to say no. Her story haunted Ratna and finally she wrote the play, *Marsinah: A Song from the Underworld*, around the issues of political violence and repression raised by the case. The premiere was scheduled for shortly before the Asia Pacific Economic Conference hosted in Jakarta and was performed, unhindered, before an audience of six thousand people. After the conference a second run was planned for Jakarta but was banned by the government. No letter of explanation or reason was given.

The factory worker Marsinah had become a potent symbol of injustice and the denial of even basic rights in Indonesia. Under pressure, the murder case was re-opened in May 1995. The police, reluctant to interview military officers, maintained that those previously convicted remained the main suspects.

This second investigation was suspended in September 1997 without any convictions.

In response, Ratna wrote another play, *Marsinah Accuses*, a monologue in which the young murdered worker describes the brutality of her torture and death. She planned to bring it to a number of cities in Java and Sumatra. Just before the premiere in Jakarta, the authorities came to the arts centre and tried to stop the show. Ratna asked to see the paper forbidding the performance. There was none and she performed, the theatre surrounded by four trucks of military.

In the next two cities there were no problems. As she continued her tour, the military were ahead of her, telling the venue owners that the play was political and dangerous and could make people angry, but the show went on. Each night was an endurance test for her as an actress, as she tried to concentrate and prepare for her role.

In Surabaya, the nearest city to Marsinah's homeplace, the military reaction was shrill. They rushed into the theatre screaming, turned off the lights and closed down the playhouse. Ratna again asked to see the official letter forbidding the performance, there was none. Ratna said 'no'. Hundreds of police fanned out as far as one kilometre from the theatre to stop people attending. Still eight hundred theatregoers broke the blockade screaming for Ratna. At ten o'clock that evening she was allowed to address them. Afraid of trouble she told them to go home, that she would be back.

Ratna took up the issue with the Human Rights Commission. The Commission agreed that the authorities had no right to cancel or ban cultural occasions and that permission was not needed. So when she arrived in Sumatra, and the military officer tried to ban the show, Ratna decided she would not be stopped again. Having told the officer that he could kill her but she would not leave the stage, the officer withdrew. Outside in the starlit night, the armed police blocked the roads to the theatre – still people came from all directions. They broke through small gaps or jumped over walls, at some risk, to attend Ratna's show and she played to a packed, appreciative house.

Shortly after I met Ratna, she was arrested with other

activists for taking part in a peaceful public meeting and detained for over two months. As they bundled her into the police car she demanded, 'Where is the warrant?' Just as President Suharto resigned, Ratna was convicted of ignoring a police order to halt a meeting, sentenced to time served, and released.

The end of the Suharto regime brought new information about Marsinah's murder. The army officer previously convicted in connection with her death admitted the young woman had been sexually assaulted and killed at a military location. Later the police admitted the possibility but said they had no authority to question the military. This third investigation failed to bring to justice Marsinah's killers or those responsible for the torture of the previous defendants. New information ascertained that truck drivers found Marsinah alive after being tortured; one of the truck drivers that night had contacted the police and she died in police custody. The Human Rights Commission has agreed with the government to re-investigate the case.

Ratna continues to give Marsinah a voice, I finally saw the play when she brought it to Dublin.

A Taste for Nutmeg and Cloves

2000

The second time I met Jafar Siddiq Hamzah was when we ran into each other in the dining room of a hotel in Jakarta, the capital of Indonesia. He and three other men from Aceh were enjoying a very Indonesian breakfast of *nasi goreng*, fried rice with vegetables, topped with an egg. Aceh, where they came from, is part of Indonesia, the archipelago of islands that stretch over 5,000 kilometres from the Asian mainland into the Pacific Ocean. Strung out like a necklace, at the centre is the island of Java with Indonesia's capital city Jakarta. At the extreme end, at the clasp of the necklace, is Aceh – right at the tip of the island of Sumatra.

After joining me, Jafar explained that they were about to set out for the Indonesian parliament, on this island over 1600 kilometres from their homes in Aceh, to request a referendum on independence. At the opposite table, the other men finished up their breakfast. They were dressed the way men in Ireland, in poorer times, could be seen at the church gate on Sunday, spruced up, hair oiled, shoes polished spick and span, nails scrubbed, immaculately clean collars. They had an eager, boyish enthusiasm and optimism about the task in hand. When I went over to wish them well in their quest they asked: Would I come? Why not, I'd get a taxi. No, no, we'd all fit. The five of us piled into a very small car, all elbows and laps, and headed off to petition the Jakarta parliament.

When we arrived at the legislature, other Acehnese had turned up, as arranged – development and human rights workers. The delegation from Aceh could get nobody of note to meet it in the modern, multi-storey citadel. The officials did not refuse straight away, the Javanese being more mannered than that. The delegation went up to the second floor, the elevator going 'ping' as the door opened onto a corridor and we were told to wait in a less than welcoming room. After a while we were shown up to the fifth floor and were again left waiting.

As we lingered we discussed what was happening in Aceh. I had just come from there the day before and knew how important the referendum was to these Acehnese men. The province of Jafar's birth, Aceh, has a splendid location guarding the Straits of Malacca, an important waterway for trade between Asia and the Middle East. The Venetian traveller, Marco Polo, came here in 1292 and noted that Aceh had six busy ports and that the inhabitants had converted to Islam, the faith carried on the winds by Arab traders.

The first Sultan conquered the coastline of Sumatra, took charge of the pepper and gold producing areas and created an empire. For almost five hundred years Aceh controlled much of the northern Malaysian peninsula and became a prosperous trading state. Merchants from Arabia, Persia and India came to exchange their wares for local products and goods brought from China. A letter sent from the Sultan to Queen Elizabeth 1 in 1585 modestly declared: 'I am the mighty ruler of the Regions below the wind, who holds sway over the land of Aceh and over the land of Sumatra and over all the lands tributary to Aceh, which stretch from the sunrise to the sunset.' It began a trade agreement with England that lasted almost three hundred years. The sultanate was also a renowned centre of Islamic learning.

Imagine Aceh then and the hustle of human effort and activity at the bustling seaports as the devout pilgrims set sail for the spiritual journey to the holy city of Mecca. The trade in worldly goods when the Chinese junks arrived with raw silk and fine porcelain from the Orient. The argosy of Levantine ships, their sails filled with wind as they paraded through the Persian Gulf and the Red Sea with merchandise for Europe, Egypt or Turkey. The ships sweetly reeking from the cargo of sandalwood and spices, laden with pepper, gold, ivory, tin and tortoiseshell, bound to satisfy the tables and boudoirs of the wealthy and inspiring the august poet, Alexander Pope, to write of the English aristocrat Arabella Fermor's toilet:

> 'Unnumbered treasures ope at once, and here
> The various offerings of the world appear;
> From each she nicely culls with curious toil,
> And decks the goddess with the glittering spoil.
> This casket India's glowing gems unlocks,
> And all Arabia breathes from yonder box.
> The tortoise here and elephant unite,
> Transformed to combs, the speckled and the white.'

Everything changed when the Europeans arrived in the region; their taste for nutmeg and cloves would have immeasurable consequences for the peoples of the archipelago. The Portuguese came first but the Dutch, their merchant ships lured by the promise of scrumptious spices in exchange for fire-arms, linen, velvet and glass, established a trading empire and became colonial masters, eventually transforming most of the string of diverse islands into the Dutch East Indies.

The Acehnese remained independent until 1873, when Holland declared war. The Dutch met with fierce resistance and while they took command of the capital, Banda Aceh, they never fully succeeded in penetrating the interior. The Dutch East Indies finally shook off the colonial yoke in 1949 and became the Republic of Indonesia; the capital was Jakarta, on the island of Java. Aceh was promised special autonomy but became amalgamated with the province of North Sumatra and integrated into the new Indonesia.

The string of islands in the Republic of Indonesia have a

rich variety of customs and civilisations. The population of over two hundred million is made up from more than three hundred ethnic groups speaking some three hundred and sixty-five languages and dialects. Diversity spans the peoples and cultures of the archipelago: the tribal customs of the Dani in West Papua or Dayaks in Kalimantan, the Hindu temples and decorative art of Bali, the classically Malay culture with its Islamic influences that embraced most of the Sumatran coast, the Javanese refinement and mysticism. Aceh has a distinctive culture of oral traditions, poetry and dance, and has made a significant contribution to Malay literature, especially religious writing.

While the islands are rich in cultural diversity, for political reasons the Jakarta government emphasises national unity and the importance of being Indonesian rather than Acehnese or West Papuan or Balinese. There is of course no such person as a native Indonesian since the country is an artificial creation born out of Dutch colonisation. The privileged circle that prospered and held power under President Suharto were Javanese. Many of the outer islands consider the Republic of Indonesia a Javanese colonisation, and Indonesian nationalism as another oppression. The experience of the different peoples in the Indonesian archipelago, under the arrogance and brutality of this administration, has spawned conflict and claims for independence.

The Acehnese experience has been insufferable, fanning the desire for an independent state. The first difference Aceh has with Jakarta is religion. While most Indonesians are Muslim, Indonesia is a secular state, not an Islamic one. Historically, Islam developed differently throughout the archipelago. The Muslims arrived in Aceh and Northern Sumatra in the thirteenth century. Early evidence comes from the writings of Marco Polo and the finding of Muslim graves that date back to the period. They also arrived in Java, but came across the influential Hindu-Buddhist court, and went through a process of cultural assimilation that made the Islam of Java different in style from that of Malaya or Sumatra. Politically, since the State and religion are separate, Muslims in Jakarta have had to accommodate those with secular or nationalist agendas. In Aceh, where ninety-eight percent of the population is Muslim, Islam is regarded as a religion, a civilization and a social system. Islamic leaders are a respected political force and favour an Acehnese Islamic state; this has branded them as fundamentalists.

Aceh also has economic reasons for breaking away. Like many of the outer islands, the territory remained underdeveloped and poor because of discrimination by an elite based in Jakarta. Java has few natural resources and as if it were a giant hoover at the centre of the archipelago it has sucked the natural wealth from the other islands, with little return to the indigenous populations living there. Fortunate enough to be one of Indonesia's richest provinces in terms of natural resources, Aceh has minerals, oil, gas and forestry, but less than five percent of the revenue from these resources is returned to the Acehnese. On even a brief visit there the lack of economic development is evident, unemployment is high and a considerable portion of the population lives below the poverty line. Large corporations moved into North Aceh after natural gas was discovered and their displays of wealth alienated the indigenous population excluded from the profits of industrialisation.

The most difficult problem for the population is the level of fear in the province because of the presence of the Indonesian military. The separatist group, Gerakan Aceh Merdeka (GAM), has led the armed struggle for independence and this resistance has been countered by heavy state violence. The years from 1989 to 1998 were particularly harsh when Aceh was declared a Military Operational Zone and the military was given a free hand. To control the four million inhabitants of Aceh, the Jakarta government sent in thousands of marines, air-force personnel, and the most ruthless contingent of the army, the red-bereted Kopassus. They let loose a reign of terror against the guerrillas and the civilian population, including children. The armed forces are to blame for killings, disappearances, torture, rape, internal displacement and the burning of property, including family homes and schools. They have behaved with impunity. Besides the army's appalling human rights record, there is the daily harassment that people are subjected to such as 'sweeping' operations. During these operations, which I have seen, jeeps, loaded with police that look like heavily armed military, halt buses and physically search passengers. This means that even short journeys can take many hours. Passengers are shouted at while they are lined up against a wall with their hands in the air; the men are ordered to roll up their trouser legs to show that they are not concealing weapons, the shopping bags are roughly gone through. The scene is frightening to watch let alone live through every day. The sea breezes that drift over Aceh now have the tang of despair and death.

This was where Jafar Siddiq Hamzah came from. Raised in a traditional rural Acehnese family, his education from elementary school was in Islamic Studies. His mother, educated in an Islamic boarding school, hoped that he would become a prominent religious leader, knowledgeable in Islamic law. At university, he found the authoritarian campus environment under the Suharto regime oppressive and he became interested in law. His interest in law and justice also stemmed from what he described as a 'profoundly painful experience when I was a child of being forcibly separated from my father, an elementary school teacher, who was sentenced to six months' imprisonment in Lhokseumawe Prison, North Aceh, followed by five years of exile to South Aceh, just because he refused to join the government political party, Golkar'.

After finishing law school, he started as a volunteer for a legal aid organisation and then became a member of staff with a salary of 50,000 rupiahs per month (US$12). He was sent on a fellowship to study human rights law in the US. He wrote of his time there: 'My short experience of living in a democratic country like the US reinforced my belief that the repressive political situation in Indonesia is profoundly abnormal, and that propels me to devote my studies, my life and my work, toward social justice and democratic change in Indonesia, along with working to stop human rights violations carried by the Indonesian military regime in my homeland, Aceh.'

He returned to work in legal aid in Aceh but his outspokenness created difficulties with the military and police and after they intimidated him, he decided to leave Indonesia again. He continued his studies in New York, and set up his organisation, International Forum on Aceh, to lobby and create awareness about the situation in his country. In the same way that Jose Ramos Horta had based himself in New York and lobbied for East Timor's independence, Jafar hoped to highlight what was happening in Aceh and to harness the goodwill of the international community. He knew this was an uphill battle because Western governments had supported the ruthless President Suharto and prospered from the sale of arms to the Indonesian military. After the chaos that followed the crumbling of the Soviet Union the West fears what would happen if Indonesia, the world's fourth most populated country, unravelled. The preferred solution is to preserve the territorial integrity of Indonesia and ensure the country moves towards democratic reform. There are also trade and investment considerations. Aceh's location at the vital Straits of Malacca, the waterway that provides passage for over forty percent of international trade, keeps Western states interested in its future.

The United States, Europe and Australia speak of supporting human rights and democratic reform in the region, but strategic and trade interests undermine these efforts. The profitable arms business particularly compromises human rights aspirations. A key paradox of international relations is that the five permanent members of the UN Security Council (the United States, the United Kingdom, France, China, Russia) charged with the heavy burden of world peace are also the biggest arms dealers, giving them, or vocal sections of their countries, a vested interest in war.

Where Indonesia is concerned the removal of the military from the centre of power, and control by the democratically elected civilian government, is crucial for the country's transformation into an effective democracy and for the end of human rights abuses. It is little consolation to human rights activists that Australian politician Gareth Evans belatedly wrote in a newspaper article: 'I am one of those who has to acknowledge, as Australia's foreign minister at the time, that many of our earlier training efforts helped only to produce more professional human rights abusers'. Human rights groups were saying this at the time, but their message was ignored.

The East Timor crisis in September 1999, which garnered so much public sympathy, led to the US and the European Union imposing a ban on arms sales. The following January the EU ban was lifted, despite violence in Aceh, West Papua, the Moluccas, and fears of a creeping coup by the military in Jakarta. So vigorous were the rumours that three days before the lifting of the EU embargo, the US Ambassador to the UN, Richard Holbrooke, sent a robust message to the Indonesian military that any coup attempt would be condemned and lead to international isolation.

Those in Indonesia who supported democratic reform were dismayed at the EU's position, their view articulated by the Indonesian Minister for Maritime Affairs: 'We all have a sense that elements of the army are trying to effect a creeping coup d'etat. They are subverting the work of the government by perpetuating a controlled and limited state of unrest.' He went on to accuse Western countries of hypocrisy in making money from selling arms to Indonesia. It was in this international arena that Jafar hoped to plead Aceh's case.

The attempt to make the case in the national arena of the Indonesian parliament was not going well. Since I had another appointment I had to leave. Later I heard that after being shuffled in and out of rooms and kept waiting, the petition for a referendum in Aceh shrunk on polite but deaf ears.

* * * *

The first time I met Jafar was at Medan airport, the day before we ran into each other at the hotel. Medan is the stopover for flights from Banda Aceh to Jakarta. He came over and introduced himself in his low key, gentle way. I regret now that I was so discouraging when Jafar asked me if I thought Aceh would get a referendum and independence like East Timor.

'No', I said, too emphatically. His wince was barely perceptible and I tried to explain. The night before I had had dinner with a man from the US state department on a fact-finding mission, and he said that the Americans would never let Aceh leave Indonesia. Talking to Jafar was like speaking with 'David' after supping with 'Goliath'. Maybe I should have pretended to him that the US Goliath showed weakness, when all I heard was his certainty, imperial resolve and invulnerability. Jafar with that winning smile had shyly put forward arguments based on justice, fairness and international law, and modestly proposed that Aceh would get peace and freedom. Jafar told me how heartened the Acehnese were by the referendum in East Timor, supervised by the United Nations, that led to independence. Over half a million people had attended a rally in the capital Banda Aceh two months after the Timorese vote and demanded to be heard in a referendum. They gathered under the striking Grand Mosque whose stark white walls and coal-black domes brilliantly landmark the city.

I told him that I did not believe that the authorities in Jakarta would allow independence, because they feared a domino effect throughout the archipelago that might lead to the break-up of Indonesia. The politically dominant island of Java needs the outer islands to support its burgeoning multitude since more than half of Indonesia's population lives there, and because of its own paucity of natural resources.

I was so negative about his country's future and he was so quietly resilient and determined. Still we parted on good terms and he gave me his card with his e-mail address and the web site details of his organisation.

At Medan airport, the only other western travellers had been the tall, strong-boned American oil workers of the multinational corporation, Exxon Mobil. The company's Aceh operation makes a major contribution to the Indonesian economy. Jakarta receives millions of American dollars every month in taxes, revenues and foreign exchange earnings from the plant and the military receives money to provide security and protection for its facilities. Human rights activists have raised questions about the use of members of the Indonesian military for security when they are also the perpetrators of human rights abuses. Such is Exxon Mobil's importance to the Indonesian economy that when the company announced, in March 2001, the suspension of operations in Aceh because of the bad security situation, the Indonesian Stock Market fell. Extra troops were sent to Aceh to strengthen armed protection of the gas field and liquefaction gas plant installations. The shutdown of one of Indonesia's primary sources of foreign exchange was an additional reason for the Jakarta government's decision to renew military operations. It has been suggested that the military's determination to destroy the armed resistance group, GAM, is partly driven by the need to reassure Exxon Mobil that the situation is sufficiently stable for them to carry on operations.

Jafar was one of thousands of human rights defenders scattered throughout the world who campaign for justice based on human rights and the rule of law. They show indefatigable courage in the face of immense and dangerous odds by daring to raise their heads above the parapet. It was they who turned Indonesia's economic crisis into a push for democratic reform and an end to Suharto's rule. This happened as the globalisation of information technology was spreading. Closing down access to information and ideas strengthens tyrannical rulers. The millions of people on the various islands within Indonesia were unable to share their experience such was the level of censorship and control by the authorities in Jakarta. The development and spread of the Internet and e-mail makes it more difficult for dictatorships to stifle free expression and to curb the exchange of ideas and influences that inform people and allow them to question the status quo. Aceh's capital, Banda Aceh, has a cyber café, and some non-government organisations have computers and websites, which means they can globally link up with solidarity groups and post on their own sites news about what is happening there. The web has also spawned a kind of global techno-activism, where those concerned with such issues can spread information quickly about the behaviour of governments and corporations.

In Asia the dispersal of business cards is voluminous; on a given day start with an empty pocket and by day's end it will be mushrooming with dozens of assorted cards from people engaged in every kind of activity. Aceh is no exception when it comes to the easy, eager dispensing of such cards. Now they often include web or e-mail details.

Realising the power of the information revolution, Jafar's New York organisation had set up a web page. Back in Ireland, I was researching on the Internet when I saw his name mentioned in connection with a gruesome death. I hurried home to check the business card, hoping I was mistaken. It was the same name but still disbelieving, I kept searching until I saw a photograph – it *was* Jafar. It was not a photograph of his corpse, which would have told nothing; they had tortured him and shattered his face so that he was unrecognisable.

Dental records and the marks of an old operation had been used to confirm his identity.

I learnt from the Internet that family members said he had received death threats. Suspecting that he was being followed, he telephoned relatives every two hours to report his whereabouts. Then he didn't ring – he just 'disappeared'. Known in the international human rights community, a campaign of calling, writing and e-mailing the Indonesian and US governments began as soon as he vanished. Demonstrations were held in New York and Washington, but the Indonesian military and police refused to search for him. At first the police declined to even take a missing person's report, until a thousand students and a group of four hundred lawyers demonstrated outside the police station. When investigators came, they harassed and threatened his friends and colleagues.

It seems that Jafar was abducted on a busy street in Medan, melted into the middle of a hot, tropical day. There was no word for almost four weeks until his naked, mutilated, decaying body, bound in barbed wire and bearing the marks of torture, was one of five bodies found in a ravine. The corpses had started to rot; villagers noticed a foul odour and discovered the human remains. Locals know the area as a dumping ground for victims of the Indonesian military and police. The bodies had multiple stab wounds; the injuries, according to human rights advocates, fit a pattern used by the military to suppress those who expose abuses relating to the conflict. There was no attempt at burial; Jafar's corpse was just strewn by the wayside. He was thirty-four years old.

News of the murder was reported all over the world from the Aceh paper *Serambi* to *The Jakarta Post*, *The South China Morning Post* and *The Los Angeles Times*.

Large crowds congregated for Jafar's funeral at the family home in the village of Blangpulo, in the shadow of the Arun gas refinery near Lhokseumawe, Aceh's second largest city. He was buried close to his parent's graves, where he had recently visited. The resistance group called on the Acehnese people to come and pay their respects, even though Jafar was not a member of GAM; he was anti-violence and had been instrumental in negotiating a ceasefire. The US embassy issued a press statement expressing concern and sympathy that Jafar was sadistically murdered, and stating that the US would support efforts to bring peace to the province of his birth. They have since renewed their relationship with the military, the prime suspects in his murder.

Holding someone accountable for Jafar's death is proving elusive, as is usual in Aceh where a culture of impunity pervades.

I still have his card, one edge curled from when I thumbed it in disbelief.

In May 2003, martial law was declared in Aceh, once again putting the Indonesian military in control of the province and the lives of the Acehnese people.

Regiment of Widows

2000

When I arrived to meet a group of women in Aceh, one immediately asked if I had not been stoned for walking along the main street without wearing a headscarf. Having come from Jakarta, the capital of secular Indonesia, it had not occurred to me to cover my head in this furthermost part of Indonesia. Many Acehnese women willingly wear the headdress from deep religious belief but being obliged to wear it publicly and being punished for not doing so was seemingly a relatively new development after the introduction of Syariah law in the province.

In the distant past women in Aceh held positions of equality with men at the highest-level, as State leaders and commanders of war operations. Sixteenth century widows of men who died in war joined the *Armada Inong Bale*, the 'Regiment of Widows', an armada made up of two thousand women mariners and hundreds of warships with heavy artillery. The warrior fleet cleaved a course through cobalt seas with a reputation as the strongest flotilla in the Malacca Straits. A century later Mecca decreed female rule contrary to Islamic practice and women's role as decision-makers was curtailed. Even so, Aceh's reputation for strong resistance fighters had its female legends.

In the nineteenth century, during the struggle against the Dutch colonisers, Cut Nyak Dhien, a national heroine, was the fiercest of the women who fought, and many of the wives of those Acehnese men who co-operated with the unwelcome intruders from Holland deserted their traitor husbands.

Today, the story of Acehnese women is a moving, painful, tale of rape, death, war and sorrow; of burying husbands, of birthing and burying children; of being used, repressed, suppressed and oppressed. Of desiring safety, peace, homes, loving husbands, good doctors, decent food, schools for children, normality, monotony, banality, a humdrum life without fear, greed or subjugation. The women Acehnese are tired of being at the centre of the chaos and sidelined from decisions.

In this land of beautiful rain-forested Aceh, women are at the mercy of the mayhem of war. Tortured, raped, taken as hostage, killed, they are used by the Indonesian military as a terror tactic to weaken the separatist movement, Gerakan Aceh Merdeka (GAM). The military call to houses looking for the men. If they are not at home, they suspect they are fighting with the guerrillas, and wives and daughters are taken away. In societies like Aceh that strongly follow Islam, Muslim men are seen as protectors of women; the women are taken to draw out the husbands or to deliver a severe psychological blow and sap the morale of the guerrillas. The women in Aceh say that if the army killed them it would be fine, but the intimidation and painful torture that they endure until their husbands are found is intolerable. For the Indonesian soldier the women are dehumanised, seen as primitives and rebels. Underlying the physical violation is the idea of woman as a commodity, the property of her husband, and a possession to be despoiled. The assaults plant an emotional landmine that lingers even after the battle has been fought.

The women have gathered evidence that the intimidation is widespread and systematic. In villages near the mountains the men are gold diggers and make their living from sifting through the soil for the valuable ore. The work takes them away from home for long stretches of time. The wives get visits from the military who do not believe that their husbands are prospecting. The women are tortured because of the men's absence; kicked, burnt with cigarettes and matches and beaten with electric cables.

One wife in North Aceh was six months pregnant when soldiers came to her dwelling. Her husband was not there so the soldiers assumed that he was in the hills with the resistance group. She was taken away to a torture chamber. When her husband came looking for her he found that they had opened her stomach, taken the baby out and brutally killed her.

If the army suspect that a woman has information her children may be tortured in front of her. In one home a two-month-old baby was hung by the legs and beaten and thrown to the floor. In the village of Alue Lhok, the military arrived searching for the guerrillas; male relatives were tied up and beaten, three women were raped and seven sexually assaulted. Afterwards women often feel unclean, ashamed and fear rejection by their family.

Sumiati Binti Hazah, a woman with polio, was followed home from her small trading kiosk and raped until she lost consciousness. She was too afraid and ashamed to tell anyone until she realised a few weeks later that she was pregnant.

The Acehnese woman waits – with apprehension and tension; waits for the knock on the door that means torture or rape; waits for news of her husband. Usually the military do not bury the murdered corpses and when she hears that more lifeless bodies have been found, she goes to the side of the road or the plantation to check if her husband is one of the abandoned dead lying there. If he is, there is the gunshot wound, or perhaps marks from ill-treatment or swollen hands from being tied up.

If a woman is widowed it is hard to make a living. The day begins with the struggle to survive; the night ends with the shiver of loneliness and the silence of heartbreak. There are hamlets in Aceh where sorrow and weeping have become commonplace, known as 'widows' villages', because only women and children remain, the men abducted, killed or fled into the jungle.

The Acehnese woman waits for the day the house or the shop or the market stall may be burnt; or the day the whole village may be charged with supporting the GAM; or the day the children may be taken away; or the day she may have to flee her home because of the conflict and the search tactics of the military. The entire community may leave because of security threats, frustrating the growing and harvesting of crops and leading to food shortages. Camps of displaced people under plastic sheeting, malnourished and worn out, line the main roads and the courtyards of the mosques. Even here there is no stillness, the familiar call to prayer interrupted by the ringing of gunshots in the surrounding hills.

She also waits for justice but there is no justice here. It is too intimidating to indict an army that has licence to behave with impunity in a place where the judiciary is too weak and morally bankrupt to uphold the rule of law. What reigns here is the misrule of fear.

She is a woman who supports and fears the resistance group, the GAM, who have violated human rights, executed women accused of being military informers or of fraternising with the security forces; the GAM who have taken her young and turned them into child soldiers. Some women have joined the guerrillas brandishing AK47s, gathering intelligence or running as couriers between units; village women have been trained by the GAM in civil defence. In many cases the women have lost parents, been subjected to rape and torture and have nowhere else to go.

The dominant political view in Aceh is that the small province wants a referendum on whether to remain part of Indonesia or to become independent. The Jakarta government is opposed to independence, fearing that it would signal the break up of Indonesia. Civil society groups, which emerged after the fall of President Suharto, are the main supporters of the referendum, as are the Islamic leaders, the Ulemas; the GAM see it as a way of achieving the goal of independence.

Women in the refugee camps and the rural areas say that they support a referendum on independence. Rumours promise that when Aceh is independent everyone will get two million rupiah and that schools, welfare and medicine will be free, everybody will have a prosperous life; they have been given hopes and dreams. When asked what they want the women say schools for the children, peace, the terror to stop, not to dread the knock on the door at night that will take them further into the nightmare. When they say they want independence they mean they want peace.

In the capital, Banda Aceh, the women I met have organised themselves into a human rights organisation to highlight the excesses of the Indonesian military. They have a distinct, alternative view to the prevailing referendum demand. Indonesia is a secular state; religion and state are separate. Acehnese religious leaders, who are very influential in the province, prefer the idea of an Islamic state with independence meaning a stronger role for Islam in Aceh. The women have caught glimpses of what this would mean, enough to make them wary. Jakarta has already allowed Islamic or Syariah law in Aceh. The women distrust the interpretation of the law because it has narrowed their human rights and tried to suppress their activities. They say that two men are placed on the main street of Banda Aceh and if women pass with no cover on their head their hair is cut or stones and vegetables are thrown at them. They are not against Syariah, they are devout Muslims, they say, but disagree with this interpretation of Islamic law. They do not want to be forced to wear the veil. Imagine, they say, if Syariah is brought in even stronger and women cannot go out of their homes, the windows are cemented and Aceh becomes like Afghanistan under the Taliban. Afterwards when I met and asked one of the religious Ulemas about the stoning he put it down to 'a kind of enthusiasm' after the introduction of Syariah law. The women also suspect that Jakarta's support for Syariah law is a way of creating what they call a 'horizontal conflict'. Women have got involved in the opening up of civil society after Suharto's departure and have become strong critics of human rights abuses. They were the first group to attempt to take military officers to court and to produce witnesses that would press charges and speak out. If Syariah law sidelines them, it could very well suit the government in Jakarta.

The women consider that their interests may be better served within a secular, democratic, reformed Indonesia that upheld the rule of law and punished those who violated human rights. Given a choice it would be better to be part of a new democratic Indonesia rather than an independent Islamic Aceh. If the human rights abuses were to stop, women in Aceh would have more freedom in a wider Indonesia.

The women have also run into problems with the resistance group who control swathes of the territory in Aceh. Whoever has a gun, they say, has power and authority, whether they are guerrillas or the Indonesian military, and the GAM is waging a very violent campaign. If a body shows up in the middle of the street, or a vehicle is taken, or if someone is intimidated for money, it may be at the hands of the GAM. The movement deny this, but locals know that they are sometimes responsible; the women say that the guerrillas are part of the climate of fear and if they have power, they may create even worse terror and chaos. People are caught in the middle of the war; for example, tormented by the military if they refuse to fly the red and white national flag of Indonesia, and sanctioned by the GAM if they do.

The resistance group feels that the women are diluting the independence claim by throwing up these concerns, a fissure in the cry for breaking away from Indonesia. They resented the women holding a press conference to advocate for peace. For peace, the women pray, march in the streets, distribute flowers and the message, 'stop violence against women'; they have suggested to the GAM commander that a special zone of peace should be set up for women.

When meetings were held to discuss the conflict or the political situation, few women were invited. So the daughters of the women who made up the Regiment of Widows acted. They held their own All Women's Conference, and women throughout Aceh gathered to publicly discuss their concerns. The participants were harassed and received death threats from both the guerrillas and the Indonesian security forces. Their priorities were justice and peace, fair representation in decision-making and equal economic rights. Finding themselves adrift in a society collapsing under the weight of violence and spiralling with a dervish-like descent into chaos, the women have moored themselves to the raft of peace. Unlike the reactive widows who took their role from the profession of their dead husbands, these women are proactive, carving out their own identity and advocating peaceful solutions to the province's conflict and problems.

The women of Aceh want peace and the right to walk through the streets of Banda Aceh, tossing an uncovered head without being stoned. Otherwise, on the independence issue, the demure demur.

Brazil

The Charcoal Workers

1998

Brazil takes up almost half the land in South America and most of the other South American countries touch its borders. The coastline is edged by the Atlantic Ocean; the world's largest river, the Amazon, flows through the interior. Mountains and wetlands with lagoons and marshes full of kite, hawk, egret, stork, kingfisher, parakeet, toucan, macaw, iguana, jaguar, and cougar; jungles and forests with spider monkey, armadillo, alligator, turtle, boa constrictor and over 1,800 species of butterfly populate this nature lovers' paradise.

The first people in Brazil were the indigenous Indian tribes, later joined by Portuguese colonisers and black Africans, brought over as slaves, followed by immigrants from Europe, Asia and the Middle East – each contributing their own distinctive traditions. The intermingling of people and customs has created a unique culture; interesting and exciting but laden with inequality. The majority of the population lives hedged along the Atlantic coastline; vast inland areas are inaccessible and sparsely inhabited.

Central West Brazil is the most thinly populated part of the country. This outback is home to the Pantanal, a wildlife fantasia, and to many of Brazil's remaining Indians. Road building has opened up the region to large ranches of cattle as well as fields of corn, soybean, manioc and cotton. It is also home to the charcoal workers.

To get to the mud kilns, snake off the asphalt onto the dirt roads, leaving the huge ranches behind. Next, drive several kilometres along a serpentine course of rutted tracks, deeper towards the forest, into the nether region, towards the fangs of smoke rising up in the air. Then, in the sizzling heat, follow the curling smoke to a dry expanse of flatland where the dusty ground is black and grey with ash. On each side are twenty-five mud and brick ovens, shaped like beehives. When you find them you have found the lost realm of the charcoal workers of Mato Grosso do Sul in Central West Brazil.

The charcoal worker's soot-black chest is bare, muscular and sweaty. Branded by the flames, his body bears the scars of old burns. On his head is a faded baseball cap grimy from the fire's dust and worn back to front. He wears nothing else but a pair of shorts and shoes. No special clothing protects him against the piercing heat and the belching fumes, not even gloves. He works with his bare hands.

The mud-domed kiln he is working at is six or seven feet high and ten feet wide. Inside it is like a subterranean cave of concentrated heat and fire. In front is a small entrance, about four feet in height. Through this opening the charcoal worker fills the earthen oven with wood from the surrounding forest and eucalyptus plantations. Thick chunks are placed in the lower part of the dark chamber and at the top he places the thinner pieces. Wood that catches fire easily is used. Then the entrance is closed with bricks and clay. The fire is lit and he waits for the blaze to really catch, 'with good speed', he says, 'good speed of fire with a lot of smoke and it will burn for many hours.'

To control the flow of air there are small holes in the side of the kiln. These are sealed with mud to close them off and the mud is hollowed out when the vents need to be reopened. The next day, it will take about twenty-four hours, the charcoal worker closes the first layer of holes, in the top of the oven.

After that he waits. Going by the smoke's colour, he then shuts the bottom apertures leaving only two holes, one in front of the chimney and one in the back. The infernal furnace has to be kindled through the night; he gets up in the deep, black silence, walks softly across the darkened terrain to see how it is going and to check that the wood is burning at the right temperature. It looks like he doesn't have to know anything, but there is great skill in gauging what holes to shut and when, there is great know-how. Burning the wood with a minimum of oxygen makes the charcoal. If he doesn't do the right thing at the right time, too much air blows into the kiln and the wood is eaten by fire and turned into ashes. If enough air does not reach the oven he is left with smouldering stumps of half-charred wood.

In front of the bee-hived kilns are piles of lumber ready for the fire and behind the ovens is the finished product, plastic sacks of charcoal. It is hard, physical labour and he has to carry heavy weight when loading the firewood and unloading the charcoal.

Inside the oven chimney are marks of the tar that came out with the smoke. It has a lot of toxins, which the charcoal worker breathes in when the furnace is opened to take out the charcoal. Many workers become ill, their rugged chests weakened with heaving coughs and lung disease. The pernicious vapours drift off in all directions, according to the wind. When families lived close by the children choked in the smoke, day and night. Now it is slightly better. The men's living quarters are a little further away, about two hundred metres from the ovens, and the families are not living there anymore.

The lack of shade and the baking heat from the ovens is insufferable; the hot, clammy weather outside is about one hundred degrees centigrade. The charcoal worker says the temperature inside the oven, when he starts taking out the charcoal, is usually about sixty degrees centigrade, so the heat's intensity is doubled.

His charcoal provides the reddish glow for barbecues, very popular in Brazil, and is sent to the big cities like Sao Paolo. Other kilns make smaller sized charcoal for the large iron and steel smelting plants in the State of Minas Gerais, over a thousand kilometres away, where he has come from.

The charcoal worker gets paid according to what he

produces, about fifteen reais or fifteen US dollars a day, which is much too low. Work starts at five in the morning until five or six in the evening, every day except Sunday. In this faraway place there is nothing to do and so even on Sundays he sometimes comes here and works two or three ovens to pass the time.

The landscape around the charcoal camp has become harsh – a drab, seared land of denuded forest with swathes of scorched grass and tangled undergrowth. The rustic shack where the men stay and live and sleep has nothing in it, only a couple of hammocks. It has no comfort. There is no covering on the dirt floor. Only a few pieces of clothing lie about; the men have little more than what they wear. Outside is a small stove where they cook food. Scratching around are a couple of clucking chickens that will provide dinner some Sunday. Even this mean hut is an improvement. Not so long ago they lived under plastic sheeting, which in the fierce beating heat does not bear thinking about.

The profit from the charcoal does not reward the workers. Landowners provide the eucalyptus trees, selling them to a contractor who clears the forest and builds the ovens. Sub-contractors supply the workers and decide how much they are paid and supervise the work and the camp. The wage does not include pension, social security or health insurance. The landowner and the contractor cream off most of the money. Often the sub-contractor is not much better off than the workers themselves and working on tight margins means that many exploit the men. They recruit them in the city slums, where there is high unemployment and enormous poverty, promising good wages, accommodation, food and working conditions. When the men reach the camps, the reality is very different. They have travelled a road to perdition that ends at a place far away from their homes and leaves them cut off from families and friends, penniless, isolated and vulnerable. It is difficult to escape or to find other employment; many know nothing else and cannot read or write.

There have been some small improvements to their grim, gritty lives. Before the workers got less money and were docked for accommodation, food, tools and medicine, at exorbitant prices. Sometimes after deductions they ended up not getting paid or, worse still, owing money, so that the labourer became bonded, never earning enough to clear his debt. Now the basic accommodation is free, and they can arrange their own food and medicine instead of being overcharged by a company supplier.

The biggest improvement has been stopping children working in the furnaces. One young man started when he was fourteen years old. His family were landless and needed the money. He hated having to face the oven, he says, and the fire and the dripping heat, and he thinks it is the worst job on this earth. His job was to put out the fire; he had to get inside the kiln with water and a kind of axe and extinguish it, which is a very hard thing to do. This was after the charcoal was taken out of the oven. The fire had to be put out and the ashes taken out so that the whole process could begin again. It was very hot and there were flames everywhere; the scalding heat when the water was thrown on the fire made it hiss, turning it into a sauna. Publicity and advocacy by human rights organisations, about the use of child labour in the furnaces, forced the government to introduce a scheme whereby fifty reais a month is paid for each child of a charcoal worker not working in the kilns, who is attending school.

As we spoke the charcoal worker demonstrated and explained the whole process. Then he stopped for a few minutes, his arm resting on one of the planks of timber ready for the fire. Even then he threw the odd glance at the oven, always alert, assessing what stage the burning was at. He told me that it wasn't so bad being so far from home since he was not married. There was little chance of him finding a wife around there. I left him in that oppressive heat, eyes stinging from the smoke.

Driving away on the dirt margins into the wide expansiveness of the Brazilian countryside, the mud-domed beehives become abandoned smudges on the horizon; but the smell of the smoke, the steaming heat, the bleached landscape and the wanton desolation of the camp stay with you. It is escape from a netherworld of exploitation, lacking in all humanity or joy, as hellish a place as Dante's Inferno.

Asking for the Earth

1998

The card players are squatting at the roadside amongst half-packed belongings. Onlookers peer, squint and holler as the last card is thrown in, the final hand is played. The men and their families, around three hundred of Brazil's landless people, have been encamped by the road for months. Today preparations are underway; the caravan is getting ready to go and itches with anticipation and unrest.

As he scoops up the cards one of the players explains: 'As you can see, our homes are just tents and we don't have too much to carry so it's very easy to take the tent and rebuild it in another place.' At nightfall they plan to move and invade the adjoining pasturelands, a large unproductive tract measuring between five and six thousand hectares. They say the farm has been abandoned and that nobody lives there now. 'Tonight we're going to occupy a large tract of land that is unproductive. For about ten months there have been men, women and children waiting for their land and tonight we're going to get it. Conditions living by the road are the worst possible. We have no food, no milk; there are problems with disease. We have problems with the water, there is not good water, but we are fighting against all this for what we believe'.

Brazil's record for land distribution is one of the worst in the world. One percent of the population own fifty percent of the agricultural land and much of it is underused. On the other hand, Brazil has millions of landless that want to farm. The lack of political will to tackle agrarian reform has led to the dispossessed organising themselves into a strong movement called MST, Movimento sim Terra, movement of those without land. They are asking for the earth, and if necessary, taking it by occupation. According to MST, there is enough land for everyone, and since politicians have failed to carry out reform, the MST plans to redistribute it for them. Their tactics, moving in on unproductive farms and settling families there, are radical and often lead to clashes with the large landholders and the police.

By morning the field coveted by the card players will be spotted with temporary shelters, made from black plastic sheeting inside which are beds and household things. The wire fences will be cut and the new arrivals will start planting. By morning the landowner will have heard of the night's activity.

This was the night they had been preparing for. They could not let fear in and there was a sense of communal bravado. The stakes seem high in this very real game that involves their families.

'Well, every action has reaction and we know that the owner of the land is a powerful person and he may use some violence. We just hope that tomorrow we don't have to fight against the landowner's men and his guns, which is probably a fact that should be considered. We don't have any kind of weapon, the only weapons we have are our work tools and we're ready to use them to work the land. Our fight is not just a landless fight, it is a fight of the people of the city too because if we get land and produce we can give cheaper food to the people who live in the city. So it is a fight about who owns the land and what you do with the land.'

The inequity of land ownership in Brazil goes back to colonisation five centuries ago when the Portuguese caravels arrived with explorers and adventurers. The Portuguese King divided the territory into fifteen districts or captaincies. Each captaincy was awarded, as hereditary property, to a friend of the court, who became lord of the acquired land. It was the beginning of the system of very large estates. The cultivation of coffee, cotton and sugar in vast plantations continued this type of land use, making the owners rich and powerful. At the same time social conditions created millions of landless. Some originated from the African slaves brought over by the Portuguese to work on the estates; eventually liberated, they were prevented by law from owning land.

Then European immigrants came to Brazil searching for the promised land but ended up disillusioned and homeless. Others held land but lost their farms, often to the banks, or lost jobs working the fields and ended up in slums. The cities grew fast as people drifted in from the rural areas where they could no longer make a living. Farmers with little education, they had few skills useful for towns that already had high numbers of unemployed, and it was hard to survive. The landless, tired of the lack of political initiative, are making a stand. Reversing the traditional flow towards the cities, they are packing up and heading off to settle in rural areas.

MST began when activists, frustrated with the lack of progress in reform, seized large estates. Within a short number of years a national movement had spread throughout Brazil. MST identifies estates where less than eighty percent of the land is productive. This makes it eligible for expropriation by the government under land reform legislation. Brazil has enacted laws requiring that land should 'serve its social function' but the influence of wealthy landowners at government level has hampered substantial change.

When MST families find and occupy idle land, they begin a settlement and start farming. Pressure is then put on the government to comply with the law and give them ownership of that piece of land.

Officials investigate the claim that the land has not been used productively by the original landowner, and if this is the case, the landowner is compensated and forfeits the land. The government takes the title deeds, holds them for ten years, and then gives them to the landless that have settled there. In return the families pay the government for the land by instalments.

The authorities, however, usually discourage settlement and offer little support by way of infrastructure such as water or roads.

As land in Brazil gives access to financial and political power and status, landholders are reluctant to relinquish it. The landowners have set up their own organisation and many of the occupations meet with violent resistance. These landowners have private armies to assist the police in evicting the occupiers. Members of MST have been imprisoned, assaulted, run over by trucks and murdered and leaders have been assassinated. Water near settlements has been deliberately poisoned, but the movement continued to grow.

The roadside card players were from Mato Grosso do Sul, one of the biggest states in Brazil. It is cattle-raising territory, which means large acres of land and few workers, lots of land without people and lots of people without land; one percent of the population owns eighty percent of the land. MST is strong here and has successfully taken over unused land in other parts of the state.

I left the card players and their families and travelled to another landholding in the state that had been occupied and was now a working farm. Stretching over more than five thousand hectares, the spread was owned by a Spanish count. He resided in Spain and for him the grand villa with courtyard, swimming pool and magnificent views was little more than a holiday home that he visited occasionally. Now, straddling the land, are straw-roofed bamboo huts built by the MST families who occupied it in 1993. Three years later the land was given to one hundred and sixty four families. They are well settled; fields are sprouting and clean, torn clothes are hanging out to dry.

After a relaxed lunch *al fresco*, of potatoes, salad and fried chicken set out on a long wooden table under the shade of a large tree, Ailton, one of the community, showed me around and explained how they took the land. Beneath the battered sombrero are brown, serious eyes and a demeanour that intimates he does not suffer fools. Unemployed in the city, he had found it difficult to support his family. He wanted the chance to work and to create a good quality of life for them but couldn't see how this would be possible where he was. He thought that by moving out to the countryside they could have a fresh start.

The occupation of the count's land, he recalls, was not peaceful; they came onto the farm and stayed for five or six days until they were evicted. 'The count who owned the land had police here night and day and they threw us out.' They had to leave and come back eleven times before they could legally hold onto the land. The families have little money for improvements but are growing bananas, rice and corn. The farm is a mixture of good and bad soil and they are trying out different kinds of seed, learning as they go what suits the earth best. Farmed as a co-operative, so far the enterprise is working well. It is a way of life that holds better promise for a good life.

Ailton explains that coming here has given him and his family a new lease of life. He is enjoying the challenge of making this earth, that lay fallow for so long, flourish with fresh fruit and vegetables and is content in his new role as farmer: 'We see a brighter future if we work together in an organised way, there's always hope for a brighter future. We are very happy; we worked so hard to be the owners of this piece of land.'

Rio de Janeiro

1998

On the face of it, Rio de Janeiro is not hard. Eased in between mountains and ocean, Rio has one of the most naturally beautiful sites there is. Cooled by the trade winds, the climate is pleasant although at the hottest time of the year humidity can be high. Portuguese explorer ships arrived in the unspoilt bay on January 1, 1502 and the navigators gave Rio de Janeiro (the January River) its name, mistaking the inlet for the mouth of a river. The hot sands of Copacabana and Ipanema make Rio a byword for beach life, amusement and lazy, sunny days. Overlooking the harbour, on the hunch-backed peak Corcovado, stands the famous statue of Christ the Redeemer with welcoming outstretched arms. The city's dwellers, the Cariocas, are described in guidebooks as fun-loving and hedonistic and every year organise the world's most famous street carnival. The extravaganza takes its cue from the masked costume balls of medieval Venice and the rhythms of the African heritage brought in by shiploads of slaves who came through Rio's port from Guinea, Angola and Congo to work the sugar and coffee plantations. Samba, an African musical idiom later laced with satirical, witty lyrics to acutely capture life in the metropolis, became the signature tune of the carnival. But behind the city's masquerade of exuberance and *joie de vivre* is the city's shadow side; some have met it at a tender age. Long after carnival sounds fade, the city becomes home again to children escaping domestic strife and living rough.

Rio's street children made international news when

policemen one night shot dead eight youngsters sleeping in the porch of the Candelária Church, a lovely old church precariously positioned in the middle of the traffic on the city's main thoroughfare. The murders exposed a vindictive vigilantism, paid for by shopkeepers who believed that the children lurking around were bad for business and for tourism. The death squads hired to 'cleanse the streets', a euphemism for eliminating the children, operated by and large with impunity. From 1988 to 1991 an estimated two thousand street children were murdered, usually youngsters from poor families or families of African descent. In spite of the bad publicity, the city still draws young people like a magnet.

On a visit to one of the homes that takes in street children, the sound of loud drumming came from the yard. Outside, a group were practising *capoeira*, a strenuous, full-of-beans exercise that is part dance and part martial art. Graceful and robust at the same time, the origins are not entirely precise, perhaps resembling the movements of African animals such as the Zebra, or a cock fight. The more popular belief is that it started as a martial art but then became a dance to disguise fighting among the slaves from the all-seeing eye of the slave owner. Danielle is one of the star performers; she is from Rio de Janeiro but has been living in the home for the past two years. Before that:

'I lived on the streets for four years. I decided to go on the streets when I started not getting along with my mother anymore. We were always fighting and she was mistreating me. She was drinking a lot so I just decided to leave. And I was seven years old then. When I was on the streets, I used a lot of drugs. I used marijuana and I used to sniff glue and other things and I also ripped off a lot of people. I used to rob a lot. The problem is, on the streets people do a lot of very bad things to us. They can kill us, they can rape us, so we can never really relax and sleep on the streets. We always have to be awake and we have to pay a lot of attention otherwise they can get us. So we can never relax really. You're always very uptight and worried about what can happen to you.'

After the *capoeira* a birthday cake with candles is brought out to the yard followed by a trail of clapping youngsters singing *Happy Birthday*. The birthday boy, Samuel, is thirteen today.

'I'm from Recife. I was living with my grandmother in Recife and she used to go back and forward from Recife to Rio. So one day she said, 'don't you want to come to Rio with me?' and so they talked – my father and stepmother – and they decided I could come to Rio and stay with my other grandmother; my father was dying at that time also. So I came to Rio and stayed with my grandmother but she started beating me up. She had given me a bicycle so I ran away with the bicycle. When the bicycle broke I was lost and then I met six boys and they said "do you want to be part of our gang?" And I said "yes". I was eleven years old at that time. When they went back to their homes, there was only one of them left, Rafael, and so it was Rafael and me.

'I used to beg for food in a small snack bar and they would give me something, a hamburger maybe. And sometimes I used to watch parked cars and I would get some money. Just once I had a problem with the police because my friend Rafael was not very nice to me and he gave me in to the police and then I was beaten up by a policeman but I wasn't arrested. I've been in Rio for one year and eight months now. I wouldn't like to go back to Recife with that family. I would like to go back to my real mother, she's called Rosemary and she lives here in a faraway district. I would like to go back to her – she is my real mother. They say that I can't live with her because she can't afford to support me. She has three other children and when I was small, when I was three years old, she left me in Recife with my father and stepmother. So when I came from Recife to Rio my mother came and she wanted to hug me but I wouldn't hug her because she left me when I was three, she left me in Recife with that other family.

'People say it's very dangerous for an eleven-year-old but there's many kids that are eight, nine, ten, eleven, twelve that are on the streets in Rio. The dangers of the street are killing, robbing, sniffing, smoking.'

The furore about killing street children galvanised human rights organisations to press for child legislation to protect them. As the legislation was debated in parliament hundreds of street children descended on the capital Brasília, taking over the congress and demanding that the legislation be passed. They sat in the aisles raising their hands to symbolically vote 'yes'. Their message was clear: the killing had to stop, they were not disposable; they were citizens of this country. Brazil now has very progressive child legislation but a gap remains in implementing and enforcing the law. The children themselves stayed organised and formed a national movement of street boys and girls which meets every three years to exchange views and information about rights.

The children most at risk of ending up on the streets come from Rio's poor communities that live in the mountains, in *favellas*. The cheap houses cling to the hillside like mussels to a rock. In one that I went to, the houses scramble on top of each other up the mountainside and are accessed by a narrow outdoor staircase. One hundred and sixty thousand people share sixty thousand square metres of space. The houses of brick have improved over the years but extensions are added on without regard to the basic foundations so there is always a fear of buildings toppling over. Basic services of decent water, sewage, good schools and health facilities are lacking. Walking around with one of the residents, we passed a bakery that had just been robbed and the two banks, he told me, had also recently been robbed. Drugs have added to the violence and dealers have turned the children into addicts or used them as couriers. The police, he says, have agreements with the drug dealers – if paid off they are nowhere to be seen and if not they show themselves in force. Improving conditions in the *favellas* and allowing the possibility of an education and a decent future, he believes, would help keep children at home and off the streets.

Back in the centre of Rio an energetic band of youths who

grew up in a *favella* is playing its own cocktail of music based on traditional samba, mixed with reggae and a dash of hip-hop. The African influence is strong since many from the *favellas* are of African descent. The band, creative and talented, explodes onto the stage full of verve, versatility and vigour. *Capoeira* is an art form when in the right feet, and the boys give a wonderful exhibition. It has taken nine months to put this show together; they write their own songs, about the reality of where they live. On the stage, using lights and sound effects, gunfire is musically simulated to create the background to a song about a massacre in the *favella*. Backstage the songwriter explains that his uncle was slain and he dipped into a bad mood, a kind of depression. The words came from all his feelings about what had happened. The boys in the band grew up in a *favella* known for violence with poor wooden shacks and occasional brick houses. One says it was 'a sack of poverty'. A strong social and community spirit and the setting up of a cultural centre in the favella has reduced the violence and kept the youths in the community. They have pride in where they come from and insist that they want people outside to see that the place is changing and can produce artists, musicians, composers and dancers. With that they run on to the stage for the second half of their electrifying performance.

The band was refreshing and exuberant. Danielle and Samuel were bright and resourceful – survivors of Rio's harsh streets. They were studying and hoping to create some future for themselves from the ashes of disadvantage and neglect. Rio still gives the best street carnival in the world. Like the two-faced mask worn by revellers, one half of the city can still be entertaining and glamorous; the other sinister and frightening.

Guarani

1998

The supreme god Tupa created the sun and the moon and they watch over the Guarani people of South America. His home is in the sparkling sun, the centre of radiant light and the origin of the world. He married the beautiful Arasy and she lives in the shimmering moon. One morning Tupa and Arasy set about creating the firm earth and the liquid sea, the inert mountains, rushing rivers, thick forests and the magnificent menagerie of animals. Tupa took clay, the leaves and juices of plants, the blood of a night bird and a centipede. Soaking them with spring water he made a paste from which he sculpted the first human couple and left them out in the sun to bake. As they dried they stirred into life. Tupa and Arasy looked at them and the first figure, formed as a woman, they named Sypave. To the other, shaped as a man, they gave the name Rupave.

Tupa told them how to live in love and peace, and gave them the Earth. He created a spirit of good and a spirit of evil to show them the road to follow in life. Braided from this beginning is the religious mythology of deities, monsters and mortals that form Guarani culture and spirituality. The gods mingle in the mountains, the great stretches of land, the dark mysterious caves, the rolling hills, jungles and forest, the sweet air, the sable dew, dreamy sleep, mischief and the cemetery. Gods protect the thick clusters of ripening fruit, all animals big and small, wild blossoms and plants, insects and humming bees. The human population slowly grew and for thousands of years the men and women of the Guarani retold the creation stories under the gaze of the bright golden sun and the pale silver moon that shone down on their South American forests.

The tribe were semi-nomadic warriors inhabiting settlements of communal dwellings, each of which accommodated a hundred people or more. Surviving by fishing, hunting and gathering, they practised shifting agriculture, growing maize and mandioca on different plots from one season to the next. Men cleared the sun-drenched fields and women tilled them. With no wheel, plough or metals, tools and weapons were made from wood, thorn and bone. Life was woven with spiritual belief, in harmony with the flora and fauna around, and they became knowledgeable about natural medicines; they had a vital affinity with the living world. The Guarani language echoes the sounds of the forest and their songs, dances and myths are a rich body of folklore.

Caarapo in Mato Grosso do Sul, Brazil, is the village of Marcos Veron, an elder of the Guarani. He is small and stocky and his weathered, nut-brown, lined face tells he has lived his life outdoors. He is gracious in his invitation to come into his home – a small, simple bamboo house with a clay floor, no furniture, and well-used pots and pans. Strung across the room are a couple of handmade hammocks for himself, his wife and children to sleep in. A bow and arrow, used for hunting animals, leans against the wall. Life is hard and people here tease out a living but they are psychologically, culturally and spiritually bound up with this sacred land of their ancestors. Marcos says of his people's relationship with the land: 'The land is everything for us. The land, to tell the truth, is our life. The land is our mother, our father, our everything. Without land we can't survive, we can't eat and we can't preserve our culture.'

Despite the still watch of the sun and moon, the Guarani Indians had the misfortune to be discovered by the Portuguese and Spanish in the sixteenth century. It was a painful experience that has tinged their lives to this day. The tribe has suffered for five centuries from disruptive, confusing contact with colonisers and Christian missionaries.

The Guarani-Kaiowa Indians who live in the southern part of the State of Mato Grosso do Sul, are the largest indigenous community in the country. Once upon a time a million and a half Guarani ranged across one hundred and thirty five thousand square miles of forests and plains in four South American countries. Now in Brazil there are just thirty thousand.

The Mato Grosso, in the middle of South America, is part of the great rainforest. Large and difficult to get to, it is the home of thousands of species of animals, plants and insects. Until the early twentieth century hundreds of tribes lived there.

Having lost their ancestral territory over centuries of colonisation and exploitation, the Guarani now live on tiny parcels of land encircled by cattle ranches and plantations and crops of soya and sugar cane.

'Living on the Guarani lands now,' says Marcos, 'are big ranchers, especially coming from the south with a lot of money and some agribusiness industries. They cut down all the trees, they just plant grass for cattle, and the Indians cannot go there, not even to the rivers to go fishing.'

Colonisation began in the year 1500 when Pedro Alvares Cabral set sail from Portugal in search of India and the promise of pungent, lucrative spices. A navigational error brought him to the coast of present-day Brazil; realising his mistake he sailed on to find India. Thirty-two years later Martim Afoso de Souza came to the vast territory. Martim, an explorer and a Jesuit missionary, established a base from which adventurers and Jesuit priests set off for the interior to colonise and convert.

For the next four hundred years Portuguese and Spanish explorers combed the Mato Grosso for gold and silver, while missionaries set about converting the local tribes. Rapacious colonisers exploited and enslaved the indigenous people; greed, humiliation, deprivation, murder, rape and disease were commonplace. The Jesuits gathered the Indians into settlements and taught them religious instruction until the eighteenth century, when the order was thrown out, and the settlements abandoned.

Brazil's independence eroded the Guarani's position as they came into conflict with the non-Indian community that moved and settled near the tribes' lands. The Brazilian government encouraged the plantation of Mate tea in the region, and large pieces of the Mato Grosso were sold to tea planters and ranchers. With the settlers came roads, making it easier to enter Indian areas. This affected their physical and cultural survival and brought diseases to which they had no resistance. The government then decreed that any land not sold would be kept under federal control, effectively giving the Brazilian government ownership of Indian territory. The peoples who inhabited Brazil for centuries do not own any part of it; they live on and use government land designated for them. The ancient tribe are now vagrants and squatters on their own land.

As Marcos says: 'The white people took from us the best part of the land, the best soil, the best forest and what was left was much less than half of what we had and the land left to the Indians is not so good.'

The Guarani were gathered into reservations as the new owners cleared the forest of trees, and the indigenous populations, with little regard to their rights. The Indian reservations vary in size and conditions and the Guarani say that the land is not enough to support the traditional life of hunting, fishing and farming. Around Marcos Veron's home at Caarapo, which means Root of the Tea Tree, the Guarani still live on the land of their ancestors, but it used to be much larger and used to stretch, they say, to the four rivers.

Ranchers and plantation owners exploit them as cheap labour. In Caarapo they survive day-to-day, planting food to eat inside the village, and going out for fifteen, thirty or forty-five days at a time to earn money. Outside the reservation, they work on farms and big ranches, or for the distillery, cutting sugar cane for money to buy clothes or whatever they need.

Marcos laughs and explains: 'We don't have any gold factory here.' So they need the work. 'Cutting the sugar cane is very hard heavy work. Many of our people get sick because of the dust that comes out cutting the sugar cane. They cut their hands, legs and feet because the tools are very sharp. The Indians don't earn much, but the ones in charge of the Indians get more money.' When they are ill they buy medicines in drug stores, but mostly they use medicine that they still produce themselves from native trees and plants.

The Guarani here dress in denim shirts, jeans and t-shirts. Some wear beads around their necks. Sometimes they perform traditional dances and rituals, adding beads and vivid feathered headdresses splashed with red, yellow, turquoise and violet. The synthesis of style is uneasy, reflecting their situation. The plumed headdress is a reminder of a prouder time when it was donned by heads that were assured and held high; a time before men with balding pates, bowing to an ungodly king or an ignoble God, destroyed a gentle feast of life and all for greed. God and nobility were here already in the Guarani lands, in every harmonious breath and singing bird.

A hand shaker filled with beads shudders out a rhythm, a repetitive chanting prayer in the Guarani language. The hand instrument is shaken until the sound hisses like a rattlesnake. Blowing through a hollow bamboo pipe creates a bird sound. The shaking beads and the pipe become an altercation or conversation between a rattlesnake and a forest bird. In a piece performed during festivals, the dancers circle in a soft, stomping movement. Sadly, the lethargic dancing and chanting here has lost its power and vitality, and the air of forlorn hopelessness is barely lightened by the play and energy of the children. They have their own school and are taught through the Guarani language.

In 1988, Brazil's new constitution recognised that the Indians formed a social group, and that Brazil was a multi-ethnic nation. The constitution gave land rights to the native population and undertook to demarcate all indigenous lands within five years. This paper assurance does not provide security. Government efforts to balance protection and return of Indian lands with economic development usually favour the settled population, reflecting the stronger political power of that community. Indians are seen as obstacles to progress, development and wealth. It is not simply a question of Indian rights versus the rights of rich and powerful landowners; many non-indigenous farmers are poor people settled in Indian areas during efforts at land reform. They worked hard tilling the land and are afraid of losing homes and livelihoods. Their meagre prosperity has been at the expense of the indigenous community.

The constitutional protection was undermined in 1996 when a change in Indian Land Rights legislation permitted any person, company or local authority to lay claim to part of a reserve, if they showed documents proving it was theirs. This allowed those already profiting from mining and deforestation to legally challenge the Guarani's rights to the land.

Disinherited from sacred ancestral lands, able to survive only by labouring for those who stole it from them, the Guarani have found hunger, disease, poverty and alcoholism. Despair shadows the young; hardship, hopelessness and humiliation have driven them to suicide. Suicide was rare among the tribe until the 1980s. Now the rate among the Guarani is greater than the rate for Brazil's population. Marcos Veron links suicide with the lack of land because, he says, 'if the Indians are reduced to a small plot of land they have no place to live, to survive, and they lose hope of life'.

His own son needed money to provide for his wife and children and went to work on a ranch. After a month he was sacked and the landowner refused to pay him. Marcos saw him heading to the forest and followed him. He arrived just in time to cut down the rope from which he was trying to hang himself.

Recently the restless resentment of the indigenous people in Brazil has been stirred into action. Several communities have occupied old ancestral lands. Marcos's people have proof that the land of the surrounding ranchers in Caarapo belongs to them because of the many Indian cemeteries there. The burial grounds give the Guarani a claim under the constitution. Marcos says he himself is a living testimony to the land they once held.

Sixty-six years old, he remembers the places where the Indians stayed and lived.

'We are trying to retake the land that was taken away from us because the piece of land we have is becoming too small and the population is growing, the number of families is getting bigger. We will try and retake the land by ways of law. If we are unable to retake the land by ways of law we will do it through our law, which is to enter the land and not to leave it. We will not accept other land from the government because we were born here, we lived here for many centuries and that's the land that belongs to us and we don't want any other land. We want this land that belongs to us.'

The Guarani have already occupied Lima Ry, Field of the Limes, and settled almost three hundred people there. The makeshift encampment with black plastic sheeting is uncomfortable and hot in the deadening heat of one hundred degrees, but they've begun the patchwork planting of food, rice, beans, peanuts, orange pumpkin and yellow corn and they have dug a well. They took over this land because they know that their parents and grandparents are buried here; the cemeteries provide proof that their people once dwelt here. A few years ago the Indians were taken from this land and dispersed to different parts of the state. Now they have gathered together again and returned because it belongs to them. One elder reckons that the land belonging to the tribe is about ten thousand hectares. When they came, there was nobody living in the house, so they took it over. Violent evictions sometimes follow the occupations. At Lima Ry, the Guarani occupying the land are angry and defiant but Marcos says that they want no violence: 'We don't want any problem with anybody. What we want is our land where we can live in peace. If the ranchers come here the Indians don't want any violence and if they tell us to get out we will try to stay. If there is no other way we will go to the side of the road but we will never go back to where we were, we will stick together and eventually we will enter the land again.'

Recently a farmer came and told them to get off the land

and they refused. He came with food and told them to stay on one side of the fence. They want more than this piece of land and they will wait until the farmer gives in. They have been at Lima Ry for two months and so far nobody has come from the authorities. They expect to stay here, to take root here and want the government to do something, to build an infrastructure so that they can work the land. Throughout the State the Guarani are on the move, packing up and leaving the reservations to come and join them.

In January 2003 Marcos Veron led a group of one hundred Indians in a takeover of traditional Guarani lands. The following day the rancher sent in gunmen to reclaim the ranch. Marcos was beaten unconscious, left on the roadside and died. The tribe insisted on burying him at the ancestral burial site on the ranch. An anthropological investigation has confirmed that Marcos's people are the original inhabitants and that the land should be handed over to them. Having staked their claim and lost their leader, the Guarani are refusing to leave the area and are demanding the return of the ranch.

Philippines

The Sweet Potato Will Not Be Able To Grow

1998

The universe was the sea and the sky and a large bird that flew between the two. The bird grew tired of flying since he had no place to rest and he started an argument between the sea and the sky. The bird told the sky that the sea wanted to drown him in waves; he told the sea that the sky wanted to hit her with stones. The sea responded by throwing waves of water up into the sky. The sky moved upwards and upwards but when he saw the waves rising higher he threw soil into the sea. The soil quietened the sea and then shaped itself into seven thousand islands that became the Philippines.

Or a great volcanic eruption created the fragments of land in the sea. Or the islands are the tips of a submerged land bridge that once joined China to Australia, passing by Borneo, Indonesia and New Guinea. Tossed into the South China Sea, the formation had a pristine beauty of volcanoes, notched mountains, limestone caves, coral reefs, tropical rainforests, mangrove swamps, overspilling waterfalls, thousands of plant species (including eight hundred kinds of orchid) and the richest concentration of marine life in the world. The islands fit into three groups: Luzon, the Visayans and Mindanao. The largest island is Luzon in the north, with the capital Manila; the second largest is Mindanao in the south.

Attached to Mindanao, reaching into the sea like a beak

pecking at grain, is the Zamboanga Peninsula. The original dwellers of the peninsula, the Subaanen people, lived there in comfort for a long time, and then the Muslims came. They adapted to the Muslims and then the Spanish came. Mindanao was opened up as a land of promise after the Second World War and large numbers of the Visayan people moved in from farther north; the Subaanen moved away to the mountainous parts of the peninsula.

The tribe's number is hard to gauge since census takers often miss the far barrios where they live, and many Subaanen births are not registered because of the expense involved. The estimate is about half a million people; here in the district of Midsalip about twelve thousand. The land is quite poor, badly affected by logging, and the tribe's tenure is insecure. Ancestral rights are recognised under the Philippines constitution, but no law gives them authentic papers that prove this is their land.

The Subaanen live in groups with cultural leaders called *mesalaggetaw* and Shaman healers. They live by tilling the soil but they are not just farmers; their religion, way of life, everything is one with the land.

Kota is one of the tribe's most gifted musicians and is keen to keep the tribe's culture alive. He has a dreamlike quality; his flute, cut from a tree in the forest, sends notes soaring like a songbird, a tour de force on one controlled breath. Kota explains that 'the Subaaneen own the land, but the real owner of the land is God, because if we want to work on the land we ask permission of God.'

All the tribe is involved in farming, men and women; says one woman: 'We till the ground and carry water and this time in the hot season we glean after the thresher. If we didn't glean after the thresher we'd have nothing to eat.'

At each stage of planting or reaping they perform a ritual out of respect for the earth. Spirits are in the ground; land is not just a resource – a Western way of appraising it. The Subaanen have a relationship with their land; the land is alive for them.

A string instrument, also made from wood of the forest,

accompanies Kota's flute with its deep sighing music, and the owner says ruefully: 'Before there were people here at all there were fish and elements and birds; now the people have come and the poison has come and the birds are not there anymore. In the time of my father and my grandfather at every step, from clearing the ground to the harvesting, we did our ritual but now there will be no rice growing because how can it grow on stone if the land is taken from us? Before, we sowed many kinds of rice.'

In Subaanen culture the life of the person, from the time they are in their mother's womb until they die, every stage is marked with a ritual, a *pekanu*. Every stage of planting and harvesting has a *pekanu.* Rites are celebrated as the sun is rising, catching the very first rays of light or at the time of the rising moon. *Suk Penaguy* greets the newborn three days after birth; *Su Kanubata* prepares the child for life as a Subaanen; the wedding ceremony *Sug Bela'I* unfolds throughout the night until the bride and groom enter their new home; the eight ceremonies, *Sungak Pekanu Dingag Minatay* begin when a Subaanen dies and the spirit, if it has lived a good life, takes the journey to *Baya. Pekanu Pailis* precedes the clearing of the ground before planting; the end of harvesting is celebrated with the *Beklug*, a wonderful thanksgiving ceremony. In the past, when the economic situation was better, the *Beklug* could last as long as a month with feasts that included roasted pig. In these harder times, it is more difficult to perform the ceremonies because there is not enough rice or livestock.

The Subaanen live on the steep slopes of the forest on land that is no longer very fertile. Over many years the rich, tropical forests were logged by companies who did not keep promises to replant trees. During the rainy season, since the large trees are gone, there are landslides and since the trees are no longer there to regenerate the soil, the soil is thin.

'The forest is important,' Kota interjects, 'it's where we do our rituals and we do rituals for the trees before we cut them. We don't cut them all. When the logging companies came they didn't ask the Subaanen if we wanted them to come to our place. We want to live and work on our land and we don't want our land to be destroyed.'

The tribe are so dependent on the forest that they decided to take on the loggers and kept a picket on the road going up the side of the mountain for a whole year, hampering the work. If it were not for the picket in Midsalip the trees would have been felled until everything was gone but the protest finally succeeded in stopping the logging. Unfortunately, the effects of the logging are felt every year as the soil gets thinner and thinner.

Deforestation has made the women's job of gathering firewood and water more difficult. One woman points out that she is near water and far from firewood, another is near firewood and far from water so 'the laundry isn't done sometimes; it doesn't get done for days because it is very tiring.' The Subaanen themselves have worked to restore the land by terracing the steep slopes and planting trees. In some of the barrios the fields are becoming fertile again.

At the centre of the Subaanen world and culture is Mount Pinukis. From the beginning the tribe had great respect and reverence for the mountain and the guardian spirit they believe lives there and protects them. In Subaanen sagas, Pinukis reached to heaven, and it was the pathway from heaven to earth; God came down on Pinukis. It is a sacred place, the place where the Shamans go to gather plants for medicine. The holy mount is at the centre of an ecosystem and the point where all the rivers of the Zamboanga peninsula spring from.

Kota explains: 'For us Pinukis is special because all our ancestors are buried there and it is the source of all the waters so it is important to us that Pinukis is not destroyed.'

The threat to the mountain and the Subaanen way of life now is from mining companies interested in gold. Since they have no papers under law to claim their land, the tribe is more vulnerable than the lowland settlers. They have no place else to go, unless they become beggars; with little education, they are not prepared for a life apart from farming. Mining would be the death of the Subaanen culture. If Pinukis is spoilt, the centre of their religion, their medicine, food, water and air is destroyed.

Kota says: 'If the mines come, nothing is going to grow, the sweet potato will not be able to grow, what are we going to do? We don't want the mining companies to come in here because our way of life will be destroyed.'

Where will they go, the tribe ask, what will they do? If miners come they have the right to cut down all the trees they want. An enormous amount of trees are needed to build all that is required for mining operations. It would mean the end of the forest of Midsalip; the end of all the medicines, all the birds and all the insects that are there at present. The Subaanen have their own cures for sickness, for snakebite, for rabies; the knowledge is with the medicine men. Women make medicines from local vegetation – syrups for colds and fevers from plants such as oregano and hot peppers; ointments for skin diseases, sores and itches; oil for massaging chest colds from plants and coconuts; cures for rheumatism and ulcers. These will be lost forever because only a few people have this wisdom and it is usually passed on from generation to generation. If the next generation is begging in towns and the forest is gone it means the extinction of something that cannot be replaced and that is gone from the world forever.

If mining was confined to one area, perhaps the tribe could again adapt, but the applications from foreign companies cover many thousand hectares. In the past they could evacuate and find other land, but land is now too expensive.

The Subaanen have tried talking to the mining corporations. Some companies have come and held meetings but they have not really consulted with them. They came with slide presentations and they spoke in English; the Subaanen could not understand what they were talking about and the companies made no effort to speak or to listen to the people.

Kota attended the meetings: 'We went to Midsalip and the room was full of people but they didn't talk to us. The Subaanen have drawn up many petitions and many letters asking, please let us stay on our land. We have a right, even under the mining act, we have the right to stay on our land. Just please let us stay because the graves of our ancestors, our medicine, our land, our food, our air, our water is all going to be gone.'

This has not been heard; the companies say they have heard it, but they have not. The corporations have promised schools but these are of little use if land, water and livelihood are devastated. The Subaanen have held rallies, at great personal cost. If they work for a day they get around 40 pesos, about a dollar and a half, sometimes less. It means they have barely enough, and to give a day to protest is a great sacrifice. Still they have done it and put their lives on the line. They have been threatened, but still they campaign; some have got up and spoken in public in their own language and in the Visayan language to say they do not want mining on their land. At one large rally in Midsalip, over a thousand Visayan and Subaaneen came; the Subaaneen came from even the very far barrios. Some walked for hours; some came the day before; some came without food. The government officials that were invited failed to come; the Mayor who was invited to speak said nothing; the local officials were not to be seen. Kota nonetheless was happy and encouraged with the turnout at the rally: 'Many people came to say that they do not want the mine. It's okay for rich people, they can buy rice; we have to grow our own.'

The Subaanen know that they cannot hold on to their life as it is because the forces coming from outside are strong. Government development, they believe, is assisting their extinction; they are like a dying species of bird. The tribe want positive development in which they can share, and a voice in how the land that is so holy to them will be protected and preserved; where precious Mount Pinukis can remain intact as a symbol of the sacredness of the earth, and where respect for the total life of the Subaanen, the air, water, soil, what is under the soil, where 'all is one', will be protected.

The Subaanen say they have no need of gold. 'Why would

we need gold? Haven't we a right to decide about the earth that we live on?' As tests were carried out on part of the mountain to check for deposits of the yellow ore, the Subaanen performed a *pekanu* and were delighted when the results were negative.

According to the Mining Act, the government own the resources of the country and the tribe are surface dwellers. According to Subaanen beliefs they are surface dwellers in the sense that they have a sacred relationship with the land; they are caretakers for their lifetime. According to the mining company they are surface dwellers in that they can be thrown away, they do not count – what counts is the gold. Philippine mining legislation was drawn up with the advice of the mining companies, not with the counsel of indigenous people. One of the most liberal mining acts in the world, companies have been rushing here from all over the globe; foreign businesses have applied for access to about one third of the surface area of the Philippines. The short-term gain is the immediate dollar, but in the long run the people will lose out. This kind of investment is not an answer to the country's economic problems because when the land is gone food will have to be imported; the Philippines already has to import rice. What will happen, ask the Subaanen, when more of the land is taken and more rice has to be imported? In the short term the mining companies will build a few roads, in the long term it spells disaster.

The Subaanen persist in the fight to hold on to their place on the earth in spite of language difficulties, lack of money and access to modern methods of communication. There was a sigh of relief when one of the larger corporations, Rio Tinto Zinc, dropped its plans to begin mining in the area. Other companies have lodged applications for permission to mine in Midsalip but the tribe took great heart from Rio Tinto's withdrawal and it has given them the courage to keep up the struggle. Their resilience and ability to endure hardship is remarkable. Having moved down the Zamboanga Peninsula they have run out of space and can only stay vigilant against those who would take what is left of their land and livelihood away.

'We have no place to go, what will we do?' ask the Subaanen. 'Will they give us a place on the moon?'

Moonlit Manila

1998

A big moon reflects on the water in the harbour but makes little impact on the cityscape of bright lights, high-rise and neon. Malate is prevented from slipping into Manila Bay by the seashore that runs alongside it and the Rizal Park, a sixty hectare green open space with ornamental gardens and wooded patches. Lively at night, it has hotels, Dunkin' Donut and restaurants that specialise in Filipino food or barbecued chicken; a long established popular restaurant is the Aristocrat (house speciality: deep-fried pork knuckles). Beside the Aristocrat is a longer-established four-hundred-year-old church that is a national historic monument, Nuestra Senora de los Remedios, Malate's parish church. Strolling along the park and the seashore is the parish priest, Father Micheal Martin, his parishioners either going about their business or settling in to sleep.

'You've got to ask the question here, looking at a hotel beside us which is twenty storeys and they're constructing another one over here to the left, it's forty-two storeys high, and then there are condominiums which are like just buildings of about a hundred houses all put together. We've got that in this area plus really dense housing, squatters' areas. They provide an awful lot of basic services in the area. They clean out every building and they polish nearly every shoe in the area and they serve a lot of the food to people, everything like that. But they are regarded as disposable. The ultimate test is the value of the property underneath their feet and that's about real estate. Change is coming about here and I really don't know how long communities of poor will remain in this area. There's tremendous hope and vitality in people and an ability to bounce back and to survive with little.'

On the fringes of the Rizal Park some families have set up home and are bedding down. Others catch a little sleep in the pushcarts that are used as cheap local transport throughout the city. A Filipino variation of the rickshaw, a small covered sidecar in which the passenger travels, is bolted to a bicycle or motorbike.

'There would be about ten families who sleep in this park every night; and maybe another sixty who live in these pushcarts, because a step up from being on the beach is a pushcart. And a step above that would be to be with some of your relatives, sharing the room with them, and a step above that would be to have a little place rented that you can call your own and a step above that would be in a house that you call your own but the land under it isn't your own and then you can go from there up.

'One old lady always slept over at the door of the church. She was a lovely old lady and she sold flowers there every night. If I had visitors it would seem a bit embarrassing, like why should she have to sleep there?

'But the truth is that there are people who have the great gift of opening their door and bringing people in and then there are the rest of us who are caught between our hearts and our heads and our gut.'

As we walk by some of the parishioners are still working, offering various services to the night's insomniacs.

'There's a woman here selling coffee, soft drinks, usually cheap food for taxi-drivers, people like that. They come along here and pull in. Frequently I come along here, sit down, talk to her, have coffee, eat a bit of bread or whatever. As you can see there's a table with bread on it, three thermos flasks, a pitcher of water and then there's a whole lot of glasses. The poor get served at the side of the road, that's generally the way it works, but Filipinos are very hygienic, very clean if it's possible at all. I mean the food will not be bad but, naturally enough, they won't know the source of some of the pork and some of the chicken and in general what you'll get, well, it will be from lower down the food chain shall we say.'

The priest knows his congregation, their circumstances and where they came from before arriving in Manila. Many of those living in poorer conditions have come in from the provinces hoping to earn money. He has lived and worked in the Philippines for many years and speaks the language; the encounters are warm and friendly with a bit of bantering good humour.

'President Marcos's wife was from her province, that's why naturally enough we joke about that. We look down at her feet and remember that when Marcos left the Philippines his wife left behind an extraordinary number of shoes. Anyone who I meet from the province always jokes about it. She has five children, look at the big smile, would you wonder. She's selling flowers, sweets, cigarettes. This is a good place for doing business. The police apprehend anyone who's selling, so she just keeps moving. There's legitimate business for which the police will normally extract something and then there is the illegitimate business, which is the flesh trade, and we think the authorities are making a rip-off on that too. Naturally, if something is illegal that makes you so much more vulnerable. She says if we protest we'll be put in jail.'

A cheerful young street vendor who put up a makeshift roadside stall has just returned from working in Saudi Arabia as a domestic help. The money sent home by millions of Filipino emigrants is an important part of the economy.

'There are eleven in the family so she sells at night here. Her family lives in an isolated village in the mountains and they have some rice for livelihood but she helps them to send her younger brothers and sisters to school. So she sleeps during the day and she works at night. In Saudi she worked inside a house for an Arab family and slept three hours at night. She got two hundred dollars a month working for a family there and three hours' sleep per night. She came home after a year and a half. She says you're half collapsing because of the work and then they'll get angry with you as well. Her name is Griselda.'

From out of the dark a voice hails 'hello father' and as he limps over Ray is introduced. He has been married twice but is now on his own.

'He's a technician actually, in electronics. Sometimes he fixes refrigerators, radios and TVs, because he's very enterprising. He has two children. Ray has had polio since he was a child and so people in the church bought him the equipment for fixing radios and TVs and that went well for a while but then the income wasn't big enough, especially with children. It was coming near Christmas, so Ray said you can make more money sitting at the church door begging. When people saw him sitting there they bought him a wheelchair. Some of the people who see him limping by now say, "hey you're the guy in the wheelchair", so there's all kind of ambiguities introduced into his life because of the wheelchair. He's full of hope despite his disability.'

Like every other city round midnight, Manila has love for sale, and across the road of loud traffic and hooting cabs streetwalkers have just arrived to begin the night's work. Father Martin points to one group.

'There's a negotiation going on over there. That taxi is dropping the girls to work and quite frequently the taxi drivers are employed to bring people here. People also rent a taxi, come here, pick up prostitutes, take them off to the local motels where, just up the street there, you pay for the hour or for two hours or whatever. That looks like a load of girls going off somewhere.'

Down one side street, half in leafy shadow so that cruising police will not see her, a fragile looking young woman with a bad cough is out looking for business. It's a cool rather than cold night, but she's shivering.

'She has one child who is three years old. She's from the provinces and her parents don't know. She just got out of a taxi now and she paid 60 pesos, almost a pound, to get here. She says she gets 500 pesos from a customer and that means that she can live and look after her child. And she's no idea who the father of the child was because she's been on the streets for a long time. Many, many are here because they were abused within the extended family or they were married off to someone. Generally people don't choose to work the streets; it's either sheer economic necessity or they don't see anyway out of their own abuse. Her parents of course don't know that this is how she makes a living. They think that she has other work. For three days it's so cold, she says, she's just coughing but she doesn't think that she has TB or anything like that. She's twenty. She told me that when she makes some money she goes home and visits her parents in the province and stays with them. Then she comes back here again. Mostly eleven o'clock at night she'll come here. She would love to meet somebody who would respect her and says if it were that way, it would be great. She's afraid in case the police arrest her. So many times she was arrested. If you pay 200 pesos they let you out. You can go home immediately if you pay 200. Do you hear her cough? She thinks it's just from the cold.'

Crossing the eight-lane highway with its ceaseless traffic leads to the seawall. The traffic is a steady soundtrack of noise for anyone trying to sleep here. Out in Manila Bay, which at sunset throws up beautiful red skies, ships have moored for the night. Further along is the container port with cargo vessels and cranes that stretch like giraffes in the skyline. Down from there is the passenger port, a hive of activity by day as people queue up to be ferried to their homes in the provinces. The inter-island boats, some of them aged craft, come to the pier, load up and head out to sea again. The couple of kilometres of seawall that fence off the sea extend from the Rizal Park to a large area of reclaimed land. Along here are the men in charge of the smaller boats.

'Now if you glance in behind the wall there are people who hear us talking so there are heads coming up. They may belong to the boatmen because outside the wall there's five boats and another dozen further down.

'When women are needed on the boats they ferry them out. But they'll be coming along then to have the boats blessed as well to make sure that they do the job properly. If anybody comes along here who wants to go out to the boats, they'll take them.'

The three young ferrymen are chewing on something meaty, which they immediately offer to share.

'What have you got here? Aah Adidas! Adidas! You know what this is? Chickens feet – they call it Adidas. It's after the Adidas athletic wear. People love those; five pesos for each Adidas, it's eaten with vinegar.'

Father Martin takes some and thanks them.

'Filipinos will share everything with you, whatever they have. So these are the men, these are the people who are watching over their sisters and brothers and mothers and wives.

'There are quite a few people who live along the beach. It is a place where people find some sort of refuge. So people who elope and have no place to go, they may come here. Some who are mentally retarded; groups of homosexuals or lesbians sometimes end up here. Women who are beaten by their husbands may end up there. But the gap is enormous between those at the bottom and those at the top. There is a middle class but it's small. Here the vast majority of people are near the bottom, the vast majority. It's a tough life.'

Father Martin knows many of their stories.

'Two men are just asleep there. He's quite mentally disordered that fella; it's a pity on him you know. Her six children are in Santa Maria. Now she's ashamed to go home because she left her six children there. Her companion here now, that's not her husband. She said her husband's in jail in her province, just north of Manila; and why is he in jail? He was stupid, she says. She's here for two months living on the seashore.

'She's ashamed to go home without any money, if she had a bit of money she'd go home. Anyway we'll talk about it another day. It's quite personal and while her male companion now is accommodating, I think I've seen him here with other female companions. I don't think there's any malice, I think people are finding companionship in a lonely situation. People are very natural.'

Father Martin notices that one man is injured.

'What's that? Broken leg. What happened? An accident.'

'One foot is paralysed from polio and now the other is in a plaster because he had an accident. He is sitting with one of the groups of young men; the men who like men along the beach, the men who find comfort and solace in the companionship of other males.'

We move on along the promenade, which has benches for sitting on.

'Sometimes, you see how the cement benches have a hollow place underneath them, sometimes people sleep there. It's one way of keeping the rain off. Other people work the streets and then they come here and they sleep quite late at night. There's another group here who live up trees that are suitable for making a kind of a tree house. The others say the drug pushers live up the trees, I don't know.'

Parts of the seashore are like an open-air living room with residents going about normal evening activities. In the open space people somehow manage to make their own niche.

'They're having a meal. She's preparing a drink for them; she's pouring the sugar from a plastic bag and putting into a glass. One of the things here is that food has to be got out of the way otherwise it will be eaten by ants or rats. Ants would be the biggest scavenger but rats come up the sewers and you can't keep them out. Since the history of the world the rat has been the constant companion of the poor.'

There are a significant number of people sleeping; Father Martin notices one man with socks on 'so he's not too badly off', sleeping under the coconut tree. Another man's sleeping on the actual sea wall, totally oblivious. Some people are reading; others are playing chess.

Quite a few people are under the trees and a few families

are sleeping. One child is sleeping on a piece of cardboard that isn't big enough; a family of five are sleeping beneath the coconut trees and have a big piece of plastic.

'This is filthy dirty although they have recycled anything that is capable of being recycled. Flood control from this part of Manila comes out here so it brings out all the garbage from the streets. If there is anything worthwhile it will be gathered and sold then as junk. It's terribly, terribly dirty. Manila being tropical it just has to have a great drainage system but no drainage system could take the rains when there's a typhoon, nowhere on earth could you get rid of the amount of water that comes down as fast as it needs to be got rid of.

'Now you can see, people have the minimum of clothes, the minimum of security or privacy. See the children sleeping there. Probably right now after the rain it's not oppressively hot, it's cool enough tonight but the children are sleeping with almost no clothes on them, no roof over their head, open to mosquitoes, probably not as many this near the sea, more inland and in slum areas. But God help them, just look down there; the cats going around scavenging for anything. If you moved in there the dogs would start barking. That's one of the good things, dogs protect people from intruders.'

An old man is sleeping on a wooden bench, like a piece of plywood. He probably works on one of the boats.

'Some people actually sleep on the boats. Where it's possible at all they have pieces of bamboo strung together and then they put plastic on top of it. Some of the plastic, as you see, is substantial enough. I mean it's like the cover we would use for a truck. Some of it is like the black plastic that we'd use for covering silage. But others are fairly improvised, I mean it's little more than a piece of bedding, little more than a piece of paper. This one here is like a big umbrella or one of those round table things outside a café. This is how the poor survive.'

A mother has four children sleeping beside her. Two one side and two the other side of her. The street lamp, which is defective, is going on and off in the background. She is fixing the children to try to help them sleep.

A man is sleeping on top of the sea wall, trying to get a bit of a breeze because it's cooler there.

'Visually this is a very powerful scene but it puts a knot in your gut to see that people have so much to contend with here. The only good thing is the climate. The climate for a significant part of the year is gentle, you can sleep out. Not that I recommend it to anybody.

'Even though there is little privacy, nonetheless there's great dignity. People hold themselves with great dignity. Now last year there were two children kidnapped from here, not kidnapped, because who would kidnap, I mean there's nobody to pay anything for them, but they were stolen from here. This caused terrible pain and there wasn't anything that any of us could do about it. They say themselves it could only be someone who's been around here who has watched their patterns of behaviour who could have come along and taken a child from here; so they were very hurt that anyone would do that to them. This is home, this is the only home that the people know. The children were never found, not a word about them, probably sold off… life is hard, life is hard. Just keep walking.'

Further down is a police detachment. Their job is to keep some kind of order along here, which according to Father Martin the majority do. 'There would be many policemen here who would have a great sense of integrity and honesty and would treat people fairly, but there are so many of the others.'

We turn for home.

'You've got to put the challenge of the poor to the rich here in Manila just as much as we've got to do it to the rich world. So we try to create an opportunity where the poor can, with dignity, say things in a stronger way than they can otherwise do. Hopefully, the conscience of some people will be touched and hopefully, society will be enriched because the voice of the voiceless is heard a little better.'

Disposal

1998

On a hill of rubble the buff cardboard flap lifted and the box began to move. A head emerged and dirty arms struggled through, levering out a skinny little body that wriggled free from the confines of the cardboard. The seven-year-old ears perked up listening to the distinctive motor sound of the garbage truck making its way into the rubbish dump. Other small bodies sprang from the bumps of rubble in response to the distant burr of the motor. The dumpster had picked up waste from the expensive hotels and rich residential areas of Manila and brought it here – the open pit at Payatas, in Quezon City, Manila.

As the truck trundled into the site it changed down a gear then noisily dislodged its load. High up in his cab, the driver gave only an occasional glance to the scene and the chasing pickers below. Fleet-footed, running like the wind, skidding to a halt only when they reach the emptying lorry, the children know that the best foraging time is immediately after the garbage men have disgorged their cargo. Then the scraps of food from the restaurant and hotel tables are freshest and have not had a chance to be contaminated or filched by sniffing dogs or gnawing vermin. Bread and leftovers they devour immediately, but the hungry hunters will cook up the meat again before relishing it.

It was a couple of days after the night stroll when I came to the homes of those who live further from the centre of town – even more on the margins than those in Malate. The child scavengers are as young as four or five, but they know already how to pick up garbage in order to live. Some go to school, but many stay searching through the flotsam and jetsam to trade whatever they find for money or food. The swift sweep over the hills of scattered debris provides excitement, but more importantly food for the families who live here.

From a distance the mounds of motley-coloured litter look like daubed dots from the disarrayed palate of an Impressionist painter. Move into the picture, and among the dots are the couple of thousand of Manila's poorest people who make their living by scavenging on these marginal hectares of open pit at Payatas. The rummaging families rely on the dumpsite for everyday survival. Some have been swept here after eviction from inner-city slums that were cleared for development; others have drifted in from rural areas, driven by poverty or conflict, not able to exist where large, rich landowners and multi-national corporations control much of the land. They migrated to the capital city, with empty hands and heavy hearts, hoping for a better future for themselves and their families, sometimes joining relatives already living here.

At the dump they trade broken dreams for the rough, dirty work of collecting abandoned cardboard boxes, disused rubber, iron, thrown away plastic from bags and shampoo bottles, paper, wood, glass, metal, all the discarded trash of a consumer society. The items are sold to recycling agents to buy food. Junk for food. With experience come increased earnings. Those longer at the job can deftly earn about 300 pesos a day; the new prospectors fumble to find junk worth only 60 pesos because they have not yet learnt the value of rubbish and how to properly mine these hills. Here the fat of consumerism is broken down to the lean of livelihood.

Some have made tents from sacking, or flimsy, fragile shacks from the cardboard boxes, plastic and sheets of corrugated iron. There are modest makeshift businesses, small sari-sari shops that sell simple foods like rice and vegetables at five to ten pesos a serving, and the everyday necessities that the citizens can afford to buy.

The residents say that the foul smell that souses the site and that clings to body, hair and clothes is not so bad, but the new people can be spotted holding handkerchiefs to their noses until, over the weeks, they get used to it. They have to because this is the only work here and there is nothing else available to them. Outside there are too many people chasing too few jobs. Poverty and lack of education or training make it difficult to find formal employment or alternative work. Rats crawl through the dross and heaps of expended rubbish, and hordes of cockroaches and flies find it a natural habitat. At night the mosquitoes settle and feed on the sleeping bodies.

From time to time bulldozers pack the fresh garbage to make room for more and level the rubbish so that the dump does not become another 'Smoky Mountain', a notorious waste site that became an embarrassment to the Philippine government and was finally flattened.

* * * *

On July 10, 2000, Payatas became submerged in waste as the piles of garbage buckled under the wet weight of heavy rains that had poured for days and just stopped. The rainfall was due to a typhoon that had battered the northern Philippines the previous week. The mountain of city rubbish came loose and crashed down on the shanty town of huts and shacks that stood on the compacted rubbish below, burying the dwellers. The collapsing debris burst into flames, ignited by fallen power cables and stoves in the huts. More than two hundred people, including children, died beneath the smouldering rubbish heap and many more were injured or missing. Hundreds were left homeless.

Evacuation centres were set up which gathered clothes, food and other supplies for the victims, including towels from a Christian organisation that read, 'God is our refuge and strength.' Emergency assistance and rescue operations were put in place to dig people out of their garbage graves. Buried beneath the city's trash, Payatas appeared in the world's newspapers and on television. Pictures showed bulldozers removing crushed corpses and shocked survivors from beneath the tons of rotting trash. Amidst the rubble and dirt came the smell of defiance, as the dump dwellers demanded that the local authorities be held accountable for the disaster.

The Payatas trashslide was the tip of the squalor, deprivation, inequity and injustice that is life for many Filipinos. Throughout Manila, slums and shanty towns have to fight fire and flood, eviction, disease and poverty. The forsaken who survive in Payatas are hard-working, resilient and resourceful; still they are Manila's unwanted surplus. Unwelcome in the city and driven by poverty and hunger they have ended up here – society's unwanted sweepings.

South Africa

Hangdog

1994

It is disturbing to see a grown man look hangdog, bent over until he is almost on all fours and every inch of his doubled-over body is wrapped in worn clothes and fear. In contrast, the farm dog running alongside him is cocky and confident with a well-cared-for coat. The farmer barks a command at the man and he lops on, his body contorted in such a way that it seems he is wearing chains but he is not. The farmer affectionately rubs the dog and pulls it towards him as he eases into the garden bench. His wife comes from the house carrying a tray with tea and rusk biscuits, her grey hair pulled back into a tight bun. They are a severe couple, these Afrikaans farmers from Kwazulu Natal. The wealth is in the land because the house, with its heavy Dutch style furniture, is austere, almost shabby and their clothes – shorts, shirt, boots and socks for him, cotton dress for her – are plain and useful.

For all their stoicism, master and mistress harbour their own fears in April 1994, the month when elections will hand South Africa over to black majority rule. He is from the incumbent National Party and we, Ibrahim and me, are UN observers come to talk to him. He registers no embarrassment, seems hardly aware of the short scene with his servant and his dog. Ibrahim, from Somalia, has caught my eye but says nothing; what we have observed is ingrained normality.

Later in the week, an open-backed truck pulls up at a local hostelry where I am having a lunchtime sandwich. In the back of the truck, in the hot midday sun, is a man with the same hangdog posture and look of bowed fear. A farmer and his wife step out of the cab and come into the bar. The farmer orders a steak meal for two and as he turns away he points to the vehicle and orders that something be given to the man crouched in the back. The hostelry owner tells him that the man is welcome to eat inside, as the premises has no prohibition on colour. The farmer, with a dismissive hand gesture, again orders that food be sent out to the truck and he and his wife disappear into the restaurant.

A few minutes later a bowl is taken out to the waiting passenger in the truck. The farmer appears at the door leading to the restaurant and asks what is happening with the steak lunch. He is assured that it is on its way. Several more minutes pass; the farmer comes through the doorway again, points to his watch and complains about the delay. Again he is reassured that the food is coming. The heat beats down on the truck outside; the figure in the back has finished eating but remains alert and does not rest.

Finally both the farmer and his wife come over to the bar, furious, and demand to know how much longer they will have to wait, they are in a hurry. In the exchange the farmer has become belligerent. The bar owner tells him that he doesn't like his attitude and that he will not now serve them. Angry protests fall on deaf ears and the couple are forced to leave. As they do a waiter passes them in the doorway, carrying in the empty bowl.

Zimbabwe

Tongue of Fire

2000

Chenjerai Hove lumbered into the Meikles hotel in Harare, bristling with emotion at what was happening in Zimbabwe. It was Easter time; invasions of white-owned farms were escalating and the first white farmer, together with the farm's manager, had been killed. It was the beginning of an ugly election campaign – even though the election date was yet to be announced – by President Robert Mugabe's ZANU-PF party. A formidable group, the Movement for Democratic Change (MDC) led by Morgan Tsvangirai, was presenting a real challenge to the government. A couple of months earlier a referendum to change the constitution was lost, effectively a vote of no confidence in the government. It was a chastening defeat for President Mugabe and in the lead-up to the coming elections no opposition would be brooked.

The restive Hove is a highly regarded Zimbabwean writer. He was born in 1956 and grew up in rural Rhodesia around an African extended family. These roots taught him about his county's culture and customs before the traditional landscape and society was disturbed by colonialism. He became a teacher and while working in the rural areas he was deeply distressed by the brutality that he witnessed during the War of Liberation, a war that went on from 1967 to 1980. The strong empathy he has with rural people is apparent in his work as he records their experiences first under colonialism, then during the liberation struggle and finally in independent Zimbabwe. Through fiction, poetry and essays he describes the brutishness and greed of a colonisation that left the native population abject; and the suffering and loss they experienced during the struggle for independence. He writes fearlessly about violence in the new Zimbabwe and the sense of betrayal, anger and disillusionment with a post-colonial government that has reneged on its pact with its people. His writing covers a broad spectrum, exploring many facets of Zimbabwean culture, politics, the land, nature and tradition.

When he finishes reading part of his poem *I Will Not Speak*, about the situation in Zimbabwe, Chenjerai Hove explains: '*I Will Not Speak* is a very traditional poem where the wayfarer says I will not say what I know, but what I know is this. You denounce it before you say it. What I know is this, but I will not say it – it's a way of announcing that I am now going to say it. I will not speak when I see this corruption, but I have seen this happening. It used to be performed at the chief's court. When the chief is trying a case and the chief is very corrupt, a poet who is a wanderer will stand up and say: let me tell you what I will not say, I will not speak about this, about the king doing this, I will not speak; I will keep quiet. I will not speak about the king sleeping with so and so's wife, I will not speak – and he goes on and he has spoken it. It's an art form.'

As for the present Chief of Zimbabwe, President Robert Mugabe, the wayfarer Hove will not speak: 'Our president is totally out of touch with our country. What happened, he was in prison for many years and then in 1975 he was released for some sort of negotiations. They talked and they didn't agree and Mugabe ran away to Mozambique. He came back in 1979 in a motorcade; so the guy was in prison for nine years and he came back to go into a motorcade. The Harare which he knows is twenty years plus nine, which is twenty-nine years ago. Even when he wants to shop a little bit for public relations he goes to Babars, which is just down the road, and everybody has to be removed from the shop. So he has been in a prison, because this motorcade for me is a prison, he has been in prison for twenty-nine years: nine years of involuntary imprisonment, twenty years of voluntary imprisonment and he doesn't know which country he's running. He's completely out of touch with the realities of this country, with even the realities of the world.'

Hove has what he calls in one of his books a 'tongue of fire' that just has to speak out. This has incurred the displeasure of an administration that does not tolerate criticism or dissension. 'You know I always invent phrases. We have freedom of expression. What we don't have is freedom after expression. After you've said what you've said. I did an article for *The Independent* a few weeks ago and they published today. What happens to me after that is something else but we have the freedom of expression, not the freedom after expression. You have the editor of *The Standard*, Chavunduka, and he was tortured after they expressed themselves about an issue and it's like that with everybody. You've seen what has happened to *The Daily News*, wanting to kill the editor. The freedom of expression, everyone in the world has got that, what people don't have is the freedom after expression, which you don't have here.'

Editor Mark Chavunduka and reporter Ray Choto published an article in *The Standard* claiming that members of the Zimbabwe National Army had been arrested for inciting a coup. Both journalists were taken by the military, even though Zimbabwean law does not allow the military to detain civilians, and were tortured. The men's tormentors demanded that they reveal the sources for the story and told them that President Mugabe had signed their death warrants.

The editor of *The Daily News*, Geoffery Nyarota, has consistently denounced corruption and criminal activities among top government officials despite arrest, death threats and bomb attacks. The paper was critical of the ruling party, ZANU-PF, for acquiescing in the war veterans' takeover of white-owned farms, and divulged that police transport was made available to the invaders. On Good Friday a bomb exploded in the building where *The Daily News* offices were situated; fortunately they were closed at the time and no one was injured.

For his fiery words Chenjerai Hove has received threats. 'I know the system; the only thing that they will not do to me is to have an obvious death. They have threatened me, they have bashed my car and tried to kill me in my car, but now I am used to that, I don't panic. What they do is try to intimidate you because you have written. So all these dangers of my being outspoken, I know them and I don't bother anymore. I know the secret agents following me and I go and tell them "hey how are you doing, you have to write a report, what are you going to include" and that's how I survive. What they don't dare do is put me in prison. If you can kill him, kill him quietly somewhere and make it look like an accident. Just up the road they bumped into my car, the guy just sped off. Fortunately the guy dropped a number plate and for six months I was going every other day to the police station asking "who is this guy?", until one constable said "hey you go home and relax, this is a secret service number plate".'

Uppermost in Zimbabwean minds this Easter are the farms and the 'war veterans', so inevitably we talk about the takeovers. Chenjerai Hove explains the importance of land here: 'For us Zimbabweans land is life, water is life, the sky is life, the mountains are life. When I talk of Zimbabweans I am talking about all Zimbabweans. That is why at the moment, with the farm invasions, the commercial farmers are very sad because for them the farm is life. They might have a slightly different interpretation about what a farm is or what a piece of land is but for them land is life, especially farmers of Afrikaans origin. They have nowhere else to go – this is their country, this is their land. It's a matter of thinking and knowing that the white commercial farmers and me share the same attachment to the land. We believe where your umbilical cord is buried that's where you belong. And their umbilical cord is buried in this soil; my umbilical cord is buried in this soil. So we have absolutely the same attachment to the land. Now, the difference is that what a white commercial farmer would want to do with the land and what I'd want to do with the land. He wants to plant as many seeds as possible of maize, of tobacco, of wheat, and make as much money as he can. We as black Zimbabweans want to have a piece of land so that when I die I can be buried there. Whether I am making much maize or wheat from it doesn't matter but I have to have a piece of land where I should be buried. So we have the same attachment to the land but for different reasons, but it is attachment to the land.'

At independence in 1980, agriculture was divided into three sections: large commercial farms that were owned by white farmers and which employed black farm workers; smaller commercial farms owned by black farmers; communal lands on which most of the black population lived. The transfer of land to the majority black population has not been as widespread or successful as hoped. Twenty per cent of the land still belongs to four thousand white commercial farmers, the rest distributed among seven million.

* * * *

Before meeting Chenjerai Hove I had stayed a few days on a farm in the rolling hills of northern Zimbabwe, the heart of tobacco farming country. On the drive from Harare on Good Friday all had seemed quiet enough. When I arrived, the farm was going about its usual business. These farms are large, the nearest neighbour several minutes away by car; particularly at night they seem remote and isolated. The farm is owned by a fourth generation Zimbabwean, although it is not inherited. He was a farm manager for several years before buying what he described as scrubland and turning it into fields. Sixty people have permanent homes there but with seasonal cotton pickers about two hundred adults are currently on the farm.

Word coming through about violence in other areas is not reassuring and several local farms have had visits from 'war veterans', including the one I am staying on. It's a nerve-wracking time; in the house every news bulletin is anxiously watched. They rely on foreign stations BBC and CNN coming in via satellite dish since the government controls the national news. The house telephone rings constantly and now and then a disembodied voice breaks through in the corner of the room with the latest situation report from bush radio. Under a prevailing sense of siege, it is important for the farms to keep in touch with each other.

Travelling around the district on Easter Saturday, there was an underlying uncertainty and anxiety intertwined with normal rural life. The cotton pickers were harvesting the fluffy white blossom. A young pregnant woman's baby had decided it was time to enter the world and she was rushed to hospital. A local sculptor was in a field chiselling out the shape of a flower from the distinctive local serpentine stone. Sitting with him a while as he tapped on the work in progress provided an oasis of reassurance. Among the community itself there was no hint of animosity and as neighbours met along the road they waved and greeted each other warmly.

On Saturday night, the week's work over, the black farm workers drank beer in the compound's beer hall. Loud drumming music played from an old cassette player; the occasional body threw dance shapes. The workers were concerned about the strangers who had arrived and the effect the land invasions would have on their livelihoods. The farm labourers' entire lives are attached to working on the large commercial farms. They work and live there in families, relying on communal services for electricity and water.

When asked whether he would like to own his own farm, one farm worker replied: 'I can't say I would like to have a farm because to run a farm is a very hard business, because it needs cash, knowledge and everything to do it well or to flourish well.' Another answered: 'It would be so nice to have a farm but money is the problem. It's not possible.'

In Zimbabwe, a dual system of agriculture is in place, commercial farming side-by-side with subsistence farming, and meshed together are European and African traditions and ideas about land. The European tradition emphasises legal tenure, and land ownership is legally documented. In the African tradition ownership is not recorded and the community manages the land. The African is given a piece of land for his lifetime, no more. In European terms, the value of the land is easily transferred for cash. Many living in communal areas do not really believe in this valuation. Another difference is in the usufruct value of land – how land is used. In the communal land system a fundamental principle is that you hold land as you can use it. Africans use land to feed families and bring what surplus they have to market, usually a staple crop such as maize. African farmers also grow commercial crops, such as cotton. Essentially, land can be held as long as it is utilised; it should not be left idle, even for speculative value. Legally in Zimbabwe, land can be held as long as the title deed is held, whether or not it is used. This throwback to the European colonial legacy means that a portion of land owned by the white commercial farming sector is underused. With title deeds as collateral white farmers have access to credit for investing in irrigation or machinery; good land, infrastructure, water, resources, finance have all been focused on the white commercial farmers.

I asked the farm workers how they felt about the invasions that had taken place on the farm. 'The invaders came three times. The first group it came and it was supplied with food and water and a place to stay. And what they did, they just pegged their pieces of land which they are supposed to own for themselves. After some days they went away. The second group came also but this time this group was a little bit harsh, they threatened the life. The group was holding axes and sticks and singing. They went to the boss's house threatening and insulting. It disturbed the work of the farm, took people from the work. The third group was harsh but not to the boss. It came making noise.' Were the farm workers afraid? 'The farm workers were afraid of those invaders, that's why they were involved in their singing and in the thrashing of sticks in the air. But this was done just because they were intimidated; it was not done voluntarily.' Are the farm workers worried? 'It makes them worried because they rely on the boss.'

The nature of the occupations differs from farm to farm. Usually there is loud noise, shouting and drumming. The veterans say they have come to peg land, that is, to mark it out. They peg, and set up small wooden structures for sleeping and cooking. In some cases discussions take place between invaders and owners and end with the veterans leaving. The presence of the occupiers is intimidating; farm owners and workers feel vulnerable and cut off.

At the church service on Sunday morning the congregation of both black and white parishioners was dressed in Easter finery. The choir sang beautifully, voices raised in hymns of praise. Afterwards tongues wagged at the church gate. Farmers, the enemy in President Mugabe's war, were uncertain what to do. The tobacco crop was ready and in the barns waiting to be graded before being taken to the tobacco auctions in Harare. The farmers were dressed for Easter Sunday but their minds were on the fields. Tongues talked of tactics; should they keep back the crop as leverage? The yield of dark golden leaf is needed for the country's foreign exchange reserves. 'If I burn the tobacco,' asked one, 'am I covered by insurance?' 'We're farmers,' said another. 'We produce to harvest and sell, not to burn crops or let them rot.' News was exchanged about recent events and the activity of the war veterans on other farms. There was word of one local farmer who had left his farm, the labourers were being held by the veterans and their identity papers had been taken. Others who had left their farms earlier in the week were returning. Reports were swapped of violent incidents and beatings, especially of black farm workers. Past the church the cotton fields were flecked with soft, white, miniature clouds; although it was Easter the women cotton pickers had asked to work to earn extra money.

Later that day, travelling to a crocodile farm we picked up two young men on the way to join their comrades. Sitting in the back of the pick-up they would not speak, cat's got their tongue; we would have to ask the leader. They would not say anything about where they had come from, what they were doing, or why.

The farm had about three thousand crocodiles ranging from small, almost cute, baby ones to the larger gnarled crocs. They are bred there and the skins are sold overseas. Veterans had come and pegged land; the two hitchhikers got out to join the occupation. The farm manager said that it didn't matter, there were so many there that two more would not make any difference. The farm had experienced four invasions, three of which were very aggressive. One set of invaders, a group of older men, were reasonable, even though they came with axes and machetes. These, according to the manager, were real war veterans. The others, younger disaffected men, he could not reason with at all. His voice sounded strained.

Since early this year an unholy alliance has formed between the Mugabe administration and the war veterans. Three years ago the relationship was less amicable when it was discovered that members of the government and ZANU-PF party had defrauded the War Victims' Compensation Fund of millions of Zimbabwean dollars. Protests by the veterans led to compensation payments. The cost of financing the payouts was disastrous for the economy but the veterans became allies of the government. The term 'war veterans' now encompasses not only the survivors of Zimbabwe's independence struggle but also jobless, dispossessed young men.

Back in Harare, the tobacco auction rooms have opened for business. The auction has been slow to get under way; only about twenty per cent of the bales are being put forward for sale. The farmer I spent Easter with is here: 'People aren't coming because of farm takeovers and the government has said that it will devalue by ten per cent. People are waiting for that devaluation before they put their tobacco on the floors because that will give them another ten per cent. About thirty per cent of all foreign currency comes from the tobacco trade. Agriculture in general accounts for over fifty per cent in foreign currency. It's bound to pick up, people have got their crops; they will sell tobacco this year. There is going to be approximately two hundred and twenty million kilograms; some of it has been burnt but the vast majority will have to be sold.'

This election year, the farm invasions are a rallying cry with a deep resonance. The Mugabe government presents its case in terms of the ongoing historical struggle against colonialism; the land issue is unfinished business. The argument has validity: the land grab during the colonial years left challenges around the distribution and the use of land for the new Zimbabwean government. How to deal with post-colonial redistribution is a complex question and raises issues about the nature of land ownership and how land is used. Redistribution needs to deal with these differences and needs to encompass agricultural training and capital investment to ensure farms maintain productivity when taken over. The farm invasions are a manifestation of a clash between a farming community concerned with government support for this disorderly re-distribution and a government which is not convinced that the white commercial farmers are co-operating with serious reform.

Mugabe's opponents argue that the matter is being handled in an irrational way and not according to social needs. Land is being used by the ruling party to stay in power and is a pretext for violating human rights with impunity. The opposition insist that the rule of law and democratic processes must be upheld.

Chenjerai Hove is critical of Mugabe's exploitation of the land issue for political purposes and the blood, violence and division wreaked on the country. 'He is going around about these farm invasions calling them peaceful invasions. For goodness sake, an invasion has never been peaceful and you can't invent a new language simply for you to keep power. It's like saying I'm going to kill you very nicely.

'We should impeach the president. He took an oath to uphold the constitution, the law of this country. He must be impeached and he's also frightened because if he leaves office right now – I work for a human rights organisation, we have big files – he is going to go to court and this is what he's afraid of, why he's inciting people to murder, to harm citizens who are critical of his system.'

The Tuesday after Easter, farmers attend the memorial service in Harare for David Stevens, the first white farm owner killed. He and the foreman on the farm, Julius Andoche, were murdered the previous week. Since then, farmer Martin Olds has been killed. David Stevens was involved in MDC and had raised questions about corruption in his local council. Hundreds are gathered at the memorial. The black workers from the Stevens farm are not; they were invited but were threatened and told that they should stay away. The vicar says that the murderers must be brought forward, not for revenge but for justice. He says that Stevens' death was not an 'incident'; it was murder, and if we call a murder an incident we have lost respect for human life. The church organ leads the congregation in *The Lord is My Shepherd*.

When I meet the Minister of Information, Chen Chimuntengwende, and ask him about the government's failure to maintain law and order and protect all the country's citizens, he is smooth-tongued and unconvincing. His glib replies about the farm invasions, violence and corruption are coolly and calmly measured.

The two farmers, he says, 'were shot because they fired first or they provoked the fighting which resulted in their death.' No one else believes this version. He maintains that the police are doing their job despite evidence that at best they are turning a blind eye to the violence. When asked about the violence directed against the opposition, Chimuntengwende replies: 'It is not true that MDC people can't wear their t-shirts in the rural areas – they do – but if they provoke trouble they can get into difficulties.' The recent deaths of five MDC supporters are 'unfortunate, we don't encourage that'.

Today's corruption scandal is the discovery that money collected as a levy for dealing with HIV/AIDS has disappeared. The government, he says, has given a directive to the

Department of Tax that if they receive such money it should be put in a particular vault and sent every month to where it is supposed to go. As I leave, the minister, keeping up the rhetoric of the historical grievance, mentions that he has read James Connolly, the Irish socialist leader executed after the Easter Rising in 1916. He says the situation in Zimbabwe is the same as it was in Ireland.

The colonial experience stays in the national psyche long after the changing of flags and twenty years of independence is a short time to change ways of thinking in Zimbabwe. This was most notable in the attitude of the black farm workers who were vulnerable and dependent and lacked the confidence to envisage a life outside the paternalism of the boss.

The land invasions this Easter are being politically manipulated because of the impending national elections and to distract attention from other issues. Chenjerai Hove believes that Mugabe will do anything to win. 'Our president loves power. He cannot imagine himself out of power. He thinks that he's the only one born with the privilege to rule, not even the privilege but the right. Ruling a country after elections is not a right; it's a privilege. ZANU-PF has never in the past twenty years had the challenge that they have now from an opposition party and as a result of that they have never had to learn the language of persuasion, to persuade voters to vote for them.

'I go to hospital to see a relative and I find the relative dying on the floor, bleeding to death. You go to schools, there are just four walls, no books. The teacher says, I do my best but there are no books. You go to a clinic in the rural areas. You find it is just four walls and the nurse is not even properly qualified and there is not even a tablet for a headache and meanwhile they are publishing these wrong articles, which say achievement in health, achievement in education. That is total rubbish and that is madness and we are in a state of madness.

'I think the president has totally lost his mind because he has totally forgotten who elected him and what the responsibility of an elected leader is. He is behaving like a dictator and he is a dictator. You know some of his friends – it was Honecker, it was Ceaucescu, it was Banda, it was Mengistu Haile Mariam, an exiled dictator wanted in his country for genocide; it was all these guys, even Pinochet, he played around with Pinochet at some point. You can judge a man's character by his friends.'

Despite intimidation of opposition members, thousands attend an MDC rally to demand change. Voices are raised loudly, enthusiastically, exultantly, bodies move rhythmically to the chant, thrusting out chests wearing opposition t-shirts (enough reason in this country to be beaten up), hands clap noisily. Morgan Tsvangirai, leader of Movement for Democratic Change, sits in a chair under a makeshift canopy; when he rises to speak he is greeted with voluble cheers and whistles. Tsvangirai has a prizefighter build and his trade union background makes him a rousing orator on the hustings. His tongue lashes out at Mugabe and ZANU-PF efforts to bully opposition supporters. Later, during our interview, he says the land issue is a smokescreen to whip up fervour and keep people from discussing the real issues of a crumbling economy, unemployment and poverty.

Economic hardship is wrapping around Zimbabwe like a damp cloak. Farm invasions have disrupted agricultural production, making life difficult for farm owners and farm workers. In the townships around Harare the scourge of unemployment is running at seventy to eighty per cent. Living conditions are squalid and overcrowded, sewerage is non-existent, the roads are deteriorating and street lighting is not working. Originally, the townships were built to accommodate the black population who came to Harare to service the city's white, rich citizens – the black maids and gardeners who worked in Harare but kept their roots with their families out in the countryside. The small cabins are more suited to the requirements of the single migrant worker in need of temporary shelter than the larger families of husbands, wives and children that now live there. Township tongues are mistrusting, resentful, angry or uncomprehending as residents cite the lack of decent living quarters, health clinics, schools, jobs, the price of food, transport or fuel. In recent years, rising food prices, unemployment, inflation and unmet expectations have led to strikes, protests, food riots and political opposition.

One man raising his family cooped up in one of the cabins explains (with just the two of us in the room, it already feels crowded): 'Food's expensive, education's expensive and the living conditions, we don't have good accommodation, we are just living in a crowd, instead of living each one in his room we are crowded in one room. My children are now full-grown and they can't get any work to support themselves. We are just living like this, no sign of improvement. If I'm not working how can I stay here, because you can't stay in town without working. Nobody can support you and nobody will give you anything.'

Did people from this township go to occupy farms?

'Yes, I heard that some people are going there but not myself. I don't know whether they can be given enough land for ploughing.'

A young man, intelligent and articulate, can get no work: 'The conditions are really tough; a lot of unemployment, a lot of people are suffering. Even those going to work, they cannot live on their wages and salaries. So conditions are generally tough, especially in townships.'

Does land reform concern them? 'People in towns, they are concerned about the land reform but they're not for the way the war vets are taking over the land illegally. They think it should be done in a professional way, a legal way where it goes through stages up until the land is redistributed equally, not like the present scenario where people are just going and grabbing land. I think they are afraid it is going to affect our economy because we Zimbabweans rely mostly on agriculture. The present scene is bad for agriculture because it's going to disturb a lot of activities on farms and everything. So people in towns are against the invasions. A small number from the community have left for the land; they are paid 50 Zimbabwean dollars a day (about one and a half US dollars), given transport and sometimes are under orders from the ZANU-PF party, not many but some are involved. Not all the people are war vets, they are just taking advantage of the scene. Many of them are young people, not really the people who went to war. Most of them are unemployed; they have nothing to do so when something like this happens they just go, take a chance.'

He wants the government to deal with the issues that affect their daily life. 'The government has moved the agenda from the main things, HIV/AIDS, poverty, unemployment, the economy, and focused on land. In this township people begged, stole and borrowed to invest in their children's education but jobs are not available.'

One young woman with an honours science degree who lives nearby is glad to have work as a cleaner in the local inn.

Tongues click in disgust at government corruption and President Mugabe's expensive military engagement in the affairs of the Democratic Republic of Congo. Zimbabwe's involvement in this costly war is more about lucrative mining contracts that benefit private companies controlled by government officials and military personnel than about any national interest.

The taxi driver who drives me back from the township has a 'tongue of fire' too. It peppers inside his mouth until he can't hold its hot coals any longer. He spits them out, like sparks from a welder's tool, as he denounces Mugabe and what he is doing to Zimbabwe. His heaving frame, wedged between the seat and the steering wheel, erupts like a volcanic mountain. 'He is now far removed from the people. There is no money, no jobs, no food even for the children.' His outburst lasts a few minutes; just as quickly he quietens.

'I'm sorry. I hope I haven't offended you. I only speak my mind to a stranger like you. I wouldn't speak to anyone, even if he is black, from Zimbabwe because you don't know how he thinks. It's not good these days to talk like this but it builds up inside your chest until you think you will burst. Even to my family and friends I don't say these things. It's not a matter of trust but you do not want them to feel under pressure, in case they are questioned. It is better that they do not know how you are thinking. So we think but do not talk about these things and this is very bad for us.'

The taxi-driver is the anonymous face of unarticulated opinion. In this society unutterable fear has led to self-censorship. People choke off their words before they reach the mouth, an accumulation of strained silences – national asphyxiation.

Chenjerai Hove continues to write critically: 'All these killings, the responsibility of a writer is to say we have the human capacity to survive. We can fall but we have the human capacity to rise; we have to recreate this country again so no problem.'

* * * *

Since Easter 2000, the crisis in Zimbabwe has escalated. There have been many more deaths and economic conditions have deteriorated further.

Eventually Hove left Zimbabwe for France, after constant harassment by the authorities. 'The threats were becoming unbearable. People were phoning my house saying I would disappear.' *The Daily News* kept up its struggle to report on events in Zimbabwe but was finally closed down by the Mugabe government in September 2003. Morgan Tsvangirai and the Movement for Democratic Change continue to oppose the Mugabe government; Tsvangirai is now on trial for treason.

Zambia

Prudence

2000

It was like grave day in Ireland, when cemeteries burgeon with people visiting the tombs of loved ones, bearing flowers and prayers. In this cemetery small crushes of people gathered together, but the graves were not old and settled, they were freshly dug. The funeral processions of slow footfalls making their way around the burial ground and the lowering of coffins into the earth told that this was not a special memorial day. It was a usual morning in the Kitwe graveyard, in the heart of the community in a country whose life's blood is being sapped by the AIDS pandemic. It was an everyday scene of death and burial in the once rich Zambian copper belt. There were so many daily commuters that local minibus companies had a decent enough business taking grieving friends and families from the mortuary to the burial place. In the town of Kitwe, rows of passengers could be seen waiting for transport to the cemetery, much like people would stand waiting at any bus stop.

The tombs were strewn with sweet-scented bouquets. The breeze played with the flowers, lifting petals and tossing them, spreading their loveliness and pleasant fragrance around so that each grave ended up with its own pot pourri of fresh blossom and old, spiky, bloom. As for the mourners, in sombre attendance under the shade of large parasols, some no doubt stood uneasily looking at intimations of their own mortality; were their bodies wracked with the virus? A shadow of despair hung over the graveyard. Here were coffins with corpses who had arrived not because it was the natural closing of the circle of their lives, not because they had lived full lives, seen their children grown and it was their time; here were coffins of people cut off in their prime, hundreds of them.

Zambia is almost ten times the size of Ireland and has around 10 million people. The Zambians are known for their warmth and friendliness; as in many African countries courtesy in everyday social exchanges has not been lost. Again, as in many African countries, Zambia is trying to cope with the challenge of the HIV/AIDS pandemic. One in six adults has the AIDS virus. Life expectancy is now thirty-two years, the lowest in the world. Decades of development, efforts to improve living standards, health and education, have been reversed. The loss of teachers has countered gains in education and the teacher ratio now is fifty-six pupils to one teacher. The disease's devastating impact on the country is due mainly to poverty, the large national debt, sexual mores, traditional values and the subordinate role of women in Zambian society. HIV/AIDS is taboo and not openly discussed; since it is associated with promiscuity, to contract the virus is to be in disgrace.

At a home for those too ill to take care of themselves, the patients are the wasting human lives behind the statistics. The hospice prepares people for the grave, making their last days comfortable. It is a new building, crisp and bright, with cheerful staff. In the hallway hangs a sign: 'Welcome. Please speak softly.' The patients are in clean beds and are well cared for. Some were put out out of their homes when they became ill; these came from the most socially and economically disadvantaged communities.

The very poor ones had no house to begin with, and when they became infected they were incapable of providing for themselves and moved from one relation to another. With Zambia's strong tradition of the supportive extended family, many relatives have taken in ill and vulnerable kin in spite of the enormous burden. Practically everyone I met earning a regular income was providing for several members outside their immediate family. For some sufferers, their relatives were as poor as they were and they came here to the hospice.

In one of the beds lies Victoria, a widow and mother of four children. Her husband had the virus and finally died from tuberculosis. She was about to divorce him when she discovered that they were both HIV positive. So she stayed with him until his death. 'He died on the very bed I am sleeping on at home. I've tried to prepare the house; life goes on.' She came to the hospice because it was difficult living with her only daughter. 'People were saying that woman will die because of that daughter and go to hospice and at least die peacefully.' She has improved since coming and now can talk, walk and eat, and she has put on weight. She gets medicine here; there was none in the compound where she lived.

Justin has been sick for over seven months. He has tuberculosis and his struggle for breath makes it difficult for him to speak. He is twenty-two years old, unmarried and has no children. His parents are dead: 'both mamo and daddy, so the family is disorganised'. Justin is obsessed with organising and leaving everything in order because there is no one else who can do it. He is a teacher and he had just started a small business, a pre-school, and it was going well. 'Then I became sick and found myself here, and the business? I can do nothing and cannot keep it going, so now the business is not running because I'm sick, so there is no income and no source of money: it is very difficult.'

Away from the cemetery and the hospice, leaving the tarmac road and moving through the tall stalks of yellow corn, entire villages and townships are hidden, unseen from the roadway. Drive over earth as hard as baked biscuit to one of the desperately poor compounds of primitive huts made from mud bricks, the roof consisting of corrugated iron held down by stones. One of the huts is home to Prudence and her eight siblings; she is the eldest and only fourteen years old. The children have watched first their father and then their mother die from AIDS. Prudence now takes charge of the family. These are only nine of the eight hundred thousand AIDS orphans in Zambia. With no breadwinner to take care of them, they barely survive on one feed of mealie-meal a day, which they get from the community and from a local non-government organisation. It is an effort to keep the orphans in a traditional family and neighbourhood environment for material and emotional support. Most Zambian homes now take care of an orphan child; the pressure that the pandemic is putting on relatives is stretching the fabric of family life. In Kitwe, with a population of around one million, there are around sixty five thousand orphan children.

The one-roomed hut where Prudence and her family live is small, windowless and full of choking smoke. It is empty of anything suggesting food or clothing, no storage presses or boxes. In the corner lean a couple of sweeping brooms made from rushes. When they run out of food and need to buy, Prudence goes out into the bush, gathers the rushes to make the brushes, then walks the ten miles to market. Every morning, like a mother hen, she gets her young brood up and ready and out because she wants them to have an education, and here even primary school is not free. She says she would love the young children to learn rather than just run about. The youngest child, finger in mouth, clings to her big sister's knee and shyly looks around. Prudence does not go to school herself because she needs to take care of everything. She has a passivity and acceptance about her situation, and says she is used to the work, cooking and cleaning for the younger ones. Anyway, she says, when the children come back from school they help her. At night they sleep on mattresses on the earth floor, spooned together in the dark. Prudence herself is waiflike with heart-tugging brown eyes and a sweet, trusting face; she looks smaller and younger than her fourteen years.

No sunlight washes the dark corners of the hut where Prudence lives. Hunched over a bundle in one corner, barely seen because of the bad light, is a gaunt, underfed, young woman. The swaddling bundle nestling in her arms is a baby girl to whom she has given birth this morning, with the help of a traditional midwife. The newborn gives a gusty cry and then a satisfied suck on the warm, damp breast. The infant is peacefully unaware of the poverty that she is being weaned into. The mother is related to Prudence and does not look well. Sitting beside her and the baby is another thin, young woman with a consumptive cough – suspected tuberculosis. All three are cooped in the corner of the clammy hut, the contagion palpable in the small, congested cabin that allows in no fresh air. Since they are on their own, with no parents or breadwinner, it is not possible to build a better home.

* * * *

Once upon a time here in Zambia's copper belt, prices for copper were high and the mines were king. The open cast mine in the nearby town of Chingola is the second largest in the world. It is about a mile deep: the vehicles below seem like miniature toys. In the early days people remember elephants along the top peering over the mine, but that was a long time ago. On the back of the mines, the newly independent Zambia, emerging from the old Northern Rhodesia, would create its national wealth. Nationalisation, a drop in world copper prices, inefficiency and corruption led to huge losses and government subsidy of the mines. Instead of wealth, the country remained mired in poverty, and now carries the burden of an unforgiven multi-billion dollar international debt. Prudence is in the hands of the World Bank and the International Monetary Fund, which are advising the government how to get the economy on track. The mines have been sold to private interests, stemming the drain on the exchequer but at the cost of retrenchment and job losses for the miners. The strict structural adjustment policies of the IMF have meant cutbacks in the already impoverished education and health sectors, the latter under pressure because of the HIV/AIDS pandemic. Zambia's government has frozen wages in the public sector and raised taxes.

The IMF has its critics. The UN Special Envoy for HIV/AIDS in Africa, Stephen Lewis, pleaded in June 2004 that Zambia was at risk. 'I have argued before in cases involving the International Monetary Fund, and I argue again that it has failed to grasp the demonic force of the human and economic carnage caused by HIV and AIDS. The poorest sectors of society the extended families, the women, the children, the orphans, they have all made incredible sacrifices to keep life going in Zambia in the face of wrenching austerity. I appeal to the IMF Board to introduce the tiny quotient of flexibility being requested by the government of Zambia. To do otherwise is to give continued momentum to the pandemic.'

Lewis has also admonished large pharmaceutical companies reluctant to allow cheap generic drugs for fighting the disease.

The international community has not grasped this insidious worm that is gnawing its way through an entire continent. Words and half measures cut pieces off the worm but it slithers on with its deadly work. The AIDS virus is an enemy; to destroy it requires a coalition of the willing to wage war with all of the resources usually available for such ventures. The war would have no 'collateral damage'; lives would be saved and misery reduced.

Meanwhile, hidden by the tall cornfields, Prudence dwells in a mud hut in awful conditions. However, she is surrounded by her best chance – the other mud huts. Any relief in the bleak picture came from the Zambian people: the gentle compassion of the caregivers in administering to the terminally ill; the families who grow larger and larger as they take in those who have lost kin; the communities with slender means who support the many thousand Prudences among them.

Colombia

The End of Mr Garcia's Coca Career

1998

Mr Garcia has stopped growing coca; he says it was bad for his soul. He started because he needed the money. 'At that time you could make plenty. The price of coca was high and the cost of living very low so it was a lot of money relative to what you spent.'

Planting the crop earned him easy money because the buyers would come directly to him and offer to buy the coca raw, without any processing at all. They came and purchased the green leaves, harvested from the plants. 'Normally, because most of the coca growing area is along the rivers, there was a market day and the buyers came in with boats. You arrived with your crop and sold it to them. The people buying the coca you didn't actually know, but they were working for the drug mafias in Colombia. You didn't know who they were, but that is who they were connected to.'

When I went to Colombia I knew that it was the largest supplier of cocaine in the world. The drug comes from the coca shrubs indigenous to the massive, ranging Andes Mountains of South America. Coca has grown in the countries surrounding the great mountains – Peru, Bolivia, and Colombia – for over four thousand years. The rapture-inducing plant was part of Andean culture and religious ceremonies. The region's inhabitants chewed the leaf, stimulating a mild euphoria that reduced appetite and fatigue, relieved altitude sickness and conserved body heat, important qualities for living in the mountainous Andes. Cultivating the crop for the traditional use of leaf chewing is one part of coca growing. The other is the cash-crop business that provides coca leaves for the processing of cocaine. Cocaine was first extracted from the leaves in the mid-nineteenth century and was a popular stimulant and tonic. During the American Civil War the drug was dispensed to lighten soldiers' pain and later it was used as an anaesthetic for eye surgery and dentistry.

Physical, political, institutional and economic reasons facilitate growing the illegal crop in Colombia. Many parts of the country are isolated and inaccessible, communications are bad, the central government in the capital Bogotá seems remote and irrelevant to the outlying regions, the justice system is weak, and corruption and poverty are widespread.

Mr Garcia grew his coca in the Amazon region. In the 1950s peasants came to the area from the Andean valleys in the hope of finding land because there was no chance of land where they were. The number of dislocated farmers grew when they were forcibly displaced by the consolidation of large farms. Landowners replaced people with tractors. The displaced and landless labourers were forgotten by the State. They had to find somewhere else to work and to produce, and they came to the Amazon region. The small farmers, the campesinos, started farming using the traditional slash and burn method. They were given no advice or technology, and, even though they broke their backs working the fragile, feeble soil, many failed to make a living from traditional crops. The region was never developed and had no proper routes for transporting crops to market.

Then came cocaine, and it was a solution; the campesinos found that the cultivation of coca was the means of survival. It was profitable, and since buyers came to them it was easy to sell. They started producing and found a magnificent product, with a well-organised commerce and increasing demand all over the world, and so they went into cocaine. As coca production spread, others came to the region to produce the illicit plant, but many producers were the original small peasant farmers who had come seeking a new life.

In later years, poor coffee prices drove large numbers of coffee growers off the land and the seasonal pickers lost work. Farmers and pickers made their way from the traditional coffee locales of Antioquai and Old Caldas to the booming coca meadows in the jungles and the lawless plains of eastern and southern Colombia.

Coca is an easy product to harvest. It is a resistant, versatile shrub and it can grow either in Amazonian soils that are wet and quite infertile or in richer soils. Either way, the seeds grow quickly.

Every three months Mr Garcia used to have a harvest of small green leaves from the feeble earth. In Colombia, he says, there are strikes by rice and corn farmers because the country is importing them from other countries. Many of these other farmers have a much more difficult time making any kind of money. By comparison, coca is guaranteed. Coca farmers live better than other farmers do. Mr Garcia found that a huge amount of his harvest could fit into one big bag, whereas a corn or rice harvest would fill up a boat. Coca buyers use the rivers; roads hardly exist on the frontier where coca is grown. The lack of roads makes it more difficult to get other crops to market and if nobody buys, the farmer loses out. For the coca farmers, the drug commerce chain was always ready to get the product from them to the customers.

Then the campesinos began not just producing the plant but turning the leaf into coca paste, a short step from cocaine. They collected the leaf and chopped it up. Water and cement was sprinkled on the shredded coca leaves, then the mixture was stomped on to release the cocaine juices. The leaves were then stirred into a barrel of liquid gasoline, which drew out the cocaine. Afterwards it was mixed with water and soda to extract the alkaloids that produce cocaine's high. A solid off-white substance separated from the solution and this was the coca paste. The paste was removed and allowed to dry.

Scattered around Colombia are laboratories with chemicals that refine coca paste into powdered cocaine. The cocaine powder is dried and compressed into easy-to-carry packages. Colombia's difficult terrain and coastline make the country a natural haven for smuggling. Airstrips are located near the laboratories and most of the cocaine is flown to distribution centres near the Pacific or Caribbean coasts and then shipped out. After several stages, involving different organisations and countries, the drug finally finds its way onto the streets of cities all around the world.

So the campesinos planted coca and made money but, according to Mr Garcia, it did not lead to happiness or fulfilment. The result was a lack of values and the money was spent on prostitutes, alcohol and consumer goods.

A trip into town shows superficial signs of prosperity: shop windows are chock-full with electrical and household goods and new expensive four-wheel drive vehicles were parked outside well-frequented hostelries. All the material needs of the individual are met, but the town and surrounds seem incomplete; missing are proper services and infrastructure such as decent roads, schools and health facilities – in short all of the services provided when individuals are not just operating as individuals, but are operating as communities. The state is not in control here and an air of lawlessness, of a frontier town from the Wild West, pervades. On Saturday night the place is lively. Packed bars, accordion dance music, sentimental love songs, wolf whistles and raucous laughter compete with noisy horns and moterbikes that stopped and accelerated with a loud screech. Among the patrons there is rough, macho swaggering, heavy drinking and easily available – bought – sex.

Mr Garcia says that the money is easy, but coca cultivation brings with it a different culture. Transacting with mafia figures puts small farmers in touch with a lifestyle in which there is little respect for anything. 'They don't respect your life, they don't respect children, any of the basic values that you grow up with.' He finally found it a difficult way to live. He got out because he realised 'it wasn't a business for a good person'. It caused families to disintegrate, and 'to be a person that can live with yourself and be someone who can feel good in the face of God, and in the face of society, it is not the kind of work to do'. It was a hard internal struggle for him because of the great fear: 'If you leave it you are going to die of hunger. If you have never really learnt to do anything else and you leave coca production what are you going to do? It is very difficult to find any other crop that would give the same kind of return that coca gives. The farmers who want to get out of coca can begin to try other crops, but often they are planting and growing at a loss to themselves because the markets are not developed, and so it's difficult for them to get out of coca because there is very little support for them, or realistic options.'

People get into coca, says Mr Garcia, because it has great financial promise. But then 'it makes them a slave because they keep hoping, they keep having dreams that the next harvest will give them enough money to get out of it. But they never quite make enough money so they are always trying to produce and they are stuck in it and can never get out.' He found himself, a small farmer in the Amazon, wondering how the price of cocaine was doing in New York; he realised this was crazy.

One of the problems, he says, is lack of education. 'The people growing coca never think of the end users, they don't have it in their mind who is using this material, they give it little thought.' Many people become totally wrapped up in the culture of coca production. 'In this area, coca has been produced for about twenty years, so you have children who grew up producing coca and know nothing else. They will continue to produce coca because they have not learnt to do something else. It becomes a cultural problem. Coca farmers, people don't realise it, are also victims. They make the least money of the whole chain of production and yet they suffer so much in terms of family breakdown and the disintegration of family culture.'

Mr Garcia moved to the coca growing area with his girlfriend. The two of them lived together but the relationship broke down when he discovered that she was selling quasi-processed coca to some of the workers and addicts in the area. In another relationship, his new girlfriend again became involved in trying to make money by selling to addicts, and the relationship broke down. He says coca has a very negative effect on all the families living in the area. 'It's very easy to fall into the trap of making money and living in a very immoral way.' That is what happened to him and is one of the reasons why he decided to get out.

Drug commerce is drenched in blood and violence. Mr Garcia says it is risky for the planters because the government launches programmes to try and stop the illegal cultivation and there is a lot of repression and guns involved. Since there are large amounts of money in the coca business, it is inseparable from Colombia's corrupt politics, weak institutions and armed conflict involving its army, right-wing paramilitaries and left-wing guerrillas. The government is not in control of entire regions: guerrillas and paramilitaries hold vast swathes of land in the country and drug money has financed the armed groups who have made alliances with the drug traffickers. The war makes drug production possible and the drugs in turn pay for the war. Add to this the intervention of the United States, with its war on drugs, and it makes for a potent cauldron of motivations and interests.

The Colombian government has tried to eradicate the plant, but its methods are problematic. Farmers grow fields of basic food crops as well as the lucrative coca and it is impossible when fumigating from the air to distinguish between the meadows of plants. Everything is sprayed and ruined and the crops cultivated for food are even more vulnerable than the resistant coca plant. Fumigation not only destroys the coca plant, but also the livelihood of farmers trying to grow alternative crops.

The Amazon has a unique and wonderful ecosystem, with an on-going recycling of organic matter, which regenerates the soils and keeps the ecosystem alive. Government proposals are often based on monoculture, the growing of one alternative crop, and do not take into account the distinctiveness of the Amazon. Coca peasants, according to Mr Garcia, are open to growing alternative crops provided they can make a living. They dislike the danger, the violence and the social problems that come with coca.

The patience and fortitude needed to develop an alternative farming lifestyle is evident during a visit to Alexander's farm on the edge of the Amazon jungle. Coca was never part of the young farmer's family life. His father always thought that it was better to be poor than to have people chasing you because you were doing something illegal. The December day is warm and bright. The breeze is as gentle as the brush of a soft-winged butterfly. Spectacular rainforest skirts the farm. Tall trees stretch into an endless sky and sunlight shifts through the forest. From branches and boughs comes the chirping of birds and insects, the birds calling each other with a shrilling woo-woo. Out here, on the edge of the rainforest, Alexander and his wife have set up a plain homestead. The youthful couple have the energy and drive that early pioneers must have had when heading for the frontier, and great determination to make the farm work. They labour long hours in the fields and at home set about preserving whatever they harvest. The whole enterprise has an air of keen industry, the kitchen full of different shaped glass bottles and jars that hold coloured and textured mixtures. Since it is a long trek into the nearest town they need to be as self-sufficient as possible. A solid, understated individual, Alexander shows off his holding with a shy pride.

The smell of the tawny ground is moist and earthy but the land is poor. It has taken hard, steady toil over the last two to three years to see the thin soil darken and become enriched. From earthworms they make their own organic compost. They are experimenting with plants and Amazonic fruits, trying to get the Amazon's diversity working for them. Herbs, cabbages, beans, peanuts and fruits, such as papaya, are growing. Alexander offers tropical fruits I have never seen before or since.

One is a cob, like corn, but the kernels taste like chocolate; the outside shell has a sharper taste, giving the whole an exotic sweet and sour flavour. Herbs such as mint and oregano are grown to make preventative medicines. There are not a lot of options around here for healthcare and the family use plants that they know are good for them to avoid illness and the need for a doctor. Around the plantain trees they have sown beans, which can take up nitrogen. Eventually the bean will fall to the ground and re-fertilize it. Another bean plant, when eaten by ants, acts as a poison; eventually the queen ant eats it and it destroys her community. The bean is a natural pesticide and stops ants preying on the plantain trees. The family also keep chickens, feeding them plants full of phosphorous, which is good for egg production. Great-looking, healthy turkeys gobble and strut their stuff about the place.

Walking through the rainforest in the splotches of sunlight, it is full of the rich resonance of life, exultant tropical birds, parrots and hummingbirds, fabulous butterflies and diverse, interesting flora. At a clearance the sound of water reveals a series of ponds, the beginnings of a fish farm. The fish now feed the family and, as the stock increases, will be brought to market to sell. Results are slow but satisfying. Alexander believes that coca farms are the future deserts of South America because they strip the earth of all its nutrients. It is difficult, he says, to convince farmers who get good money from coca to change, but as their land deteriorates and they see farms like his beginning to work, and maintain their fertility, they become more interested in diversifying.

Driving away from the farm, the waving Alexander becomes a diminutive figure against this grand, glorious landscape; while his life is hard, it isn't unenviable.

The soul-searching Mr Garcia managed to get work in rubber production and was relieved to have his coca-producing days behind him. He now spends some of his time trying to get others to do the same.

Both Alexander and Mr Garcia believe that in the long-run

coca growing is not sustainable. The easily-grown coca shrub damages the environment, leading to deforestation, soil erosion that turns the earth into desert, air and water pollution – in short, destruction of the habitat. The use of chemicals to process the harvest into cocaine is destructive too, and so are efforts to eradicate the coca crop. Aerial fumigation intensifies the environmental impact on the land, the animals and water. It affects the forests, driving away the fauna and destroying valuable species of plant life. It displaces families involved in production who then seek out new areas for coca cultivation. So the plantations move from one province to another, and this is possible because the conditions for growing are still there. These conditions are poverty, displacement, conflict, the absence of State control – and of course a voracious appetite for cocaine throughout the world.

The latest programme is Plan Colombia, an assistance package from the US to the Colombian government ostensibly to fight drugs. The drug war is entangled with the civil war and its heavy toll of killing, displacement and human rights violations. Since 2000 the US has contributed over $3 billion to the programme. How effective the plan will be in reducing the availability of narcotics on city streets remains to be seen. The drug business tends to move on rather than go away. Until the early 1980s, Peru and Bolivia were the chief cocaine producers; when anti-drug measures were put in place, production shifted to Colombia. The white powder may very well end up as a profitable export from other Andean countries.

Displaced in Bogotá

1998

The most revealing book I read before going to Colombia was fiction: Gabriel Garcia Marquez's *One Hundred Years of Solitude*. It explains how the landscape defines the people, binding them in regional mindsets and loyalties, and how geography cut off parts of the country for centuries, giving local inhabitants intermittent contact with outsiders. How Colombia is not really a nation but a gathering of regional statelets, and the difficulty this creates in exercising central authority.

The landscape so well articulated by Marquez is mountainous and rugged and extraordinarily varied, ranging from the Andean highlands to the Caribbean lowlands, the grassland plains of the Orinoco basin and the Amazon jungle. Three mountain ranges run south to north, with deep valleys and basins in between: the Western, Central and Eastern Cordilleras. (Central Cordillera is where much of the renowned Colombian coffee is grown.) The country is huge, the size of France, Portugal and Spain put together. Over half the territory is made up of almost deserted grasslands and jungle with few roads and sparse population.

Colombia is in the tropics but its climate is influenced by altitude. The highlands, where Bogotá is located, are cool and wet for much of the year and cold at night. The Caribbean coast and the Amazon jungles, which have jaguars, pumas, wild boars and monkeys, are hot and wet with mangrove swamps, palms, scrubland and coral reefs. More species of bird live here than anywhere else in the world.

The inaccessible geography facilitated Colombia's violent history. 'La Violencia', the communal violence of the 1940s and 1950s between Liberals and Conservatives, left around two million people displaced from their homes and lands. Guerrilla groups, the FARC and ELN, grew out of this culture of violence and have waged a war against the State since the 1960s. The sheer remoteness of parts of the country enabled them to hold and control bands of territory. As a counter to the insurgents, right-wing paramilitaries have formed and the conflict is a chess game of who holds territory – government, guerrillas or paramilitaries. Caught in the territorial moves are the pawns, the civilian population. Whole localities may be forced to leave; sometimes individuals, teachers or community leaders are targeted. Over a million people have been displaced; obliged to leave their homes, they head for regional towns or for the capital.

Bogotá sits at an altitude of 2,650 metres, on the edge of the Sabana de Bogotá, a fertile mountain-belted basin. The oldest part of the city, La Candelaria, has cobbled streets of attractive, carefully restored old houses. Churches from Spanish colonial times, universities, museums and theatres make Bogotá the country's political, economic and cultural capital. The growing metropolis has elegant residential districts, modern commercial centres and an industrial area. The city is also dirty, noisy, polluted and dangerous. When people in Rio de Janeiro, a very dangerous city, heard that I was going on to Bogotá they were appalled and warned that it would be hard to escape without being mugged, kidnapped or killed. Perceptions from afar are always exaggerated and other places look far worse than home.

Sprawled up the Bogotá mountainside slopes are the shanty towns where about seventy-five per cent of the population reside. This is where the cheapest housing is, on the periphery of the city, and it is where most of those who arrive from the insecurity of their homeplaces find precarious refuge. Displaced and living hand-to-mouth, they explain why they were forced to abandon comfortable homes for uncertainty and squalor. Gloria, Hector, Juan and Olibert came from different regions, each with its own set of circumstances.

In Casanare, Gloria, her husband and three daughters lived well. Casanare is part of Los Llanos, low-lying savannah that bake hot and dusty in the dry season and are flood-prone during the rains; the grassland rolls for hundreds of miles across the Orinoco basin before merging into the jungles of the Amazon system. The rolling grasslands have oilfields, which may improve the economic status of the region but which are also a focal point for the struggle between guerrillas, economic interest groups, paramilitaries and the security forces. Gloria had a government job with the welfare department and her husband was a mechanic – they lacked for nothing. The family lived in town in a good size house, each had their own room; it was very comfortable. Here they live on top of each other in one grubby room that includes the kitchen. The small room is in one of the poorest areas in Bogotá, up the side of a muddy hill, where rent is cheapest. It was not so bad at first but her husband died a few months ago and she is alone now with her three girls. The family left Casanare because the guerrillas wanted to take her two elder daughters, wanted them to become fighters, and this was not what Gloria had in mind for her children. She wanted them to go to school, to have a good life. For the sake of the children, she and her husband came to Bogotá.

Where she lived many young people have been forcibly taken by guerrilla groups, the ELN and the FARC, and recruited into their ranks, taken into the woods and trained for war. Gloria is not exactly sure why they like to bring them in so young but maybe, she says, it is easier to psychologically manage them. Her daughters are fifteen, thirteen, and six years old. She worries they may not be able to continue with school because they have no money left to buy uniforms and books.

The beautiful home in Casanare has been left totally abandoned, utterly empty. She wanted to sell it, asked her mother to sell it for whatever price she could get, but nobody wants to buy it because of the conflict between the guerrillas and the paramilitaries. The paramilitaries, she says, moved even more into Casanare and killed a lot of people, so no one wants to live there anymore. Who will buy it? Nobody.

Hector left his region, Uraba, on the Caribbean coast, when he received death threats from paramilitaries. Uraba is a steaming lowland and Colombia's main banana-producing region. The landless and unemployed have come down to Uraba from the highlands for decades, clearing out plots for subsistence farming or seeking work on the plantations. This part of the country has many armed groups, guerrilla and paramilitary, struggling for control. Political violence and massacres by paramilitaries are commonplace and hundreds of banana workers have been killed as a result of the bloody feuding.

The paramilitaries were looking for both Hector and his brother. He was threatened because he was a community leader and had influence locally. They found them in a bar and shot and killed his brother, but Hector got away. The paramilitaries, he says, don't like rivals. They want total domination and want to do things their own way, so they eliminate anyone who might compete with them. Rich people in the area pay the paramilitaries; anybody with a lot of money is paying two or three hundred people in these groups. Those with money are involved in various forms of trafficking, because Uraba is right by the border; they traffic in drugs, guns and contraband appliances. Some big plantation owners are also involved. There are a lot of large economic groups in the area, a lot of money and a lot of paramilitaries. Hector maintains that the army and the paramilitaries are essentially the same thing; they patrol together, they do many activities together. State organisations take no action against the paramilitaries, he says, and evidence has been gathered by human rights groups about complicity.

Hector had property in Uraba; he lived a middle-class existence. He had a house in town and a farm nearby. On the farm he grew plantain and he was also studying at university. Neighbours have appropriated the land and taken over the animals that are there; he has lost it for the moment. He needs to go back for a couple of weeks to try and sell it off, but for his own safety, he's going to have to get a non-government organisation to help him do this.

In Bogotá, Hector took the initiative to get two to three hundred displaced families together to raise funds to help themselves. The government has money, he believes, but it is eaten up in corruption, and little of the money that comes in from international groups filters down to those who are displaced. They are trying to get hold of some of this money for assistance with food. So far they have been able to put together some shelter for people, but there is little else they can afford to do. Right now it's difficult to send a lot of the kids to school because they don't have money. The State is obliged to provide children with an education, but as the families cannot afford uniforms or books, in many cases the kids just can't go.

Juan used to live in Uraba as well; he lived there for 18 years. He was a banana worker and at first it was fine. In the earlier years the guerrillas controlled the area; they knew him and he had no problem with them. Then the paramilitaries came. Again, at first it was okay, they also knew him; it seemed to be alright between them. Then they started to say that he was a guerrilla or a guerrilla sympathiser. Then he heard from the guerrillas that he was supporting the paramilitaries. Besides working in the banana plantations he had a couple of hectares of plantain, which his wife farmed, but one day a group of paramilitaries came to his house. They shot at his wife as a warning to make him leave the area. Before this there was another incident. He was on the highway and three men surrounded him; they were also paramilitaries and they wanted to know who he was. They were searching for him but he said he was somebody else and they let him go. He has children aged sixteen and seventeen, and he was concerned that they would be targeted too. He had a son in Bogotá, and decided to come here for the safety of the family. He had to abandon his land. Here they live on handouts from non-government organisations. He tries to make money by shredding paper but that earns very little; from a huge quantity he maybe can get maybe 1,500 or 2,000 pesos, the equivalent of a dollar or two, for a lot of work.

Oliberto comes from the Cauca, in the south-western part of the country, on the Pacific Ocean. It is a place of lush vegetation, volcanoes, mountain creeks, hot springs and caves. 'The reason I came was because I received death threats from a guerrilla group called the FARC.' He supposes that the reason he received these threats was because he had ideological differences of opinion with the local guerrilla commander. It also had something to do with his involvement in the marches by coca farmers. At that time he was the negotiator and he was co-ordinating the marches. The guerrillas were not involved and it was very much a farmer activity. The guerrillas reacted against him being in that position, and because they objected to him negotiating, they would not allow food to come into the area. He came to Bogotá because he had friends who could help him out here. Eventually, he was able to get a bit of money from the Ministry of the Interior to help with the rent. He lives in one room and gets work from time to time to allow him to survive, but he lives badly. He lives alone, which, he says, makes it easier. His family is in Venezuela. At the time that he left his province they were on vacation there, and stayed when they realised that they couldn't go back home. He could join them, but says he loves his country and wants to deal with the problems he has here. The Colombian government, he says, have a responsibility to deal with his problem and the problems of other displaced people. So far they have not done much; the only organisations that have done anything are the non-government organisations.

The damp, dilapidated dwellings where they now live seem transient, as if their real lives are suspended elsewhere. Suspended in the abandoned comfortable home in Casanare; in the hot banana plantations of Uraba; in the diverse wildness of the Cauca. These tenants, in this shanty town, have come from all corners of this stunningly beautiful country, looking for some security and peace, but they would much rather have found it at home. Against these odds they have a remarkable ability to 'go on' and to make the best of things. Gloria, keenly protective of her three daughters, is determined to keep them safe and get them an education. Hector, the community leader, is galvanising his new community of displaced people to try and improve conditions. Juan, who is older and seems depressed, takes whatever work he can to support his family. Olibert wants to stay and sort out the problems within Colombia. The political landscape seems opportunistic and uncaring, but these people are rugged, determined and enduring.

The Occupied Territories

Eid in Jenin

2002

In April 2002, the Israeli government sent in tanks to crush the Palestinian population residing in Jenin refugee camp on the occupied West Bank. I had spent three months in the West Bank in 1996, working on the Palestinian elections, and the following year I returned to record reports for radio. In the November after the 2002 Israeli attack, the daughter of a friend, Caoimhe Butterly, was shot in the leg by an Israeli soldier. I travelled with her mother to Jenin to visit her and we stayed in the camp.

Journeying through the West Bank is always beautiful. Leaving Jerusalem behind, the road goes through beige, undulating hills with flocks of sheep, goats and dark downy camels arching across the terrain. The Judean hills become desert; then down into the Jordan valley and the ten-thousand-year-old town of Jericho, the oldest town in the world; into countryside of olive and fruit trees and Arab villages, until you arrive at Jenin. This time, there were many more checkpoints, curtailing movement and causing delays.

Jenin hospital is on the edge of the camp, a basic bare-bones hospital crowded with patients, hard-working staff and visitors bringing in food and company. The iconography on the walls up the stairwell and along the corridors is unsettling in a place of healing. The large posters have snapshots of dead young men superimposed on pictures of the Dome of the Rock, the sacred Jerusalem mosque, or overlaid on shots of the piles of rubble heaped around Jenin after the April battering. Photographs of guns and babies are added, placed in the arms of the martyrs and creating a collage that seeks to evince sympathy, understanding and defiance.

We were staying with a family in the camp, and Ramadan, the Muslim fasting period, was coming to a close. However, this year the people of Jenin refugee camp only marked the festival of Eid al-Fitr, the traditional feast held at the end of Ramadan. It could not be said that they celebrated it. The air around the camp held sadness and loss; the atmosphere was subdued. The inhabitants visited each other with heavy hearts. Women wept quietly in doorways; men rubbed away tears from their eyes. The day began at five in the morning when families made arches of palm fronds to decorate the graves of loved ones who had died during the year, especially those brutally murdered during the cruel April days when Israeli bulldozers and tanks flattened their houses. The cemetery graves are marked with headstones of bright stone, artificial flowers and pictures of the dead.

At seven o'clock, people gathered on a swathe of wasteland where once homes had been. The site of the damage was a large crater; hundreds of men stood dwarfed in its centre. Before the rows of men were coloured, patterned prayer mats. Teenage boys held green flags which said in Arabic: *Allah is great, Allah is one*. The Imam plaintively led the prayer; the men responded, kneeling on the mats and bending forward. As the sun rose higher, it cast a bright light on the backs of the bowing men who folded and unfolded on the mats. Standing apart, on the verge, was a knot of headscarfed women in long tunics who also prayed. A small boy smiled and handed out chunks of pink and white Turkish delight. It was a mournful, moving, dignified prayer meeting. Surrounding the crater were semi-demolished houses, providing a backdrop of interior walls that were once the walls of sitting rooms, bedrooms and kitchens. Patches of white and blue wall tiles were like a mosaic, or a large hanging plate. From one wall, a white bath leaned out into the empty space. The surviving houses were pockmarked with bullets. When the prayers ended, mats were rolled and carried under arms as the men quietly disgorged from the crater. They embraced, planting kisses on each other's cheeks.

Back at the home where we were staying, the women were getting on with their daily chores, sweeping outside and preparing food. Baskets of dough were brought out to the courtyard, kneaded, put in the outdoor oven and taken out minutes later puffed up with hot air in the familiar shape of pitta bread. Relatives and friends called in, drank fresh cups of Arabic coffee, and exchanged news. The camp's residents had hoped that the Red Cross could arrange visits to the prison for Eid, but it was not possible. One woman commented that at least her imprisoned son had half the camp keeping him company there.

In the afternoon, Israeli tanks drove along the top road of the camp; they fired erratically into the air and at the houses nearby. For the families living on the top road, Eid would be spent indoors; there would be no getting out for the traditional visit to relatives. One tank was perched overlooking the camp, a stern reminder and symbol of occupation. I watched from the rooftop of the house. The seventeen-year-old youth beside me also looked up at the tank in the distance, clenching and unclenching his hands by his side, his pent-up anger palpable. With the corner of his eye he spotted a small cup on the ground beside him. He looked at it, deliberately swung back his leg, took aim and kicked the cup across the rooftop, shattering it into smithereens. He then called his younger sister, pointed to the broken delph and impatiently indicated that she should clear it up. She responded angrily, but swept up the debris. From the surrounding buildings other young men stood like livid statues with fixed stares and watched the tank.

The evening passed quietly. A tray of green and black olives, tomatoes, aubergines, avocadoes, plump dates and nests of sticky pastries was passed round, and a bowl of tufted persimmons, pears and sweet oranges. An aromatic beverage, made from adding hot water to cinnamon and spooning flakes of coconut and toasted almonds on top, was served in dainty porcelain cups. A woman pointed to a bare dining table and explained that normally they would bake for days to prepare for Eid and that the table would be laden with festive foods, but this year 'we can't swallow'.

Maha , a relative of the family we are staying with, is a woman bereft. Her voice has the deadpan tone of depression, as if any inflection or modulation would require an effort that would overwhelm her. She says that in the April attack 'they took everything that was sweet in our lives, the persons we loved'. Her mother was baking bread when she heard noises out in the street and as she looked out through the window, she was shot. Her thirteen-year-old son, Maha's brother, lay by her side for fourteen hours as she bled to death. An ambulance came three times to get her, but each time it was turned away by soldiers with guns and coarse language. Finally, she died. The soldiers told everyone to get out of the house but insisted that the corpse must stay. It was one week before her family could take her out and bury her. Another of Maha's brothers was visiting Jordan and when he tried to return home he was turned back because he was from Jenin. Another brother was killed and another imprisoned, without trial. Her two children, a girl of six and a boy of four, talk all the time about tanks and soldiers. She bought them paints but they drew tanks and soldiers; she gave them Plasticine and they made tanks and soldiers. Maha's house was hit by a missile from an Apache helicopter, and burnt to the ground. She and her husband have had to rent in the town outside of the camp. Eid for her was motherless and homeless and her relatives are scattered.

This was the Israeli plan for Jenin, to break up the bonds of community. Before April, thirteen thousand people lived in the camp. At this festival time, in November, there were about eight thousand. The others are dead or homeless or scattered throughout the town of Jenin, which is just outside the camp, or in nearby villages. The expulsion from the camp brought back old memories and fears of 1948 when thousands of Palestinians lost their homes and villages and were never allowed to return. The homeless residents of Jenin refugee camp have had to rent other homes in nearby villages or in the town; others have crowded in with relatives, and some have chosen to stay in their semi-demolished houses.

Night came and people slipped away to rest. Then at about 3a.m., as the moon hung over Jenin camp, the tanks rolled in. Everyone was in bed, but they heard them and the houses shook as they moved along the narrow, empty streets. Soldiers fired shots. Rifle butts pounded hard on the doors and Israeli soldiers shouted, 'wake up, wake up.' Residents were forced out into the cold night. The soldiers passed by one house, going through the small well-tended garden of orange and red roses and entered the hallway, firing shots into the ceiling. They trashed the house, overturning armchairs and settees, pulling out clothes from wardrobes, breaking up the music system. In the kitchen, olive oil, flour and herbs were thrown onto the floor and kicked around with heavy jackboots. 'Happy Holiday', they said to the family, and laughed.

Nobody was killed in Jenin camp that day, although the loudspeaker from the mosque broadcasts that a twenty-year-old man was killed in a neighbouring village and the news has gone around the camp that ten people have been killed in Gaza. 'They were just like us yesterday,' says the owner of the house we are staying in, 'you remember when we were sitting outside just having some food? And the Israelis killed them.'

Occupation is more than a tally of dead or injured bodies. It is the perched tank, the rude awakening, the cynical greeting that convey a psychological message that says: we are powerful and you are powerless. We will decide the parameters of your lives, the quality of your sleep, the integrity of your homes.

Next day, women went to the House of Condolence to offer comfort to another young widow. As is the custom, the women of the house – mother, widow and sisters – sat against the wall of the square room, on thin mattresses that are beds by night and seats by day. The dead man had been wanted by the Israelis and there were whispers that a collaborator may have told them where he was.

'If I find him I will drink his blood,' said the dead man's mother.

The young widow, her paleness accentuating the dark rings under her eyes, sat holding her six-week-old baby. 'The army kills one, and we bring another to birth,' said a woman who gave birth to twins on the day that her own husband and his brother were killed.

In another house that we visit, a small boy seems engrossed with the toy he is playing with. From the distance comes the noise of a tank. He looks up and asks: 'Are the Jews coming again?'

The Palestinian response to occupation is resistance. In this second intifada, resistance is tinged with desperation. Jenin camp is an open prison where the occupants have little control over their lives or their future. They live regularly under curfew and always in a humanitarian crisis. During curfew, no one can leave the house, even to get the most basic provisions such as bread and water. The illegal occupation they live under is capricious, cruel, contemptuous and inhumane. The residents of the camp are essentially an abandoned community at the mercy of the disposition of the soldiers on any given day.

Bougainvillea

2002

The house is up a slightly inclining alleyway; such is the higgledy-piggledy architecture of Jenin refugee camp. Like other Palestinians the owner has no work; his son is in prison, his movement is curtailed, he finds it hard to make ends meet. He is tired of life under occupation, especially since the second intifada when the situation worsened.

The courtyard of the house overlooks a neighbour's wall on which vibrant, deep pink bougainvillea vigorously clings to white stone – a pretty relief. He remarks that the plant grows in Africa. He knows because an Israeli soldier told him that he had seen it there.

Settlement

1997

The bulldozer sliced into the soil, violently displacing it from its roots and pushing it to one side. The uprooted life of this piece of earth will never be allowed to return. Under way is the construction of hundreds of homes, another settlement. On a steep, stony hill overlooking the building site are a number of tents. From these, the low murmur of Arab voices carries on the wind. Inhabiting one tent is Salah Tamari, an elected member of the Palestinian Legislative Council. He has been encamped here for two months and so far the climate has been kind. "At least.' he says, 'we have not been fighting with the weather.'

The hill, just outside Bethlehem, looks down on the development south of Jerusalem. The Israelis call it the neighbourhood of Har Homa, and the Palestinians the settlement at Jabal Abu Ghneim. Salah Tamari explains: 'This camp is an expression of our rejection of the Israeli government's plan to build a wall of settlements in this area. This is a violation of the peace agreement and this project will have a disastrous effect on the Palestinians and their future as a people, as a society. The issue here is land, the Israelis are confiscating more land. As you can see, in this area there is no land left for three major towns in the area, Bethlehem, Beit Jela, Beit Sahour. The villages around this area were also deprived of their land. This wall of settlements and bypass roads would isolate the north of the West Bank from the south of the West Bank, and each of these areas would be sliced into smaller pieces, which would result in turning Palestinian society into small communities living in isolated islands, surrounded by settlements and bypass roads. So for the first time ever, the unity of our society is in danger. This situation never happened before. This project will also isolate Jerusalem and seal it off from its Palestinian Arab neighbourhood.'

The land of Palestine, spreading over Israel and The Occupied Territories, is a little smaller than Belgium, around twenty-eight thousand square kilometres; The Occupied Territories measure about six thousand five hundred kilometres. Jews, Christians and Arabs claim long historic links to this picturesque landscape of gently sloping hills, desert, orange groves and olive trees. For Judaism, it is the Promised Land of Moses; for Christianity, the birthplace and region of Jesus Christ; and for Islam, the holy site from where the Prophet Mohammed ascended into Heaven.

The Ottomans ruled Palestine from the sixteenth century until the empire disintegrated after the First World War. In return for their support during the war, Britain promised the Arabs in Palestine independence. At the same time, the British government considered the establishment of a national home for the Jewish people in the region. After the war, the mandate system was introduced to prepare colonised peoples for independence and Britain was given the mandate for Palestine.

Jewish immigrants had been coming to the Holy Land because of persecution in Europe, and immigration increased during the horror of the Holocaust. In Palestine, hostilities between Arabs, Jews and the British intensified. After the Second World War, the United Nations recommended the partition of the land into a Jewish State and an Arab State, and the creation of an international zone in Jerusalem. The Arabs rejected the plan, but the Jews agreed and established the State of Israel in May 1948. The new Jewish State was not accepted by its Arab neighbours and Egypt, Syria, Lebanon and Jordan invaded. After this first Arab-Israeli war, Israel gained control of some of the territory assigned to the Arabs in the partition plan, and the fleeing Arabs became refugees. Jordan took control of the West Bank; Egypt controlled the Gaza Strip.

During the Six Day War in 1967, Israel occupied the Gaza Strip, the Sinai Desert (which was returned to Egypt in 1978 under the Camp David Agreements), the Syrian Golan Heights, the West Bank and East Jerusalem. The military occupation was condemned by the UN in Resolution 242, which emphasised 'the in-admissibility of the acquisition of territory by war', and called for the 'withdrawal of Israeli armed forces from territories occupied in the recent conflict'. The 1967 occupation is illegal under international law.

Settlements, the transfer of Israelis to Palestinian lands, began after the occupation. Israel's Labour government promoted settlement for security purposes; this included annexing parts of Jerusalem, creating a 'security belt' twenty kilometres wide running the length of the Jordan Valley, and annexing the entire Judean desert. The legal system was reorganised, extending the jurisdiction of the military to civil matters. Large areas in the occupied West Bank were rezoned and a special department created to register land for settlement.

Before 1967, the Ottoman Land Code applied to land ownership. Land surrounding the village was 'common' and since villagers knew which lands belonged to which families, there was no need for formal registration. After the occupation, non-registered property was declared State land and was transferred to Jewish settlers. Land was expropriated for 'military purposes', and the term included settlements and bypass roads. The properties of the Arabs who fled during the war and who were now refugees were deemed abandoned.

At the end of the Labour government in 1977, twenty-one settlements had been established in the Jordan valley, ten in the remainder of the West Bank, seventeen in the Gaza Strip, twelve in East Jerusalem. The Likud government that followed expanded the settlements and the number of Israeli settlers reached over one hundred thousand. Despite assurances that settlement activity would be frozen under the Labour government of 1992–6, the number of settlers rose to one hundred and fifty thousand. Likud's return to power under Benjamin Netanyahu in 1996 increased settlement activity. House demolitions and settlements continued under the short-lived government of Ehud Barak. Between 1967 and September 2000, the beginning of the second intifada, the settler population in Gaza and the West Bank, excluding East Jerusalem, reached two hundred thousand people.

Israelis cite political, religious, ideological and historical reasons for the settlements. Settling the land of Jewish forbears is a central tenet of Zionism. Gush Emunim, an organisation of religious settlers, spearheaded West Bank settlement, advocating the divine right of the Jews to possess the biblical homeland; the settlers are asserting the right to inherit the land given to their forefathers.

The most common justification for Jewish settlement, however, is that it is necessary for Israel's security. Settlers maintain a presence in vital areas and so are entitled to a protected, physical environment to sustain them. The settlements are *de facto* annexed territory; they apply Israeli civil law and are served by the Israeli infrastructure and administrative structure. Settlers elect their local council, vote in elections to the Israeli parliament, the Knesset, pay taxes and national insurance, have the same rights as any Israeli citizen and are tried under Israeli criminal law. The settlers are allowed to carry arms and commit acts of violence in the territories with impunity. Military law only governs the Palestinians.

In another tent, pitched on the hill beside Salah Tamari's, are Jewish activists from the group Peace Now who believe that the construction of the homes below are damaging the peace process. Relations between the two tents are cordial, sharing a common aim to stop the bulldozers from doing their work. Not all Israelis agree with their government and some see settlements as a security hazard and an obstacle to a comprehensive peace. They say that peace is ultimately the best guarantee of Israel's security.

Palestinians consider Jewish settlements the essence of

occupation and settlers are viewed as 'legitimate targets'. Planting Jewish settlers in densely populated areas of the West Bank struck at the heart of Palestinian demands for sovereignty. The settlements break up the demographic and geographic continuity of the West Bank, making it more difficult for Palestinians to create an independent, viable state. Carved up by a grid of settlements, checkpoints and roads, the territory has been likened to the South African bantustans created during the apartheid era. Settlers have altered the demographic balance in key areas, especially East Jerusalem, and perpetuated the displacement of Palestinians. Those who cannot tolerate these conditions emigrate, advancing Israel's goal of annexing the occupied areas.

The aggressive nature of the settlements is evident on a visit to the West Bank town of Hebron. Hebron is considered a holy place because it holds the two-thousand-year-old Tomb of the Patriarchs, a stone edifice that sits on the cave where Abraham, Isaac and Jacob and their wives are believed to be buried. The ardent settler population living here numbers around seven hundred and fifty, while the Arab population is one hundred and fifty thousand. Hebron is a Palestinian town. Just down the road from the important tomb, the Jewish settlers live in a tight enclave amidst provocatively arranged Israeli flags and blue Star of David graffiti. They have named it King David Street; the Arabs call it Martyrdom Street. The community began in 1979 when Miriam Levinger and a group of women took over a building and refused to leave. Israeli soldiers are stationed there to protect the Jewish occupants and Arabs need a pass to enter. Barricades of cement and wire and military checkpoints divide the town, making movement circuitous and difficult for the Arab inhabitants.

Israeli settlements violate international law and the Geneva Convention, which states that 'the occupying power shall not transfer part of its own civilian population into the territory it occupies'. The Israeli government has supported the settlements by expropriating land and by offering financial incentives. In demolishing Palestinian houses, Israel is again in breach of the Geneva Convention, which prohibits 'any destruction by the occupying power of real or personal property belonging individually or collectively to private persons'. The confiscation of land and the appropriation of water for the settlements violate Palestinian rights over their natural resources.

Under the UN partition plan, the city of Jerusalem was given special status and was to be administered by the UN through a trusteeship, but this never happened. Jerusalem is important for Jews, Muslims and Christians. It is the City of David with its striking Wailing Wall; the Mount of Olives with the Garden of Gethsemane and the world's oldest grove of gnarled, wracked olive trees that stretch back centuries; the Via Dolorosa or the Way of the Cross; and the home of the Temple Mount, with the magnificent Dome of the Rock and El-Aqsa mosques.

During the 1948 Arab-Israeli war the western part of Jerusalem was taken over by Israeli forces and the Jordanians controlled the Old City and East Jerusalem. The whole city was occupied by Israel in 1967, and while the UN declared the occupation illegal, it was formally annexed.

Since then, Jews living in East Jerusalem have risen from a negligible number before the 1967 war to around two hundred thousand. Israel has tried to limit the Palestinian population in the city by confiscating land; revoking residence permits for Arabs and then expelling them; demolishing Palestinian homes; introducing zoning restrictions; and by denying Arabs building permits. Jewish settlement in Jerusalem is creating Palestinian islands within the city, separating old neighbourhoods from one another.

The Old City's alleyways usually bustle with religious pilgrims and market business. Lining the narrow, stoned streets are shops with brassware, Hebron glass with tints of soft pinks and mauves, distinctive deep blue and white glazed ceramics, confectionary and sweet shops, butcher shops with hanging meats, and stalls of fruit and vegetables, all stacked under a cloud of smell from sacks of oriental spices such as turmeric, saffron, cumin and coriander. In small coffee places Arabs, in either black-and-white or red-and-white kuffiyehs, smoke hookahs or gurgle on hubble-bubble pipes; and kiosks sell pitta bread stuffed with falafel or hummus. In the Old City near Christmas time during the second Intifada, the shops and stalls still diligently laid out their attractive wares, but only a handful of browsers strolled about. The echo of emptiness replaced the usual cacophony of voices and sounds.

The end of the Cold War brought moves to negotiate peace in the Middle East and in 1991 a conference was held in Madrid. In his Gaza home, Haider Abdul Shafi, elder statesman and leader of the Palestinian delegation to Madrid, is emphatic that negotiations came to a 'standstill because of Israeli refusal to stop the settlement activity'. Meanwhile, the PLO and Israel were secretly negotiating through a back channel in Oslo and, in September 1993, Palestinians and Israelis signed a Declaration of Principles. The Oslo Accord envisaged an interim period during which a form of Palestinian self-government would be established and there would be a phased withdrawal of Israeli authority from parts of the West Bank and the Gaza Strip. Further 'permanent status' negotiations would cover remaining issues such as Jerusalem, refugees, settlements, security arrangements, borders, and other issues of common interest. Settlements would not be evacuated in the interim period; settlers and vital arteries such as roads, water, electricity and communications would not come under Palestinian control.

Salah Tamari's protest about the construction of the six thousand five hundred Jewish homes at Har Homa was: 'Because the agreement was explicit about this issue, that no party should take measures that would change the reality on the ground in a way that affects the final status of the negotiations. So what they do here is a violation of the agreement, they still violate land, they still build new settlements, expand the existing ones.'

Since the signing of the Oslo Accord in 1993, the number

of illegal Jewish settlements and settlers in the occupied Palestinian territories has almost doubled. Talks in December 2000 proposed the annexation of eighty per cent of settlers and their lands to Israel, the establishment of security zones controlled by Israel and territorial continuity of both the annexed and the security areas with Israel. This proposal would divide a Palestinian State into three separate cantons and impact on its territorial contiguity. Two hundred and ten thousand Jewish settlers live in one hundred and sixty settlements across the West Bank and Gaza Strip, while another two hundred thousand live in the twelve settlements in occupied and annexed East Jerusalem.

A 'roadmap' for peace in the Middle East has been drawn up by the United States, the United Nations, the European Union and Russia, and requires a freeze of settlement activity and the creation of a Palestinian State by 2005. Meanwhile, Israel continues to build a wall, deemed illegal under international law by the International Court of Justice, which will loop in the settlements, taking even more land from any potential Palestinian State.

As a frustrated Salah Tamari had commented: 'To us peace means freedom, how can we make a compromise on our freedom? It's whether we are free or not free, there's no halfway between freedom and slavery. Occupation is physical slavery, we are sick and tired of this physical slavery; we are sick and tired of occupation. We don't want to emerge in the twenty-first century as a people under occupation. I'd rather we emerged in the twenty-first century as a people still struggling for their freedom, not a people who lost everything under the label of a peace process which is hollow.'

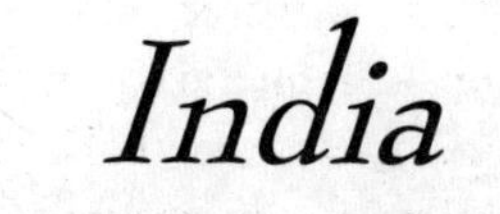

India

Human Bondage

1997

Tamil Nadu, Southern India, is awash with Hindu temples, strewn about as nonchalantly as scattered cushions. Around that corner or down this road sits a temple. Sanctuaries of prayer, ritual and procession are infused with brass bell peals, aromatic incense and bright images of the deities Vishnu, Shiva, Ganesh or Kali. The temples are built from stone quarried from the local landscape. The stone quarries are awash with bonded labourers – virtual slaves.

The Hindu system of caste permitted landlords in India to have slaves; labourers, with their families, were tied to the soil. When land was sold, slaves were valued along with cattle and other chattels. If a labourer ran away the master could go to court to complain and demand that the court fetch him back. This was prior to the mid-nineteenth century when the British started plantations in the surrounding countries of Malaysia, Sri Lanka and Fiji. The plantations needed workers, and as labourers in India were tied to the soil, they could not be taken there to work. In the 1840s, the British government introduced anti-slavery legislation, denying India's landlords the right to go to court to retrieve runaways. This loosened slaves from the grip of local landowners and brought hundreds of thousands over to the plantations abroad. The large estates became a worse form of slavery and labourers ran away.

The British then brought in a new law in 1859, a Workman's Special Contract Act. Under this Act, a labourer entered into an agreement with the contractor that he would work in the plantation for so many years, and if he failed to do so he could be arrested and punished. Indenturing workers in this way controlled them. Local landlords in India started taking similar bonds from labourers who agreed that, in lieu of money borrowed from the landlord, they or members of their families, would work until the loan was repaid. It was a change in the form of slavery but not in the plight or exploitation of the enslaved.

After independence, the Indian constitution prohibited forced labour. This prohibition was strengthened by the 1976 Bonded Labour System (Abolition) Act. The Act was intended to free all bonded labourers, cancel their debts, assist in economic and social rehabilitation and punish those guilty of employing bonded labourers or placing their relatives in bondage. Implementation of the Act is the responsibility of state governments, but bondage persists in many areas.

The segregation of Indian society into castes affects all social and economic relations. Allocation of labour on the basis of caste is a fundamental tenet of the Hindu system. Most bonded labourers come from the bottom of this social order: almost all of the Dalit community, formerly called 'Untouchables' are born slaves. In the countryside agricultural and non-agricultural occupations are controlled by rural elites who use bonded labourers. Reminiscent of the slaves who built the Egyptian pyramids, they sweat in the heat and dust of the stone quarries; at the sun-baked brick kilns; at hand looms and power looms; in the cultivation, dying, weaving of silk; and at gem cutting. From home, women and children sit rolling beedis, a local cigarette. Sometimes children are pledged as domestic servants or to factory owners.

It is all too easy for families from the lower castes to find themselves bonded for life. Hard pressed to meet even day-to-day basic needs, many have difficulty paying for festivals or social customs such as marriage or funerals, or for medicine if there is ill health. They have no collateral to borrow from the banks; all they can pledge is their labour. Unscrupulous landowners take up the pledge in return for a loan. In time, workers need further loans and advances, until they are labouring continually for no wages at all; as the debt increases, other family members work to repay the loan. The rates of interest are high, work conditions tough and they are not free to seek work elsewhere.

In many states bonded labourers have demanded compliance with the law and their release. Deep in the rural southern state of Tamil Nadu, where the land is as crusted as dried rusk, the service caste of stonecutters work the quarries. Arumugam, the president of one quarry workers co-operative comprised of former bonded labourers, was once so cowed by his employers that he only entered their presence fearfully bent in two; he now articulates the claims of his people with upright confidence. The cycle they found themselves in, he says, is typical. Contractors pay low wages, which necessitates borrowing money, this accumulates and they become bonded to that employer. 'All of us were afraid, but after a non-government organisation (NGO) came into the picture and started working in the villages, we all joined together and expressed our problems to them; and then this NGO organised all the workers around this co-operative, and we were able to get a quarry on lease from the government, and now we're working jointly. After joining this co-operative, the workers get on average 700 to 1,000 rupees and, some of them are en able to get 2,000 rupees a week. Working with the contractors, the wages were very low – 400 rupees a week – so we are able to earn more money now and we have more independence also. When we were working with the contractors, we had to work six days a week, we couldn't decide when to work and when not to work; if we needed to leave town for family reasons, we couldn't unless the contractor allowed us to; so, freedom of movement was restricted. The other thing is, we have to work from six in the morning 'til six in the evening so that makes twelve hours of work. But after joining the co-operative we're able to work whenever we feel like working and we are earning more wages also. So we have more freedom and at the same time we are able to earn more.'

Moving from bonded labour to taking charge of their own quarry has improved the workers standard of living and given them control over their own lives. Subramani, the president of another co-operative, has learnt that the rise from bonded labourer to managing a business is a steep learning curve for someone with no formal education. 'Once we started working by ourselves the contractors have created several problems against us. Recently they have also taken all our implements and we haven't got them back. Some labourers have repaid their loan to the contractor, but most of us have not repaid. We have got the lease of this quarry for a period of three years, but we have only worked for the last one and a half years. The contractors immediately filed a case against us saying that these people are illegally quarrying; they are using explosives, which is creating problems. I being the president, I have to regularly go to the courts. I was in court for almost five days a week. There were three cases filed against us, but the courts were so good that we got justice at the end of the day. For the one and a half years when we worked, we were able to get good wages; the co-operative was able to function well. For one and a half years of the lease period we were not able to work at all because these contractors didn't allow us to work, and the police didn't allow us to work. Even the people coming to load the stones in the lorries, these people were beating them. Lorries were stopped from coming to our quarries. So even though we had broken stones we were not able to sell them. So people were threatened, they were intimidated; we could not work at all.'

* * * *

After meeting the quarry workers, I went to the village of Thirupanjeeli, still in Tamil Nadu, a poor village with little opportunity for work. Gems are to Thirupanjeeli what cars are to Detroit. Almost every home has a gem-cutting machine, operated by hand and foot, and the whole family, adults and children, are involved in cutting and polishing the gems. In one home, a one-roomed hut, a corner of the small room is taken up with a manual pedal stone-cutting machine that gives off a shrill drilling sound like a dentist's tool or a knife scraping along an aluminium draining board. The hours are long and the pay is low. The village has a workshop with better quality machinery and it employs eight people; four are under the age of fourteen. Families need the children's labour to survive but they want them to learn and the hunger for education is strong. After working from six in the morning until four in the afternoon, the children are sent off to school. School is from five until eight in the evening and when I went along to one of the classes it was hard to believe that the thirty eager, smiling faces, aged between nine and fourteen years, had a day's work behind them.

The gem business also uses bonded labour. Mutulakshmi, a small, animated woman, was bonded; her task was polishing the American diamond, a synthetic gem made in the area. She has great strength of character and against the odds of not just an exploitative employer but family and social pressure she decided to break free.

'I'd been working with this contractor for the last eight years and since the wages which he is giving is very low, it is not possible to feed the whole family. So what happened is that I've taken my son to the same contractor who has given some money as advance on behalf of my son. There are times when he has beaten my son also and asked him to work. He was ten years old when he started working. There are several occasions when we have starved; the whole family have starved.'

She went to a local non-government organisation for help in getting herself and her son released. The contractor was a powerful man locally and Mutulakshmi's stand frightened her husband and the other villagers.

'And then all the people from the village joined together and they came inside my house and hit me and even my husband hit me at that stage. And these people again came to my village and said, "we'll put the fence around your house and we'll see that you are made an outcast; we'll see that nobody comes and talks to you. We'll put fire to your house." So they threatened me on several occasions. The contractors told my husband to see to it that I listened to him and stayed working as a bonded labourer under the employer. So, listening to the contractors, my husband came in and he hit me, several times. He told me that we cannot oppose these villagers because they are the only hope for us. We can only live through working for these people. So he has beaten me several times and asked me to continue working for the contractor. But I was very keen to have a new life for me and my son. My son was also beaten on several occasions. When he was sick the contractor used to beat him and put him to work. So we needed a new life, we didn't want to continue working as bonded labour.'

Mutulakshmi persisted and she and her family were finally released from bondage.

Mutulakshmi's brother Souririnjan found conditions so hard that he tried to escape. 'The wages which we receive are very low. The government prescribes 77 rupees, 50 paisos for a hundred stones, but what we get is just 14 rupees for a hundred stones. Besides that, when it is cloudy it is not possible for us to work because you need a lot of natural light to shape and polish the stones. Or when it is raining we cannot work, and when we don't go to work the employer also imposes a fine. So with all this we are not able to meet our daily family expenses, so we start borrowing money. When somebody falls sick in the house we borrow money, and we become indebted to the employers in the long term. I tried running away once because the conditions of work were very bad. Once I went to my sister's house and it took me two days to return and when I returned my employer asked me to repay back whatever advance I had taken from him. Since I could not repay immediately he slapped me and kicked me, so to escape that I ran away. My employer came in search of me and he also imposed another 2,000 rupee extra fine on me for searching for me and employing people to search for me.' Saririnjan too eventually managed to get released.

The work involved in producing a gem is divided in such a way that it involves different trades such as cutting, shaping, faceting and polishing. A person cannot buy a raw stone and produce a whole gem and sell it on the market. This allows employers to exploit the worker at every stage of the production. If someone is liberated from bondage and wants to start an independent enterprise, he has to release at least three other people skilled in the other aspects, and he needs machinery and an electricity supply. Workers cannot then sell the finished gems in the market because the diamond bazaar is well-established and managed by a cartel that will not buy from the workers themselves. This kind of manipulation and lack of willingness to give workers a better deal makes it difficult to break free, or if released, to have a livelihood; sometimes they become bonded again. It seems that, in Tamil Nadu, it will take time for mindsets to catch up with the legislation sent down from the capital, Delhi, several hundred miles away.

* * * *

In India, each state has its own legislature and local authority but the national legislature in Delhi can insist that states enforce acts such as the Abolition of Bonded Labour Act. Ensuring compliance is another matter. Besides, not too far from the capital itself, conditions of servitude exist. I visit the office of a human rights organisation that tries to protect children from unscrupulous employers. Among of its more dramatic interventions are raids on premises that keep and work children under appalling conditions. When I arrive in the office, there is a woman sitting there; her eyes are puffed from crying.

Snuggled in to her thin cotton sari is a gurgling baby. Her husband is a tailor but she says he has a stone in his stomach and has been ill for the last year. Since he cannot work through illness she has found it very hard to make ends meet. She has been crying for her seven-year-old son, Ashref. 'The school was far off and I was not having money to send him,' she says. Ashref was taken by a neighbour on the promise that he would be sent to the home of a richer man who worked in the government and given an education – again, there is that hunger for education for the children as a way out of poverty.

Ashref was put to work as a domestic servant, washing utensils and cleaning the floor. He was ill-treated and kept hungry. The mother continues, 'Ashref told the master "I'm here for study I want to go to school", and he said, "You are poor people, poor people can't afford to study so you need not to study, you have to work here".' She didn't talk about money before Ashref left, she explains; she asked no questions about how much he would get, because she sent him there for study. One day when he was hungry, Ashref was given milk to take to the master's son. The master's young boy drank the milk but a small amount was left over in the glass. It was evening and the employers were in prayer. Ashref saw that some little milk was left, so he drank it.

'The owner saw him drinking milk; he said, "Where is the milk?" The boy said, "I drank that milk." He said, "Okay I'll show you." He took him to the kitchen, the owner and the landlady both were there, they took him to the kitchen and they said, "we'll show you, how dare you to drink milk" and they saw that there is a screwdriver and they made it hot on the burner, the gas stove, and then they branded all over his body and then he was crying. Then they said, "how dare you to cry, no one will listen" and they put his hand on the burner. After that there was a big swelling.'

The neighbour-middleman brought Ashref back home. He was not able to speak. He just mumbled one small sentence, 'I had some milk and my master branded me.' He was not able to say anything else, he was not able to speak of the entire incident, and how it happened, why it happened, who did it – nothing.

The doctor advised his mother to go to the police and she took him to the police station and then to the hospital for treatment.

'The owner was also at the police station and he tried to give me a bribe of 500 rupees. I refused. I said, "I will not take this 500 rupees." They said, "No, your son will be alright very soon. You keep this money, it will be useful for you," but I threw the money and everybody was there – myself, the person who took my son, the middleman, the owner, the police, all were there and they were trying to force me to accept that money but I refused. I don't know anything about what has happened with the police. Ashref is very happy now, he's going to school. He's become fat also.'

Out on the Mahatma Gandhi ring road to the outskirts of Delhi, Ashref is at the ashram for rehabilitating the child labourers rescued in the raids. He is sitting outside in the warm sunshine calling out Hindi numbers to the class in a clear, happy voice. He is a lively bundle of big-eyed innocence with a charming smile. His slight seven-year-old body still bears the scars of branding; the distinctive mark of the head of a screwdriver is still evident, forming an uneven pattern across his soft brown skin. When he tells me his story himself I can hardly believe the petty, shrunken cruelty behind it.

'I was at owner's house and I was feeling hungry, there was a pain in my stomach. I saw that there was some milk in a glass and I drank that milk and owner saw it and then they beat me and then they branded me all over my body and face and they burnt my hand.'

All that can ameliorate the horror is that he seems so well now.

'I have learnt counting here, I have learnt the tables also, this ashram is very good and I eat too much. I'm free here and I like it.'

Other children at the ashram were rescued from servitude in the carpet industry. Mohan, ten years old, worked in a carpet factory for two years.

'I was small and a middleman came to the house and said that they will take this child to give him education, food, and they will pay him also. So my parents thought, okay, and in advance they paid one hundred rupees to my family. And they thought, okay, it's good, and they sent me and then I went to the carpet factory along with that middleman. I was in a room and I used to wake up early in the morning, at five o'clock, and used to work until eleven o'clock in the evening, and I used to get just one chapati, one roti and some dhal. And there was no lentil in that, it was just water. I used to sleep there. I used to go out with the master, I was not supposed to go out alone.'

There is something very striking about Sanjay. For someone so young, he has a quality of leadership about him. His voice is strong and he has been politicised by his experience. He was taken away from his home and his family after a visit from a middleman.

'There was a middleman came to my house and said, "Send your son, we will give him education and food and also we will try to provide him afterwards with a job," and my father at first said no. Then the middleman gave him an advance and said, "You can keep this money as an advance. Trust me, I'm a nice person and I'll send him somewhere where he will learn some skill and education and they will also pay him." I was sent with him. I don't know what my age was, I was very young. That middleman took me along with him and we reached the factory area and we slept there. In the morning that man woke all the children early in the morning at four o'clock and said, "Okay this is your school, I have brought you here, you have to do this work," and they cried, "No, no, no, no", then he took a bamboo stick and started beating them. For me it was very bad because when I went to that factory I saw my father for the last time. My father died and they didn't allow me to see my father. They didn't send me back home to see my father and every night I was thinking about my mother and they were beating me like anything. I was there for six years in the carpet factory and after six years I got free.

'When I go back to my home I'll not allow anybody to go and work in the factories. I'll go to different villages and I'll say to children, come and study here, this is a school. I'll run a school with what I'm learning here and I'll teach them and I'll create an awareness among the parents, don't send your children to the carpet industry. I know I'm very young but I'll go there and I'll organise people. People are not organised in the villages and that is why it's happening. I'll teach them and I'll make them unite.'

How old are you, Sanjay?

'I think I'm thirteen.'

Darjeeling Orchestra

1997

They had just got up from the floor of the convent school where they had slept the night; still sleepy-eyed and a little bemused, tired out after the train journey. They had come from Darjeeling, famous for its high quality tea. Tea needs land that gets plenty of rain but does not get soggy and the Darjeeling hills suit cultivation of the leaf for the popular brew. A couple of centuries ago the area was sparsely inhabited by an indigenous tribe. The British found they could grow tea there and they brought in workers from nearby Nepal. Since then, generations of Nepalese labourers have worked in the tea gardens.

The railway had taken them down through the hills and ushered them out to the foreignness of Calcutta. It was the first time any of them had been on a train; their mothers, fathers, grandmothers, great-uncles had never travelled by rail. Everything about these thirty children, eight to twelve years old, from the tea plantations was different. They had got out of the carriages, dainty and unworldly against the giant, ungainly, metal transporter. They carried violin cases with them, as big as themselves, the passport to wider horizons. Already their minds and imaginations were stretched: they had travelled by train, they were to perform as an orchestra in Calcutta and there was talk of them going to Europe.

The children had emptied out of the railway station onto Calcutta's strange, narrow, dirty lanes, filled with people crushing together; into the city of skinny-limbed rickshaw pullers, gregarious gabbling hawkers, shunned misshapen beggars, overcrowded sputtering buses with noisy horn-hooting disputatious drivers; into the smoke and stiff odours of peddled street cooking; sleeping bodies stretched out on the street; shoe-shine men with brushes and polish and neatly rolled mats that unfurl at night and on which they rest. Space in the busy city is yielded only to wandering cows, because of their religious significance.

The parents of the children in the tiny Darjeeling orchestra were also poor, labourers and farm workers who suffer from very visible poverty: little food, basic shelter, back-breaking work for low pay, no education, bad health. The homes they left are one-roomed, made from bamboo with mud walls, thatched roof and a small clay fireplace in the room, some pots and pans; the floors were their beds. The families they left cook rice, with a little dhal and a few vegetables if they are lucky. Their life is hard. All suffer too from the insidious, less visible lacks that come with poverty – lethargy, lack of stimulation, an unawakened imagination. Being poor can mean human potential is dimmed and life is limited to worrying about getting the next meal. The families must somehow earn enough for food and to buy some simple implements for their houses, like pots to cook their food. When these immediate needs are satisfied – if they are – there is a general relaxation but with no energy left to pursue anything else in life. The children sit around the houses until they are old enough to carry loads, and when they are old enough to do that they spend the rest of their lives doing this hard, physical labour, with just enough payment at the end of the week to supply the essentials of life.

The story of the orchestra started many years ago when a Canadian priest, Father Ed Maguire, went to work among Darjeeling's poor. The simple houses did not have electricity nor did they have clocks. He wondered how to get the children, who were free, interested in school. He started by having them come to school to do gymnastics and play music. 'The children were very interested at first in gymnastics because they knew no comfort in their lives, and the rough and tumble of gymnastics appealed to them. You might not think that's very important. It is important in this sense: the children had never before made up their minds to do something not absolutely dictated by necessity. When they came they were saying, "I wonder if I can do those gymnastics." The idea was to show these children that they could accomplish something. It is commonly thought in India that the very poor simply do not have the mental capacity to excel in school subjects. They believe it about themselves. The idea was to show that they could accomplish things.'

After a while he told them that if they wanted to keep doing gymnastics, to cartwheel, vault and clamber, they needed to come to school. The children got involved and started attending school regularly.

The school tried to feed them well, 'to expand that very limiting outlook on life of getting just what is needed for life today, then relaxing and not going on any further. To give them food so that they did not have that anxiety, and then to put before them activities not dictated by necessity, to develop their mind, to let them see that the world has much more to offer a human being than just the grinding cycle of working for what they need now.'

He then heard that in the Darjeeling hills the children are musically gifted. So he invited the director of the Calcutta Symphony to come and play his violin and asked him if he thought the children would be interested in and capable of playing musical instruments, of playing the violin. The director said yes, if they were given a chance, they would. So they bought violins from Calcutta at about 1,400 rupees each, brought them to the hills and started the music programme. The children began to quiver the violin strings until they could play local folk tunes and Mozart, no longer limited to thinking, 'where am I going to get food today?'

The first school lessons and music programmes started in the 1970s. As the musicians progressed, other instruments were introduced: flute, trombone, oboe, cello, tuba, French horn, bazooka, trumpets. The Darjeeling orchestra that was visiting

Calcutta played only violin and viola because of the musicians' young age, the brass instruments seemingly not considered good for their teeth. Half a dozen of the original group have gone on to become music teachers in schools that they would never have been able to attend themselves. Several others went on to get university degrees in arts, science and commerce. Two former pupils taught, rehearsed, conducted and put together the music programme for the visiting orchestra. The unassuming young man who was now the conductor had been an eight-year-old orphan living on the streets with no other prospect than to carry loads. An old, illiterate woman brought him to the school and said, 'I want you to take him, he has a fine brain.' Today he can conduct a symphony orchestra. Offers of jobs in other places with more pay have all met with the same response, 'I will never leave these children who grew up like I grew up.'

I quietly left the rehearsal after a petite eight-year-old girl finished a solo violin performance.

Soldier, Souldier

1997

He looks every inch the soldier, tall with a large frame and a mop of thick, white hair, but with his low, soft-spoken voice he sounds every inch the pacifist. His journey has taken him into Rishikesh, north of Delhi, where the majestic, sacred River Ganges heads after leaving the Himalayas. The ashram is one of the many on that stretch of the wide, garrulous river. After finishing his morning sweet porridge and tea, he says: 'Theoretically I should be dead now. Three years and two months ago I was told that I had three to three-and-a-half years to live and I feel very much alive. I wouldn't have believed that I would be in India if you said that five years ago. My life five years ago? I had a good job. I was earning good money, I was on the promotion line as you might say, but my body was doing funny things to me. I started to fall over. I'd got to pick up the telephone and find that I hadn't actually picked it up, I'd knocked it over. Or I'd spill coffee down my shirtfront.

'To start with I didn't worry too much, but then I began to get more concerned about it and I started to do a lot of physical exercise in order to try and get things right, and I thought I might have mental problems. Then I went to see a doctor about it, and they started to do a series of tests, and the results were that I have an adult form of a motor neurone type disease, which comes on in late life. When I was told about this I was totally unprepared. I knew there was something wrong with me, and in a way I was pleased that we were finding out what it was, but I never expected to be told that it was something that couldn't be cured or treated. It was an illness that was terminal, and in my case pretty painful. Of course they have lots of drugs to treat the pain, but treating the pain with drugs – it affects a lot of other things. It has a lot of side-effects. It's not really the best way perhaps to deal with it.'

'So when I was told about this situation I took it very badly. Being a former soldier, I had associated anyone who was ill as weak. I had no love or support for them, so I began to hate myself quite a lot and got very angry with myself, resulting in taking anti-depressant tablets and going on a downward spiral, and in fact going to psychiatrists to try and be sorted out.

'My life was in a very low state. And then I visited someone who lent me a book, *Touching Peace* by Thich Nhat Hanh. Thich Nhat Hanh is a Vietnamese peace activist; he's a monk. I'd never heard of him and I had a healthy hatred of Vietnamese people through my experience with the Vietnam War, and I didn't have much respect for monks or people of peace either. So when she lent me this book I threw it down on the seat beside me and didn't think much of it, but in fact I picked it up and opened it and read some lines from his book, and they were so simple, so straight-forward and sincere, that I understood what I was reading, and I continued to read that book for some time and it brought me a little peace and stability. Just a little, I was still rocky. I was still taking drugs and whatever. Then I learnt that this master was alive and quite active in France, so I didn't really think about it but deep inside me I knew it would be a good idea to go and see him. So I found out where he was and I wrote requesting permission to come and visit. I half expected to get turned down, because I knew nothing about meditation, nothing about Vietnamese Buddhism. I was really raw, but I got a lovely letter back saying, yes, they'd love to see me. So I turned up at Plum Village one cold February evening, and in fact I fell in love with the practice and with Thich Nhat Hanh, although it's been a very painful love story. This year I was thinking of going to Plum Village for the winter retreat. Somehow I got sidetracked and came to India.

'For me I think it's a little bit of an adventure. I just love standing at the train door looking at the landscape going past me at seventy miles an hour; just standing at the door, window wide open. There are so many restrictions in England where I come from. Perhaps it's the freedom, but also I think, especially here in Rishikesh, there's a deep spirituality. I don't know if it's the people or the country, perhaps it's the Ganges, but this is a very, very, easy place for meditation, especially for pain meditation, because I have quite a lot of physical pain. But here you see the beautiful coloured saris that the women wear, and you see the dirty sewage rivers, and cows, and its very different perhaps from my home.

'There's an awful lot of poverty here in India, the illness, the disease, it's almost unimaginable. If you're rich in India it's wonderful but if you're poor in India it's really terrible, whereas back in the West if you're rich it's wonderful but if you're poor, it's not too bad. I know that the poor people probably wouldn't think this, but I've seen people actually dying in a street, so perhaps our materialism isn't so bad.

'I'm not a meditator really. I sit for ages in so called meditation, but for me the most important thing is just to enjoy what I'm doing and somehow it feels really good to come to a place where I don't have to do anything. I don't have to be clever, or make conversation, or think of things, I can just sit nice and quietly and be myself. If I want to follow the meditation path of no thoughts, that's fine. If I want to think of a beautiful meadow in England with cowslips or buttercups or cows munching green grass and the stream running by, I can do that. Here in the Himalayas it's pretty wonderful, just contemplating the rising sun coming across the mountains. I think perhaps if I was to think too seriously about meditation and what I should be doing and what I shouldn't be doing then it would be difficult. But somehow it's good to know that I'm sitting in a place where generations of people have sat just letting the thoughts come and the thoughts go, and perhaps touch a little bit of peace, but as I've said before the main thing for me is enjoyment. If I didn't enjoy it I wouldn't do it.

'The wonderful thing about the path I'm on at the moment is I don't have to go anywhere or achieve anything. I suppose I've changed very much in the last three years. Whether I'm a better person or a worse person I don't know but I do know that I'm a very happy person, and I think that happiness really has to do with the fact that I've understood how not to be frightened. I don't have much fear anymore, just accepting that what is, is, and I'm just me. I'm not clever, I'm not a soldier, not a businessman; I'm just a human being with all my stupidities. It's a pretty irresponsible way to conduct a life I suppose. Luckily, I've provided for my family, and the mortgage is paid off and all those sort of things, so I'm in a pretty privileged position, I think, to just touch life and enjoy it.

'Was it difficult to let go of the military side? Yes, but I haven't let go of it. When I see a jet fighter screaming across the sky, a part of me goes, wow, and I can touch the excitement of that. Or when I see soldiers parachuting, I touch that excitement, but it doesn't affect me in quite the same way. I have moments of guilt when I'm not practising particularly well, when I think of some of the things I've done, but then if I just come back to the present moment, accept who I am, I can live with that without too many problems, I think.'

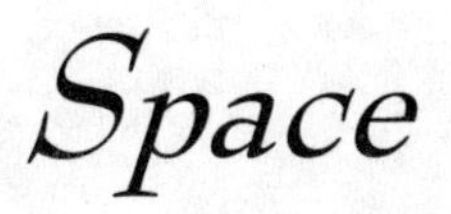

Energy and space press into each other. The great Asian crush: Calcutta, Jakarta, Dhaka. Surrounded in a street of human energies and vibrations that mesh together; part of the beckoning shout, the loud communal laugh, the intent whisper as the crowd whorls towards its business. Out in the space of a shared public arena.

Busy New York: in the midst of the crowd a palpable sense of private space, of protecting your own and honouring another's. A multitude of individuals moving along a street in separate invisible rings. No eye contact, no interlinking of the rings, any brush is incidental and brusque, embarrassing or suspicious. Out in the space of a private arena, shared with millions of other private arenas.

No

Dublin said no. London, Paris, Rome said no.

New York, Tokyo, Moscow, Bangkok, Jakarta, Dhaka, Glasgow, Auckland, Atlanta, Amsterdam, Athens, Almaty, Amman, Augusta, Austin, Antarctica, Andalusia, Adelaide, Alberta, Algeciras, Anchorage, Akureyri, Arcata said no.

Bucharest, Belfast, Berlin, Beirut, Bern, Barcelona, Barrie, Madrid, Prague, Canberra, Washington, Warsaw, Vancouver, San Francisco, Damascus, Calcutta, Karachi, Zagreb, San Diego, Santiago, Santander, Savannah, Santa Fe, Santo Domingo, Spokane, Sfax, Cadiz said no.

Sydney, Chicago, Srinigar, Istanbul, Islamabad, Lisbon, Lismore, Nice, Vienna, Winnipeg, Wellington, Tel Aviv, Kiev said no.

Johannesburg, Copenhagen, Cape Town, Kuala Lumpur, Guatemala City, Guadalajara, Ljubljana, Leipzig, Lawrence, Montreal, Toronto, Mostar, Oslo, Osaka, Oklahoma City, Hong Kong, Copenhagen, Colorado Springs, Oviedo, Mexico City said no.

Toulouse, Stuttgart, Stockholm, Sofia, Seoul, Seville, Seattle, Sao Paulo, St Louis, St Augustine, San Jose, San Juan, Santa Cruz de Tenerife said no.

Rawalpindi, Raleigh, Rafah, Ramallah, Rethimno, Reykjavik, Rockford, Rio de Janeiro, Juneau, Rhodes, Philadelphia, Dili, Little Rock, Quito, Coimbra, Gainesville, Macomb, Takoma, Yakima, Knoxville, Gothenburg, Newcastle, Luxemburg, Thessaloniki, Tallahassee, Tegucigalpa, Tulsa said no.

Melbourne, Madison, Miami, Milwaukee, Minneapolis,

Minden, Minsk, Manila, Managua, Mankato, Monza, Montevideo, Montgomery, Montreal, Montpelier France, Montpelier Vermont, Martha's Vineyard, Mackay said no.

Malaga, Lugo, Louisville, Los Angeles, Lansing, Las Palmas, Las Vegas, Long Beach said no.

Detroit, Dubuque, Boise, Boone, Buenos Aires, Budapest, Brussels, Belligen, Bellingham, Bergen, Bregenz, Bratislava, Brasilia, Birmingham, Baltimore, Babylon, Bangor, Boston, Bombay, Bloomington, Buffalo said no.

Dallas, Gaza, Cairo, Christchurch, Iraklio, Victoria, Taipei, Tampere, Pattani, Patras, Porto, Portland, Porto Codex, Perth, Pearl Harbour, Pittsburgh said no.

Halifax, Helsinki, Honolulu, Huntsville, Huesca, Umea, Edmonton, Lulea, Girona, Lyon, Hobart, Phoenix, Fort Wayne, Farmington, Fayetteville, Fresno, Fiji, Ferrol, Ventura, Tofino, Nanaimo, Newton, New Orleans, Newcastle Australia, Norfolk, Normal, Olympia, Oakland, Indianapolis, Isafyordur, Aotearoa, Rosario, Cedar Rapids, Champaign-Urbana, Charlotte, Calgary, Cleveland, Concord, Christianborg, Decorah, Decatur Trumansburg, Trondheim, Dunedin, Durban, Durham, Turin, Turku, Tudela said no.

Iowa City, Ottowa, Utah, Ithaca, Wichita, Windsor, Waterloo, Waterville, Wausau, Volos, Vallejo, Elkins Tasmania, Nashville, Asheville, La Crosse, Lahore, Laramie, Darwin, Brainerd, Brisbane, Pensacola, Johnston, St Charles, Santa Barbara, Santa Monica said no. In Singapore two women said no.

Jasper, Texas, said no. Baghdad said no.

On the 15 February 2003, like a giant Tower of Babel, millions of the world's citizens said no to war and yes to peace.

CANCELLED